I0813436

WILLIAM PHIPPS AND THE DIVING BELL BUBBLE

For William Phipps,
who suffered an unfairly bad press

By the same author

Non-fiction

The Hundredth Year

The Audit Report

The Landlord's Handbook

The Pirate Who Stole Scotland

Fiction

There's Only One Henry Green

As translator

An Armenian Family Torn Apart

WILLIAM PHIPPS AND THE DIVING BELL BUBBLE

SUNKEN TREASURE, WITCHES AND THE ROUTE TO EMPIRE

LEON HOPKINS

First published in Great Britain in 2025 by
PEN AND SWORD HISTORY
An imprint of
Pen & Sword Books Ltd
Yorkshire – Philadelphia

ISBN 978 1 39905 459 1

A CIP catalogue record for this book is available from the British Library.

Typeset in Times New Roman 10.5/13.5 by
SJmagic DESIGN SERVICES, India.
Printed and bound in the UK by CPI Group (UK) Ltd.

The Publisher's authorised representative in the EU for product safety is Authorised Rep Compliance Ltd., Ground Floor, 71 Lower Baggot Street, Dublin D02 P593, Ireland.
www.arccompliance.com

For a complete list of Pen & Sword titles please contact
PEN & SWORD BOOKS LIMITED
George House, Units 12 & 13, Beevor Street, Off Pontefract Road,
Barnsley, South Yorkshire, S71 1HN, England
E-mail: enquiries@pen-and-sword.co.uk
Website: www.pen-and-sword.co.uk

or

PEN AND SWORD BOOKS
1950 Lawrence Rd, Havertown, PA 19083, USA
E-mail: uspen-and-sword@casematepublishers.com
Website: www.penandswordbooks.com

Contents

List of Illustrations

Introduction

Fire, Brimstone, Demons and Witches

IN ENGLAND, MUCH of the first half of the seventeenth century, and a fair bit of the second half, was taken up with bickering about religion. It was not whether a Christian god existed that taxed the minds of the population; nobody questioned that. The arguments were about how He (because it definitely was a 'He') should be worshipped.

There were already deep wounds over the split, in the previous century, of the Church of England from Rome. By the early 1600s the Protestant version of Christianity had in England gained a growing, if stuttering, popular ascendancy over the Roman Catholic version.

But Protestants were not as one. Various sects had their own ideas. There were Presbyterians, Baptists, Anabaptists, Fifth Monarchists, Ranters, Quakers, Congregationists, Puritans and more. All were 'non-conformists' who chose to differ with the strict and extensive edicts and established practices of the Anglican Church of England.

There were three main streams of difference between the established church and the non-conformists. One was organisation and management of the church, with many non-conformists favouring greater autonomy for individual churches or congregations and the doing away of management by bishops (their involvement being a feature of the episcopalian Anglican church). Another was the conduct of services, embracing such features as use of music ('none', said the Puritans), who should be allowed to preach, what they should wear ('no surplices', said the Puritans), and the texts used (no book of common prayer, said most non-conformists) and language (no Latin).

A third stream related more to social reform than religion. The Levellers wanted (their version of) universal suffrage, and the Diggers, the right to farm common land.

A shared argument among the non-conformists was that the reformation of the church had not gone far enough, and that Anglican worship retained far too many of the ungodly, not to say idolatry in nature, 'superstitions' of Roman Catholicism.

Through the reverse telescope of history, the cause of much of this bickering seems less than momentous. At the time, when church attendance was mandatory and blasphemy a hanging offence, where so much in life was unexplained and death was a constant companion, it was certainly not regarded as such.

The argument had significant consequences for the country, and for New England, that part of North America where a good many Puritans and other non-conformists had fled in search of somewhere they could exercise freedom of expression. Puritans were said to be the most Protestant of Protestants. In the country around Massachusetts Bay, they thought they had identified an ideal haven for people who believed in self-sufficiency, hard work and community, self-restraint and piety.

In the twenty years leading up to 1642, it is believed over 20,000 Puritans made the difficult, dangerous and expensive trip from England to New England, uprooting their families in pursuit of their chosen lifestyle.

One such was James Phipps, a Gloucestershire man who sailed, Boston-bound, from Bristol in the 1630s. In his case, he was driven not so much by his beliefs as by his contractual duty to obey the commands of his master; James was an indentured apprentice. He settled close to the Maine frontier outpost now known as Woolwich where, nineteen years later, he and his wife Mary named their second son William.

1642 was an important date in England. It was the year that Charles I raised his standard at Nottingham, declaring war on his own people. It marked the start of the Civil War between himself and Parliament. He had become exasperated by protests against the way he chose to run the country. This included sidelining Parliament and exercising his royal prerogative to the fullest extent allowed (and beyond).

An arrogant and devious man whose many character defects included indecisiveness, Charles believed his god had given him the unassailable right to rule as he pleased and that Parliament had no other function than to rubber-stamp his financial demands. He tried to avoid having to call Parliament at all, using various dubious means to obtain money. One involved demands for 'Ship Money', supposedly a levy on coastal towns that could be imposed by the monarch without Parliamentary approval. It was supposed to be used only in times of emergency and paid only by coastal towns. The only emergency at the time was that of Charles' own making. And the only definition of 'coastal town' applied was that of Charles' own limited imagination.

The English Civil War was a tragedy in three acts. It began as a dispute about Parliamentary authority, and quickly turned into a clash between religious ideologies in which equally arrogant Parliamentarians convinced themselves that they had a direct line to the wishes of their god.

The first two acts were both won by Parliament, the second ending in the beheading of Charles. But for his continued deviousness and duplicity, the king might have survived and even been reinstated as a constitutional monarch. He did not change and was not reinstated.

The third act involved a walk-on part for Charles II (of Scotland, but not yet England) whose Scottish supporters were seen off at the battles of Dunbar, in 1650, and Worcester, a year later.

The end of the Civil War coincided with the birth of William Phipps, son of James. His life was short but action-packed. Self-educated and self-made, Phipps achieved a meteoric rise to a position of eminence.

Not only that, when, in 1687, he sailed into Gravesend, his holds filled to brimming with Spanish treasure, he set in motion a chain of events that changed England's financial fortunes. The results of his dogged determination prompted the country's transition from a land of peasants, pirates and religious ideologues into one of industrialists, financiers, merchants, and international traders and adventurers.

By raising silver from a sunken galleon, Phipps captured public imagination. Promoters of now-fashionable joint-stock companies were quick to take advantage and to come up with new treasure-hunting ventures, and new and improved diving inventions.

Investors clamoured for an opportunity to put money into what then counted as new technology. Phipps had brought together the English love of the sea, the romance of the Americas and of Spanish gold, and the possibility of instant (and legitimate) riches.

It was a much-needed change. In 1687 England was reeling from almost a century of turmoil.

In this heady atmosphere, the makings of a stock exchange were established, the Bank of England created, national finances put on a firmer footing, paper money introduced, and credit transformed. England was on its way to becoming a modern financial powerhouse.

Phipps was lauded as a hero, knighted for his troubles and made governor of Massachusetts. But politics proved his downfall. A blunt, no-nonsense ruffian of a man who put an end to the Salem witchcraft trials, Phipps succumbed to a world of intrigue that saw his free-thinking blustering approach as an affront to his Puritanical homeland.

PART I

BROKEN DREAMS

'The New-Englanders are a People of God settled in those, which were once the Devil's Territories; and it may easily be supposed that the Devil was exceedingly disturbed, when he perceived such a People here accomplishing the Promise of old made unto our Blessed Jesus, That He should have the Utmost parts of the Earth for his Possession.'

Cotton Mather

'A man's errors are his portals of discovery.'

James Joyce

Chapter 1

Predestined

PURITANS BELIEVED IN predestination. So long as they followed their god's will, as revealed by divine providence, they were the chosen ones, members of an elite few who were already destined for heaven.

William Phipps was a Puritan. He was also a carpenter, shipwright, soldier, sailor, smuggler, politician, treasure hunter, governor and knight of the realm. And all this packed into a life that was over and done within forty-four years of his birth.

Whether or not Phipps was as committed a Puritan as his first biographer, Puritan cleric Cotton Mather, would have his readers believe, is open to serious doubt. But he had the utmost belief in himself; a certainty that he would achieve worldly success. That the place and circumstances of his birth and his subsequent path to fame and fortune should have been determined by events that occurred long before his arrival on this earth, cannot be denied. There was the little matter of a Spanish treasure ship, sunk nine years before Phipps was born. There was the unplanned way in which Phipps' father ended up in New England and his parents' decision to bring up their family in so remote an area, devoid of schools and churches. And as for religion, there was the Puritan fervour that had driven the Pilgrim Fathers to create a community whose attitudes and stringent laws were at odds with those of England.

Christianity had proved itself a potent force that resonated with the sentiments of the people of Europe. A thousand years after its Iron Age creation, the religion split into two, with the Greek Orthodox Church going one way, the Roman Catholic Church another.

By the 1500s virtually the whole of Western Europe adhered to the Catholic version of Christianity. But there was dissatisfaction. Aided by new-fangled printing techniques, and influenced by the Dutch Roman Catholic priest Desiderius Erasmus, theologians such as Martin Luther (in Germany), John Calvin (a Frenchman working out of Geneva), Ulrich Zwingli (Swiss) and John Knox (Scotland) put forward their own 'back to basics' ideas. The Roman Catholic Church had got ahead of itself, they said. It used too many fancy rituals that were inaccessible to ordinary people, and it relied too much on statues and images of saints and the like, in a way that smacked of idolatry.

These ideas took hold, and the Reformation was on its way. This new, cutdown version of Christianity manifested itself as the Protestant faith that was soon adopted by many Germanic and Nordic states, England and Scotland among them (John Knox founded the Presbyterian Church of Scotland).

By 1603 James Stuart was king of both England and the separate and independent kingdom of Scotland (he had been king of Scotland since shortly after his first birthday). His accession to the English throne also made him king of the dependent kingdoms of Ireland and Wales. Not backward in writing about his beliefs (and his deep affection for other men), James' book on witchcraft (*Daemonologie, In Forme of a Dialogue, Divided into three books: Written by the high and mightie Prince, James*) had been published first in Scotland and then, on his accession to the English throne, in London. Also previously published in Scotland was his *The True Law of Free Monarchies: Or, The Reciprocal and Mutual Duty Between a Free King and His Natural Subjects*, a work in which he outlined his adherence to the notion of the divine right of kings.

James had been brought up a Presbyterian but, as a matter of political expediency, disagreed with its ban on bishops. Instead, be favoured an Episcopalian approach; that of the Anglican Church of England in fact. Soon he was busy commissioning a Protestant version of the Christian bible (1603) and the *Book of Common Prayer* (1604). And in 1605 he survived an assassination attempt by disillusioned Catholics who had hoped his rule would allow greater tolerance for their own religious beliefs. Seven conspirators were tortured, tried and duly despatched in grisly manner as retribution for their crimes; among them was the hired hit-man Guy Fawkes.

A year after that, James gave Royal Assent to *An Act for a Public Thanksgiving to Almighty God every Year on the Fifth Day of November*. Public attendance at such services was required and, according to the UK Parliament's website, 'for two centuries afterwards, special church services were held to commemorate his (Guy Fawkes') failure, under the provisions of the Act'.[1.1]

James' Protestant credentials were assured.

The *King James Bible* came out in 1611. It was a huge success. It was an English language version of a selection of religious texts originally written in a variety of different languages over a period spanning centuries. Some of the texts had originally been transcribed from versions handed down by word of mouth by generations of believers. The authorship of many was uncertain and those relating to Christianity's main man, Jesus, were all written fifty years or more after his supposed death.

The whole was put together by a committee of fifty scholars.

Despite the uncertain provenance, despite the tendency of the oral tradition to embellish, despite the inexact nature of translation, despite the inevitable politicking and compromise engendered by any large committee, the bible was taken to have somehow arrived at the 'word of god'. It was a matter of faith, not logic.

Intended for use by the Church of England, the *King James Bible* was soon adopted by other English and Scottish Protestant sects. It was studied, pored over, learnt by heart, copied out and quoted. The true meaning of each word, each phrase, sentence and paragraph was examined and argued over.

The book was so large, it contained just over 780,000 words, ten novels-worth, that support could be found within it for almost any point of view. The proliferation of Protestant sects was sanctified.

James' new version of the *Book of Common Prayer,* which came out earlier (in 1604), had not received such universal approval among Protestants. Not so much a prayer book as a guide to the conducting of services, its insistence on various rites and rituals, or 'sacraments', beloved by the Roman Catholic church, was a bone of contention. Puritans rejected many of its recommended practices. They did not like church music, stained glass windows, use of the sign of the cross, having to kneel to receive sacrament, priests wearing white vestments, celebration of Christmas Day and other events, and more.

The *King James Bible* was hailed a literary masterpiece, but the two works taken together helped to stir religious differences among Protestants. Presbyterians and Puritans in particular were outraged at what they saw as the 'Popish' preferences of the Anglican Church of England. The argument became even more heated after 1626, when James 1 died and his oldest surviving son, Charles, became Charles I of England and of Scotland. Charles had been born in Scotland and had not expected to become king of either England or Scotland. That should have been the place of his popular elder brother Prince Henry, who had died of typhoid when aged 18 (Charles was six years younger than Henry, making him 25 when he took the English throne in February 1626).

Charles was made of different stuff than the outward-going Henry. He was of slight build, diffident and devious. Even the British royal family's official website (www.royal.uk) admits Charles was 'self-righteous and had a high concept of royal authority, believing in the divine right of kings'. He was, it says, deeply religious and 'favoured the high Anglican form of worship, with much ritual, while many of his subjects, particularly in Scotland, wanted plainer forms'.

It might have added that he was arrogant, opinionated, disloyal, untrustworthy and not too bright.

Religion wasn't the only problem. Charles was not slow in spending money on works of art, music and other home comforts, nor in waging expensive wars with France and Spain. He was short of money from the start and expected Parliament continually to replenish his funds, no questions asked.

In 1628, when Charles had been in his job for just two years, Parliament demanded he agree to a Petition of Right setting out four principles: no taxation without the consent of Parliament, no imprisonment without cause, no quartering of soldiers on subjects, and no martial law in peacetime. This was a response to Charles' use of 'non-parliamentary' (unapproved) taxation, to fill his coffers. His methods for dealing with refuseniks included demands for forced loans backed by the threat of imprisonment without trial.[1.2]

Charles agreed to the petition (although later ignored the principles to which he had agreed). Even so, the argument rumbled on and, in 1629, Members of Parliament used force to prevent adjournment of the house until censorious motions against the king had been considered. This was enough for Charles. He dismissed Parliament and ruled by royal prerogative for the next eleven years (the 'Eleven Year Tyranny'). During this time, he racked up yet more causes for general disgruntlement, including the appointment of the Anglican-enthusiast and Charles-supporting William Laud as Archbishop of Canterbury, and the use of a medieval expediency called 'Ship Money' to help finance his profligate ways.

Ship Money had remained on the statute book as an emergency measure that could short-cut normal tax-raising arrangements by allowing the monarch, in times of imminent danger, to levy funds from coastal towns to be used in their own defence. Charles did not need the presence of danger nor the proximity of the sea to make his Ship Money demands.

But by 1640 he was running short of ideas for raising even more money. He needed funds to pay for action against Scotland to make it accept Anglican rather than Presbyterian ways, especially introduction of Anglican-style bishops. Backed by Archbishop Laud, Charles had wanted to impose his revised *Book of Common Prayer* on Scotland to bring the churches 'of England' and 'of Scotland' into line.

Scots people were outraged. They wanted none of it. There was riot and unrest, and creation, in 1638, of a Scottish Covenant that allowed people to commit themselves to upholding the principles of a self-ruling Presbyterian Church of Scotland. Thousands signed throughout Scotland.

Not for the last time, Charles prepared to make war on his own people. In a shambolic attempt to go-it-alone, he marched a reluctant force (of mainly drafted untrained militiamen under the command of the Duke of Hamilton) to the Northumberland town of Berwick-upon-Tweed, in the far north-east of England. It was met by a Scots army of superior force, although neither side was inclined to fight. Instead, there was a stand-off followed by a truce on terms that, true to form, Charles was not inclined to stand by.

His next move was to recall the English Parliament so that it might fund his plans for further intervention. But Parliament, many of whose members were

Presbyterian or 'independents' (mainly Puritan), refused to go along with any of this, and certainly not before they had aired their many grievances against the king. And so, to prevent Parliamentary veto of a second 'Bishops' War', Charles sent its members home. The 'Short Parliament' was no more. It had lasted barely three weeks. It was another bad play by the king.

Still determined to put the Scots in their place, Charles again tried to cajole reluctant militiamen into fulfilling their auxiliary function and march with him against the now-emboldened Scots. The aptitude and enthusiasm of his force was no better than the first time around. Their progress north was marked by disorder and unrest, pillaging and desertions. But at least Charles had the promise of men and money from Ireland, exacted from its Parliament (relying on Catholic support) by his stern Lord Deputy of Ireland, the Earl of Strafford.

Meanwhile the Scottish Parliament had been strengthening its defences and had authorised Campbell raids on Royalist highland clans and pacification of Dumbarton, a place on the Firth of Clyde on the western shores of Scotland not too far from Glasgow, where Strafford might be expected to try to land his promised Irish forces.

More Scottish troops were recruited, bringing the Covenanter force to an impressive 20,000 or so. It did not wait for the English at Berwick, as might have been expected, but sidestepped the opposition and made for Newcastle-upon-Tyne, an important east coast city. It was duly occupied.

Strafford's promise of Irish support came to nothing, his army was simply too dilatory in preparing for a campaign about which it had little enthusiasm.

The war was over almost as soon as it had begun, with Charles obliged to agree to the Scots' occupation of Northumberland and Durham pending agreement of permanent peace terms. These were subsequently set out in the Treaty of London which included reparation payments for Scotland, immunity from prosecution for those who had signed Scotland's Covenant, and confirmation that the country's Presbyterian church could continue as before.

An even more telling consequence of Charles' actions was that it made natural allies, for now, of the Scottish and English parliaments and meant the latter would benefit from the involvement of Covenanter forces in the coming Civil War. Having to accept Scottish terms was not the only setback for Charles. His attempts, backed by Strafford, to raise money from other states (including Catholic Spain) to fight his own subjects had come to light in captured private letters.

Charles was obliged to call another Parliament to ratify the Treaty of London and help himself out of the hole into which he had dug himself. But one of Parliament's first acts was to impeach Strafford. In politically motivated trials it pursued the high-handed earl for his Irish deeds until a death sentence was obtained. Despite his earlier assurances to Strafford that he would not allow him to come to harm, Charles signed his execution order. At his beheading in 1641, Strafford was attended by Laud who, three years later, was obliged to attend his own appointment with the axe.

Released from Strafford's iron grip and perhaps buoyed by the Scots success in protecting their own religion, long aggrieved Irish Catholics rose up in rebellion. One of their leaders, Sir Phelim O'Neil, immediately issued a proclamation claiming that King Charles had commissioned him to defend the country against his Protestant opponents in Parliament.

Whether Charles had ever suggested or let O'Neil believe he supported such an idea is not known, although the Irishman was able to produce some official-looking documents of uncertain provenance. Either way, given the king's recent hope of using Strafford's promised Irish force to fight the Scottish Covenanters, it was Charles' misfortune that O'Neil was believed by many.

Soon Ireland's Catholic bishops had declared the rebellion to be just and an Irish 'Catholic Confederacy' was announced.

This was too much for Charles. He wanted the Irish Rebellion put down and tried, with success, to get Scottish Covenanters to take action. Aware of Charles' devious ways, the English Parliament was not so compliant. It was wary of allowing the king to raise an army of his own; one that he might later use against it. Instead, Parliament wanted control of the army itself.

Something of a squabble ensued in which Parliament passed a Militia Bill specifying that troops could only be raised by officers that it had first approved. Charles refused to give it his assent. Instead, a furious monarch attempted to arrest those Members of Parliament he considered responsible for this affront. His attempt failed and the battle lines of the Civil War had been drawn.

Charles went off to Nottingham to raise the Royal Standard as a rallying call for support for his cause. It blew down within the week and had to be replaced.

A more sanguine man might have taken this as a cue to take stock. He was unlikely to win any protracted war with Parliament, which had control of the money and the support of the City of London and the Navy. But, surrounded by sycophants and buoyed by his own conceit, Charles pressed on.

Soon he had a not-so-secret weapon at his side; an Exocet missile named Prince Rupert of the Rhine. Rupert, 23 years old in 1641, was the third son of the Electoral Prince Frederick V of the Palatine. Against advice, Frederick, in the year of Rupert's birth, had unwisely accepted an invitation to become king of Bohemia (now essentially the Czech Republic). He was Protestant, as were most Bohemians, but the newly crowned Holy Roman Emperor, the Catholic Ferdinand II, a Habsburg, considered the crown his as of right.

Just over a year after his coronation, Frederick was thrown out after losing the Battle of White Mountain. It was a short and decisive battle which, having gone home for lunch, Frederick did not witness. Afterwards he was obliged to flee with his family to the United Provinces where he and they survived on handouts from other royals.

Rupert was therefore poor (by his standards) but well connected. Charles I, who provided him with a personal pension of £300 a year, was his uncle. Rupert had the look of a Stuart but not the laziness; in fact, he was a human dynamo. He had already set himself upon a military career when his uncle raised his banner in Nottingham. Rupert decided it was his duty to rally to the king.

Rupert was an imposing figure. He was tall and usually clad in red velvet, complete with matching cape. For headgear he had a wide-brimmed beaver fur hat, a symbol of bravado and a statement of entitlement. He traded on his courage, leading unstoppable cavalry charges from the front. But his tactics were flawed, not entirely of his own making. Smashing through enemy lines, his force, mainly composed of 'gentlemen' unused to taking orders from anyone, charged on in pursuit of their fleeing enemy, and any plunder that might come their way.

In fact, there were few pitched battles in the Civil War that ensued, although there were plenty of sieges: of towns, castles, fortifications, even private houses. It was all a slow an indecisive grind in which Parliamentary forces, seemingly in awe of the idea of fighting their own king, were reluctant to push through on any advantage gained.

But in 1644 the tide changed decisively in favour of the Parliamentarians when its own talisman was unleashed. Oliver Cromwell had transformed himself from a committee warrior to an unstoppable battlefield force. His speciality was turning likely defeat into unlikely victory. His secret was religion. Through his 'Eastern Association' he had recruited an army of 'godly' men, Puritans who carried pocket bibles in their packs and marched into battle chanting psalms. Fanatics they might be, but they were also disciplined and well trained.

Cromwell's cavalry charges were measured. To the enemy they were an unstoppable steamroller, moving forward in close order as if one. But when through their immovable but now shattered foe, they did stop. They stopped, regrouped and charged again, and again, and again.

Rupert's charges were terrifying but were one-time events. Cromwell's were terrifying, demotivating, demoralising and decisive. No wonder Rupert christened Cromwell's cavalry 'Ironsides'.

The great clash of 1644, Marston Moor, saw the Royalists, Rupert among them, roundly defeated by a Parliamentary force bolstered by Scottish Covenanters. Naseby took place the following year. It was a decisive battle in which Parliament's New Model Army, a child of Easter Association recruitment, cut through the fog to all but destroy the Royalist Army, this time commanded by Prince Rupert.

Worse followed for the prince. He was forced to surrender Bristol, taken by the Royalists in 1643. The king, resident for most of the war in Oxford, was effectively cut off from hope of reinforcement by sea from Ireland. He turned on Rupert, one of his loyal and most successful commanders, who chose to resign his commission.

The following year Rupert was back, and back on reasonable terms with Charles; just in time to witness the final days of the king's stay in Oxford. The city was surrendered and in the process Prince Rupert and his brother Maurice, who had also fought for Charles throughout the war, were banished from the country (Prince Rupert will crop up again later with more direct consequences to William Phipps).

By the time Oxford surrendered, Charles had taken himself a hundred or so miles north, turning up in Southwell, Nottinghamshire, only fifteen miles or so from where he had raised his standard four years before. The town was ten miles from Newark-on-Trent, a strategically important town held by Royalists. It had been under siege from both English and Scottish armies for the previous six months.

French agents suggested to Charles that the Scottish Parliament was likely to offer him more favourable surrender terms than the English Parliament. He ordered Newark to surrender and placed himself in the hands of the Scots army.

But Charles continued to be a slippery customer and, despite his desperate position, would not agree to all that the Covenanters wanted. After nine months as their guest, he was handed over to the English Parliament. The Scots were exasperated and had accepted payment of amounts promised at the end of the 'Bishops' Wars' as their reward.

Charles knew that many considered a monarchy to be the natural order of things and were reluctant to get rid of him. Meanwhile the English Parliament, riven by its own divisions, was unable to control an increasingly radicalised army which refused to be disbanded or be deployed to Ireland until its backpay was settled.

Seeing all this, the king made a dash for freedom but ended up simply moving location: to the Isle of Wight. Now, with unrest and uncertainty in both Scotland and England, Charles let the Scots believe he was prepared to legislate to apply the Covenant to both England and Scotland. Reconciled to a constitutional monarchy, Scotland allowed a royalist force led by the Duke of Hamilton to march into England in support the king's cause. It was met and defeated by Cromwell at Preston.

Still the king prevaricated.

Finally, his actions convinced the English Parliament, Cromwell included, that there was no alternative but to remove him from the scene. As a king, Charles embodied the state, yet somehow his trial for treason against that state was a foregone conclusion. He was found guilty and executed in Westminster in January 1649. Three months later the Duke of Hamilton met the same fate.

Later that year Cromwell was sent to Ireland to sort out the continuing rebellion. The Catholic Confederacy still hung on despite the proximity, since 1641, of competing Parliamentary and Royalist forces.

It took Cromwell less than a year to take control. He used terror tactics, treating all Irish Catholics as enemies. He believed that they had committed atrocities during the rebellion and allowed his troops greater freedom of action than in England. It worked, and a succession of Irish towns surrendered rather than have their inhabitants put at the mercy of vengeful invaders.

The price for this success has been paid in the hatred and resentment that lay at the root of 'troubles' that have rumbled on ever since. It was made higher by the decision of the English Parliament to pay off some of its troublesome army with grants of land taken from displaced, disgruntled and now destitute former Catholic confederates.

When Cromwell returned to England, he soon faced more problems. England had abolished the monarchy, but Scotland had not. Instead, it decided to recognise Charles' son, also Charles, as its king. Charles II (of Scotland) had ditched his father's former Scottish Royalist supporters in favour of a new deal with the Covenanters, supporting a Presbyterian church in both Scotland and, on a trial basis, in England.

The Covenanters had changed sides.

Cromwell marched north, and in probably his most unlikely near-defeat-turn-triumph, smashed a much larger Scottish army at the 1651 Battle of Dunbar, fought on the coast east of Scotland. Leaving General Monck to clean up in Scotland, he then marched south to intercept an invasion force led by Charles II (of Scotland).

Charles had thought he had a clever plan. The Presbyterian church had a strong following in England (and its Parliament). Having already gathered his mainly Scottish forces south of Cromwell's position, he reasoned he could beat him in a race to London, picking up Presbyterian support along the way. He had reckoned without Oliver Cromwell. A year after Dunbar, Cromwell caught up with Charles at Worcester. The outcome was familiar. The Civil War was over, the Covenanters were no more and Charles II (of Scotland) scurried back to the Continent.

Parliament dithered and Cromwell became Lord Protector of the Commonwealth. Scotland was annexed and subdued by George Monck. Britain had in effect become a military dictatorship – a Puritan state that was in a state.

Estimates vary, but somewhere in the region of 200,000 people had died as a direct or indirect consequence of the seven years of conflict. Towns had been fortified, bombarded and sometimes repaired. Parts of the countryside had been laid waste, suffering from the effects of thousands of troops marching from north to south, east to west. Raising dust and steam, these hordes moved to the sound of drum and trumpet, huge columns trampling all before them. Behind came carts, carriages and waggons, all carving ruts into soft ground, making muddy ground even muddier. And behind them came more men, women, children and animals. And behind them a trail of discarded waste.

Signs of distress were everywhere. Homeless people begged, as did those who had been mutilated. Houses had been destroyed and estates confiscated. Those people left with somewhere to live were faced with higher taxes, much higher taxes, to be paid from dwindling incomes. Trade had suffered and agricultural output too.

Ironically, many Puritans had not stayed to witness what should have been a Puritan utopia. A mass exodus began in 1620 and continued for the next twenty years (further weakening the economy). Seeking religious freedom, and believing they were unlikely to achieve this in England, some 40,000 or so migrants had made the hazardous Atlantic crossing to America. Around half of these travelled to New England, an area along the north-east coast where they might live in peace in their own Puritan communities.

Many of these migrants came from East Anglia, Oliver Cromwell's neck of the woods, and it is said that he had at one time considered migrating there himself.[1.3] Other migrants came via Bristol. James Phipps, William's father, was one of them.

Chapter 2

Coming to America

WILLIAM'S FATHER HAD come to New England as part of the 'Great Migration' from England that took place between 1620 and 1640 – an influx that was led by dissatisfied Puritans looking for somewhere they could run their lives according to their own beliefs, without the interference of kings or bishops.

The English had been looking to settle in this part of America since Tudor times. The country thought it had the right to do so after the Elizabethan privateer and adventurer Sir Francis Drake had in 1579 'discovered' New Albion and claimed it for England. It was no matter that New Albion was on the west coast of America, in what is now California, nor that the land between west and east coasts was and had been for thousands of years inhabited by indigenous people.

As early as 1585 an attempt, backed by Sir Walter Raleigh (another Elizabethan adventurer, albeit less 'hands-on' than Drake), was made to establish a settlement on Roanoke Island off the coast of what is now North Carolina. The attempt failed, as did a follow-up two years later – a 'lost colony' of which no trace could later be found.

Subsequently two 'Virginia' companies obtained royal charters and were charged with establishing colonies along the north-east coast of America. These were essentially business ventures in which the crown had a stake. In fact, James I/VI was much criticised by Parliament for his enthusiasm for handing out charters and patents which allowed him a source of income free of parliamentary scrutiny.

Colonists were expected to buy their way in, paying their own travel costs, if necessary, raising the money by means of personal indentures. The adventurers behind the companies saw themselves as part evangelists, missionaries spreading the word of God to heathen communities (this was the excuse for trampling over the rights of said 'heathens'), and part economic warriors in search of the fabled northern sea route to the orient. Discovery of such a route would bring riches to England, to the companies behind the discovery and to the communities along its way.

Current contenders for possible routes included a north-east passage around the top of Scandinavia, a northern passage (it was suggested, despite evidence to the contrary, that the North Pole was surrounded by navigable and ice-free seas), and a north-west passage around the top of, or through, North America. This latter route, it was surmised, might be possible if there was, somewhere in the interior of America, a great lake from which flowed mighty rivers to both east and west. And Virginia just might be home to the eastern branch of such a river.

In 1607 the Virginia Company of London set down a settlement at Jamestown, about 140 miles north of Roanoke Island. The eight named subscribers to the company's charter included Richard Hakluyt, a cleric, mapmaker and author of *The Principal Navigations, Voyages, and Discoveries of the English Nation*, a massive and much added-to work. He championed English colonisation of north-east America and would have agreed, and may have suggested, that the stated aim of the Virginia adventurers be to bring the 'Christian Religion to such people, as yet live in darkness and miserable ignorance of the true knowledge and worship of God'.[2.1] (This was despite the fact that the native people of North America had a tradition of living together in sharing communities much closer to the ideals of early Christians than uptight Puritans ever achieved.)

Also in 1607, the Virginia Company of Plymouth tried to establish a settlement at the mouth of the Kennebec River, near the current town of Phippsburg, Maine. It was known as the Popham Colony after its first 'president' George Popham (a nephew of Virginia Company subscriber, Lord Chief Justice Sir John Popham, who in his capacity as judge had tried and sentenced to death both Mary Queen of Scots and Guy Fawkes, although not at the same time).[2.2] Both Jamestown and the Popham Colony struggled. After various disasters, Jamestown survived, but the Popham Colony, and George Popham himself, did not.

The land granted the two 'Virginia' companies in fact overlapped. That of the 'of London' company ran between Cape Fear, now North Carolina, and Long Island, now New York State. That of the 'of Plymouth' ran from near what is now Charlottesville, in Virginia, up to the 45th parallel, which runs through Nova Scotia. Thus, both companies had claims to the middle section of these territories which covered the coast from Charlottesville to Long Island. The 'of Plymouth' company had most of what is now known as 'New England'. These were the first of many conflicting charters, patents, grants, titles and claims to various American lands.

Closely associated to the 'of Plymouth' company was the exotically named Sir Ferdinando Gorges. The second son of a West Country family with aristocratic forebears and connections (these included Sir Walter Raleigh), Gorges had made his name as a soldier. Knighted for his valour, he gained the patronage of Queen Elizabeth favourite, the Earl of Essex. On the back of this Gorges became both a Member of Parliament and commander of the port defences at Plymouth. When Essex subsequently plotted against the ageing queen, and was beheaded for his troubles, Gorges suffered a temporary career setback that included loss of his Plymouth command. He was later reinstated.

Gorges' interest in New England had been sparked by his investment in a 1605 attempt to find the north-west passage mounted by Captain George Weymouth. The captain did not, of course, discover the fabled route to China, but did bring back a description of the coastline of Maine along with five kidnapped native Americans. Three of these he presented to Gorges.

Failure of the Popham Colony dented the immediate enthusiasm of many for further attempts to colonise New England. The interest of the Bristol merchants with whom Gorges mixed had moved on to Newfoundland, where there was the prospect of quicker financial reward from its fish-rich waters. And in 1610 the snappily named The Treasurer and Company of Adventurers and Planters of the Cities of London and Bristol for the Colony or plantations in Newfoundland obtained a charter from James I giving it monopoly rights to agriculture, mining, fishing and hunting over a large proportion of Newfoundland.

Gorges, however, was not done with New England. He realised it, too, had access to rich fishing grounds that were more easily accessible than those around Newfoundland and could be fished for more months of the year.

In 1620 he managed to engineer surrender of the original 'Virginia' charter covering northern New England and to have himself granted a replacement. Operating as the 'Council for New England', it was given a huge area many times the size of England: all that lay between the 40th and 48th parallels, from east coast to west.

Gorges took £100 from each of his forty subscribers but otherwise did not attempt to raise funds for the huge task of developing this vast area. He seemed to believe his company would prosper through the sale of land and fishing rights. The latter brought him into direct conflict with Bristol merchants who objected to and challenged his right to sell fishing licences that entitled the council to a portion of catches.[2.3]

Meanwhile Gorges had forged some sort of arrangement with John Mason, a mariner and former North Sea pirate who, by 1620, had become a pirate-hunter. The two men were friends despite Mason's appointment in 1615 by the Bristol Society of Merchant Venturers as governor of their tiny Newfoundland (Cuper's Cove) colony. In this role he presumably championed the Bristol merchants' fishing rights. However, the two men had a shared interest in defence of English south coast ports. Mason had a long association with the English naval port of Portsmouth, Hampshire, which lies along the coast from Gorges' Plymouth.

Almost as soon as the Council for New England was formed, Gorges and Mason obtained patents from it for all the land lying between the Merrimack and Kennebec rivers. They divided the spoils between themselves, Mason taking, and going on to found New Hampshire, Gorges claiming Maine.

Gorges was a product of the Tudor age. He was a staunch Royalist who couched his dreams of financial reward through colonisation in patriotic terms. His disputes with hard-nosed Bristol merchants were among the factors which prevented him realising these dreams. The history of the Council of New England was largely one of a long, losing battle to enforce its rights against more energetic and active interlopers and competing claimants.

The Puritan connection with New England had started with the Pilgrim Fathers. Sailing on the *Mayflower*, members of a congregation that had first fled to the Netherlands decided to try their luck in New England. In 1620 they had arrived, somewhat unexpectedly to the north or their intended destination, in a bay they were to name Plymouth.

Theirs was the first land patent granted by Gorges' newly formed Council of New England. It was issued in 1621 to one John Pierce, in trust for the Plymouth colony. A previous 'Pierce Patent' had been issued by the Virginia Company (of London) on whose land the Pilgrims had originally intended to settle.

Many of the settlers had arrived 'weak and feeble through the length of the navigation, the leakiness of the ship, and want of many other necessaries such undertakings required', Gorges wrote in his *A brief narration of the original undertakings for the advancement of plantations in America*. But the Pilgrims soon returned to health and found the place 'so prosperous and pleasing to them' that they decided to ask the Council of New England if they could stay. It was agreed and 'they have continued ever since very peaceable, and in all plenty of all necessaries that nature needeth'.

Ten years later a much larger and more sustained migration began, both fuelled and empowered by Charles I. It was his 'Eleven Year Tyrany' and the unwanted attentions of his Archbishop William Laud that drove many to head off to America. And it was the 1628 charter that he awarded the Massachusetts Bay Company that gave them the right to settle in New England (again muddying the land entitlement waters).

Start of this second period of migration was marked with the arrival of the 'Winthrop Fleet', eleven ships that brought with them more than 1,000 settlers – families, possessions and livestock, and their own charter for a Massachusetts Bay Colony (complete with competing land rights). When leaving Southampton they had been given a farewell sermon by John Cotton, grandfather of Cotton Mather, of whom more later.

A leading figure after whom the flotilla was named was John Winthrop, a committed Puritan. Taking a lead from the bible,[2.4] he talked of founding a community 'as a city upon a hill' in which 'the eyes of all people are upon us' – in other words a Puritan example of the ways things should be done.[2.5]

A few years later John Cotton also turned up in Boston where he did in fact build himself a house on a hill, now known as Mount Cotton.

Soon there were not just one or two ships making the hazardous journey from England to New England. Ships such as the *Blessing*, *Charity*, *Confidence*, *Elizabeth*, *Fellowship*, *Hopewell*, *Planter* and the *James* made repeated crossings. Each time they brought fifty, sixty, seventy, eighty, ninety or more settlers.[2.6] In the twenty years of the migration, but mainly in the last ten, up to 20,000 people crossed the Atlantic in pursuit of a new life in New England. In the main the second-wave migrants were indifferent to the prospect of finding a north-west passage. Not all were Puritans, although a good proportion were. Not all went for religious reasons, but many did.

Their journey was far from easy. The ships were generally small, little more than vessels that today would be classed as boats or yachts. On departure they would have been filled to the gunwales with people, both passengers and crew. There would have been animals too: chickens, pigs, sheep, goats and cows in cages and pens. Sanitary and sleeping arrangements would have been rudimentary and all would be obliged to share their space with coiled ropes, spare spars and sails. There would have been barrels too, of water, small beer, salted meat, dried peas and beans, of seed corn, gunpowder and lead shot.

In rough weather it would not have been only the ships that heaved – the frightened passengers too. Banned from the deck, those below would nevertheless have suffered a soaking by sea and foam splashing through open or ill-fitting hatches and from sodden seamen seeking refuge from what was happening above. The would-be settlers, their crying children and baying and barking animals would have sat freezing and shivering in the gloom, waiting for the storm to pass. Neither were these vessels easy to handle. They were mostly square rigged, meaning they could not sail too close to the wind but were obliged to travel where the wind directed. To reduce sail, seaman would have to climb the rigging and edge along toe-ropes strung below the yardarms from which the sails were hung, balancing themselves while clinging on and pulling in and tying down the thrashing canvas.

Accidents were not infrequent and anybody falling overboard would be lost to the world in seconds. Illness, too, was a visitor, with dysentery, the 'bloody flux' and scurvy mounting constant threats.

One of those who braved such a crossing was James Phipps. The 1998 biography of William Phipps, *The New England Knight*, reports that before leaving England James had been apprenticed to Bristol blacksmith, and probably gunsmith, John Brown, and that he travelled to Pemaquid with Brown.[2.7] If so, he would have travelled with his 'master' as an unmarried indentured apprentice of about fifteen or sixteen.[2.8, 2.9]

Pemaquid, later known as Bristol, had been visited by merchant ships sailing out of Bristol, England, since the early 1600s. It stood on land granted Gorges in his 1620 patent from the Council of New England, but this did not stop John Brown of New Harbor buying, in 1625, land with boundaries that extended over twenty-five miles (the same ground on which the towns of Bristol and Damariscotta now stand). The sellers were two Indian chiefs, and the price fifty beaver pelts.[2.10]

This is confirmed in Charles Pope's *The Pioneers of Maine and New Hampshire*[2.11] which reported that John Brown of New Harbor, Pemaquid, had in 1625 bought from an Indian named Somerset or Samoset 'a tract of land extending from Pemaquid Falls to the head of New Harbor, thence to the south end of Muscongus island, running into the country north and by east 25 miles, then twenty eight miles northwest and by west, then south and by west to Pemaquid'.

It goes on to say that Brown's son, also John Brown, in 1720, when about 85 years old, testified that he had lived with his father at New Harbor, near Pemaquid, until he was about 30 years old.

Brown is a common name and there were certainly other Browns in New England. But the Pemaquid Brown of 1625 seems to be the same man who, around ten years later, bought a large tract of land from another chief. Mowhotiwormet (nicknamed 'Robin Hood' by the English) was the seller and one hogshead of corn and thirty pumpkins was the price. For this Brown became the owner of a plot extending from the Kennebec to Sheepscot River, including the land on which the town of Woolwich now stands.

This 'Nequasseag' (or 'Nequasset') land transaction was in partnership with fellow 'Pemaquid planter' Edward Bateman. Brown and Bateman soon sold on part of their holding on the western side of the Sheepscot to James Phipps (Brown's former apprentice?) and John White. James was around 27 or 28 at the time. Later, Major Thomas Clarke and Captain Thomas Lake of Boston bought other land in Nequasseag from Brown and Bateman.[2.12]

Phipps and White set about building homes and improving their land. They had chosen to live in an out-of-the-way place, a true frontier settlement of a few houses and a trading post, adjoining Indian territory and not too far from French settlements.

A few years later (1665) Samuel Maverick, a commissioner sent from England, reported that 'upon three rivers, the East of Kennebeck, Shipscot and

Pemaquid, are three plantations – the greatest has not above 20 houses – and they are inhabited by the worst of men; they have no Government, and have fled thence from punishment; for the most part they are fishermen, and share in their wives as they do in their boats'.[2.13]

True or not, James had clearly decided not to rely too heavily on his gunsmithing skills. Indians used the rivers as their highways but otherwise there was not much passing trade and probably little call for fine engraving.

But as a skilled wood- and metalworker, James had what today would be called 'multiple income streams' available to him. He would have fished, collected oysters, clams and other shellfish from the river, farmed and hunted. He almost certainly traded in beaver pelts and other goods with local Algonquin-speaking Indians, to whom, like the trading post run by Richard Hammond, he would have been both supplier and customer. Baker and Reid believe that James and his partner White were much involved in the fur trade, as to start with were Major Thomas Clarke and Captain Thomas Lake, trading from their holding across the river on Arrowsic island. James could certainly have kept in good order and if necessary repaired various implements and tools, including knives and scythes, ploughs and hoes, beaver traps and guns.

Even at this time, flintlock firearms were in everyday use in Maine by both settlers and Indians, who seemed to have had no trouble in circumventing an official ban on the sale of firearms to native New Englanders. Although the Indians were skilled at using bows and arrows, the ease of their use, even in wet weather, was outweighed by the greater range and killing power of muskets and blunderbusses. The heavy matchlock muskets used in the English Civil War, that required their own stands and had 'old-fashioned' firing mechanisms, were too cumbersome for hunting. But long-barrelled and lighter-gauged (and lighter overall) 'fowling pieces' were deadly in skilled hands. As was the shorter-ranged blunderbuss, in effect a flare-barrelled shotgun. To be fired, these guns had to be loaded with black powder, gunpowder, rammed into their barrels and placed in their priming pans. Lead shot of appropriate calibre had to be pushed on top of the gunpowder, followed by a wad to keep all in place. Flints had to be kept sharp and replaced as necessary.

James Phipps may well have traded in all that was needed, perhaps producing his own shot from ingots of lead. It could be that his constant handling of this poisonous metal contributed to his own early death (although there would not have been a shortage of other possible causes, including cuts, broken bones, burns and diseases).

In the meantime, he had married, probably a year or two before buying his tract of land. Although James would have been in his mid-twenties, his wife Mary would have been younger, perhaps only sixteen. They soon had their first child, the first of many, if Cotton Mather is to be believed. James' 'fruitful' wife, he said, 'had no less than twenty-six children, whereof twenty-one were sons.'[2.14] The figure is improbable, if not impossible, even if Mather was counting miscarriages and stillborn births. As far as is known James and Mary had six children: John, James, William, Mary, Margaret and Ann.

Why Mather should give the obviously wrong figure is unknown. But in the killjoy Puritan world, sex (or 'breeding' as Oliver Cromwell would have it), not for pleasure but for procreation, was considered a necessity.[2.15] People were begetting people everywhere, which helps account for the steady growth in the population of New England even after the 'Great Migration' had come to an end. So, perhaps Mather only wanted to emphasise the diligence with which William's parents fulfilled their godly duties. Perhaps he was just shocked by the number of children that apparently ran around the Phipps' homestead, not all of whom would have been the Phipps' own children.

James and Mary, probably with the help of James' business partner John White, built themselves a log cabin and settled down to family life. The site of this structure is known and has been excavated. The cabin was substantial. 'The core consisted of a fifteen by seventy-two-foot longhouse, probably divided into four rooms, with the southernmost twelve by fifteen foot section probably serving as a byre,' say Baker and Reid.[2.16] 'A second episode of construction made the building L-shaped. Perhaps providing an attached second home so that both Phips and White would have their own discrete living spaces'.

The addition made to the property was considerable, being twenty by sixty foot and was 'more substantially built' than the original cabin. There was also an outbuilding measuring almost thirty foot by fifteen. But the windows were not glazed, say Baker and Reid. Perhaps the family did not have the means to pay for such 'luxury', having to make do with shutters in the bitter Maine winters (when temperatures can and do dip below -10°F).

Backwoodsmen Phipps and White built their homes out of the materials available to those able to pay with no more than hard work. They would have felled and shaped trees, of which there were an abundance, stripped and cut bark, dug and splattered mud to seal cracks and joints.

However substantial the cabin, living inside might have reminded James of his shipboard experiences crossing the Atlantic when he was cold, wet and uncomfortable. Within the four rooms of the original building, children and adults would have shared their space with animals, with supplies, and probably with traps and firearms. Cooking and heating, at first at least, would have been by means of an open fire. Water was only available cold, from a well, the river or from melted snow. Lighting was by means of candles and nobody would have had their own room in which to sleep.

These were tough people, pursuing a tough life. There might be meetings with some of the few neighbours in the area, perhaps an occasional religious service in somebody's house. But in the main, locals were on their own and more or less beyond the law.

Puritan communities required parents to educate their children, which to them meant teaching them to read, memorise and recite the bible. No such requirement seems to have reached Woolwich. The Phipps children would have been expected to contribute to the daily struggle to stay alive, but otherwise would have been free to run wild.

For William this would have been even more the case when James Phipps died in his late forties, leaving a widow and six children. William's biographer Alice Lounsberry puts the future knight at 6 years old when this happened, so about 1657.[2.17]

It was the first of a series of seismic events in the life of William Phipps.

Chapter 3

Living the Dream

WILLIAM PHIPPS WAS born in early 1651 'at a despicable plantation on the river Kennebec, and almost the furthest village of the eastern settlement of New England'. So said his first biographer, Cotton Mather.[3.1]

Mather was a second-generation New England Puritan clergyman, a member of a family of well-known clerics, and a bit of a snob who lived in the relative comfort of Boston. He was a contemporary of Phipps, being some thirteen years younger, and had known William personally through his many dealings with Cotton's father, Increase Mather.

The younger Mather had his own agenda: to emphasise the self-made-man-made-good side of Phipps; somebody who with the help of God, had rocketed from obscurity to wealth and prominence. In fact, this was pretty much Phipps' story anyway (except the god bit and some illicit trading), but Cotton couldn't help but over-egg his eulogy.

Phipps was a more complex and sophisticated individual than Mather imagined, and more of a ruffian than he cared to admit (although even he conceded that Phipps 'was of an inclination cutting rather like a hatchet than like a razor').[3.2]

Phipps may not have been able to spout Latin phrases as Mather was prone to do, but he had animal cunning. And he seems to have used religion as a stepping stone rather than somebody of conviction driven by faith. He relied mostly on his self-belief in practical solutions to life.

The place of his birth was undoubtedly remote and rustic. It was 'on a point of land in the southern part of the town of Woolwich, near a little bay, called "Phips' Bay" and was not in any sense a "despicable" place', said a 1924 treatise, *Three Men From Maine.*[3.3]

Indeed, many might say that William had the childhood any boy would want. Living in almost settler-free Maine, he was unencumbered by school or church. Instead, he was free to make the most of rivers and brooks, fields and forests, to hunt and fish, discover the ways of the wild (and how to survive them) and to befriend children from other cultures and races. And all without washing.

Of course, his life was tough and fraught with many dangers and hardships. But although he could not read, he inhabited a library of natural knowledge, a university offering a myriad of exciting life-skill courses. And when confronted by something he did not know or understand, the bewildered Phipps got by with bluster and bravado.

It probably suited Cotton Mather's agenda no end to describe William Phipps as a 'shepherd'. After his father died, William lived with his mother 'keeping of sheep in the wilderness', said Mather. The inference of a start made to a path to 'righteousness' is unmissable. That William did indeed look after his mother's sheep may even have been true. A good many colonists did keep sheep. By the time William was old enough to take up shepherding, there were a few thousand roaming Massachusetts pastures.[3.4] In fact, livestock and how they were allowed to wander about was a major bone of contention with the local Indian people, one which came to a head some years later. William Phipps probably did spend some of his early years as a shepherd, guarding his widowed mother's few Wiltshire or Romney Marsh sheep from wolves, bears and possible thieves. All were to be found in the extensive New England forests comprising a vast array of tree species, both hardwoods and softwoods. They included cedars and maples, firs and pines, larch, spruce and birch, ash and elm, cherry and chestnuts.

It would not have been an easy job for a child to mind sheep. Perhaps armed with no more than a stick, it meant spending hours alone in the fields. But it cannot have been year-round work. For a good bit of the year the fields were covered in snow and the sheep housed in the Phipps' byre.

With a family to support and a farm to run, and probably mindful of the need for protection from Indians and opportunists, Mary soon remarried. The man she wed was James' old business partner John White, so no change of home was needed.

The 'fruitful' Mary eventually gave John eight children of his own. The extended homestead must have been awash with the couple's extended family, both young children and adults, as well as themselves. Shared with animals, supplies and equipment, boiling pots, hanging pelts and drying skins, and ruled over by a serially pregnant matriarch, the place was a working hub that would seldom have been still.

An inventory of the farm, compiled some years later, lists ten bushels of wheat already sown, two bushels of 'Indian corn' also already in the ground, along with nine bushels of peas. The farm had seventeen head of cattle, sixteen 'swine' and one horse. There was no mention of sheep.[3.5]

Among this medley of flesh, feed and seed, William would have found his feet. One of so many, he fought his way through his childhood into early manhood. Had, at this point, he contemplated the past few years, he would have marvelled at the changes since his father had arrived in New England.

The high rate of immigration had eased since around 1640. Even so, the number of 'English' living in New England had continued to rise. By 1668 it had reached around 40,000 people, only around half of whom had arrived by boat, the remainder being born in New England. The population of Native Americans, on the other hand, had collapsed.

As soon as Europeans began visiting the north-east coast of America, its native peoples started dying. The most devastating decline took place in the 'late few years' before 1620 when King James I of England signed his charters for 'Virginia', allowing for governance of the colonies founded there to be conducted in Plymouth and London. The king did not express sympathy at such events, but delight: 'There hath by God's Visitation reigned a wonderfull Plague, together with many horrible Slaugthers, and Murthers, committed amoungst the Sauages and brutish People there, heertofore inhabiting, in a Manner to the utter Destruction, Deuastacion, and Depopulacion of that whole Territorye, so that there is not left for many Leagues together in a Manner, any that doe claime or challenge any Kind of Interests therein, nor any other Superiour Lord or Souveraigne to make Claime hereunto, whereby We in our Judgment are persuaded and satisfied that the appointed Time is come in which Almighty God in his great Goodness and Bountie towards Us and our People, hath thought fitt and determined, that those large and goodly Territoryes, deserted as it were by their naturall Inhabitants, should be possessed and enjoyed by such of our Subjects and People as heertofore have and hereafter shall by his Mercie and Favour, and by his Powerfull Arme, be directed and conducted thither.'[3.6]

The truth was that the Pilgrim Fathers did not bring salvation with them but death. The native population had no resistance to plague or pox, nor even to the common cold. And the dying continued. Writing from Boston in 1634, John Winthrop, of 'Winthrop Fleet' fame, reported that the city had a well-provided-for population of 4,000 but that 'for the natives, they are near all dead of the smallpox, so the Lord hath cleared our title to what we possess'.[3.7]

As the local Wabanaki and related people became less noticeable (in Boston it was the Massachusett people who were disappearing), the English settlers advanced, shaping the countryside to their own tastes and needs. Trees were felled for burning and building, more clearings were made in the forest for agriculture, plots were fenced and new homesteads built. Paths became tracks that became roads, game became harder to hunt. Beavers, whose pelts yielded much income, became scarcer. Lacking the attention of these dam-building rodents, streams became swamps. Free-roaming cattle trampled their way through the countryside, eating unfenced Indian crops. Pigs excavated with their noses, digging into Indian food storage pits.

William would have noticed that gradually there was more movement on the river. Where once Indians in birch-bark canoes might occasionally have paddled by, now there were frequently shallops or pinnaces, trading vessels bringing supplies from further up or down the coast, or taking them there. And local settlers would have had their own boats, perhaps made by themselves, perhaps acquired in a trade. Besides fishing for sturgeon, shad, bass and salmon, the settlers now had somewhere to go.

As new settlers arrived in the area, they often chose to make their homes next to the network of rivers that crisscrossed the fragmented coastline. And from 1654, across the river on Arrowsic Island, Clarke and Lake were busy developing their holding.[3.8] Usurping a traditional Indian meeting spot, the two soon moved on from reliance on the beaver-skin trade to a more sustainable business model. They knew they were in possession of a strategically placed holding with river access to the interior and its wood and other natural resources. Downstream was Pemaquid and the sea. In return for beaver and moose skins, the two Boston businessmen traded knives, kettles, textiles, and other goods with Indians and settlers, says Emerson Baker in his *The Historical Archaeology Of A Seventeenth-Century Maine Settlement*.[3.9] But the number of beavers in the area was in decline, so Clarke and Lake planned to establish a new community around their fortified trading post. They mapped out lots available to settlers. They built tide-powered sawmills that converted local timber into planks and posts, and they added a shipyard. They employed a workforce of lumberjacks, carpenters and other craftsmen, besides fishermen allowing them to feed their workers. Clearly, they saw a long-term future in the area.

Chapter 4

Unforgotten and Unforgiven

KING CHARLES II was not a vindictive man. Or so he tried to give the impression in his *Declaration of Breda*. This was a proclamation, a written promise, made in 1660 by Charles before returning to England to claim its throne. It stated, among much more, that crimes committed during the Civil War and Cromwell's protectorate would be forgiven and that property rights established in those times would be respected.

In the aftermath of the Civil War, Oliver Cromwell had, in 1653, been appointed 'lord protector' (of the commonwealth of England, Scotland and Ireland). He continued as such until his death in 1658, aged fifty-nine. William Phipps was 7 years old at the time.

Cromwell had overseen a more liberal than expected regime that was making headway in recovery from the ravages of war. Pleased with his performance, Parliament had, in 1657, offered to make him king. Cromwell turned it down. His death, probably from complications arising from kidney disease, left a more than difficult recruitment problem. Cromwell's son Richard had a go at filling his father's massive shoes but failed. He was briefly put in charge but resigned in 1659. Many thought that George Monck, Cromwell's enforcer, would make a suitable successor, and should be appointed not lord protector but king. Monck would have none of it. He wanted a Stuart on the throne. And since he had an army at his beck and call, people tended to listen.

And so it was that Charles Stuart was invited to return to England as king. Of course, there were dissenters and many who sought some sort of guarantee from Charles about his future behaviour. His *Declaration of Breda* came in this context, helping to clear his way to the throne. By August 1660 Charles was indeed king, and able to give royal assent to the *Indemnity and Oblivion Act (An Act of Free and General Pardon, Indemnity, and Oblivion)*, an early attempt at truth and reconciliation based on Charles' earlier declaration. Unfortunately, the 'general pardon' was not general at all. It certainly said it forgave everyone who had committed crimes during the Civil War and the protectorate that followed, everyone except, obviously, 'any Jesuit Seminary or Romish Priest', and those who had committed crimes such as 'Buggery.; Rapes, and wilful taking away any Maid, &c.; Bigamy; Witchcraft.; Accounts of certain Treasurers and Receivers', and except for a list of named individuals.[4.1] The list had been the subject of much Parliamentary debate and had been added to considerably. It consisted, in the main, of over a hundred people who had been directly involved in the trial and execution of Charles l, the so-called 'regicides'.

Some of these, Oliver Cromwell included, had been sensible enough to have already died. They were dug up and cut up, and their putrefying heads stuck on pikes for all to see. Some of those still living were soon arrested, tried and imprisoned or hung up and cut up, with their heads placed on pikes. Twenty-one got away, taking themselves off to Holland, or Germany, or Switzerland or New England. In fact, only three regicides escaped to New England. Colonel Edward Whalley (who had fought in Cromwell's army at the battles of Marston Moor, Naseby and Dunbar), his son-in-law Colonel William Goffe, and John Dixwell. All three had been members of the High Court of Justice which convicted and sentenced Charles I. They lived in hiding and were never caught.[4.2]

That New England should be harbouring any regicides must have been one of the many things that irked Charles about his North American colonies. Another was that so many Puritans had decided to run there to avoid his father's calamitous regime. There they had established their own Puritan laws and pursued and imbedded their own Puritan customs and prejudices. Not all settlers agreed entirely with the ways things were in New England, but enough did to have created a community which by accepted convention was as good as run by Puritan ministers, men such as the Cottons and the Mathers.

Not only that, in the near-on twenty years since the start of the English Civil War (followed by Cromwell's protectorate), the New Englanders, and the Massachusetts Bay Colony in particular, had displayed a wilful independence. They had developed their own trade in obvious contradiction to English shipping and trading interests. They had even minted, and continued to mint their own money, in flagrant disregard of Charles II's royal prerogative.

As long ago as 1652 the Massachusetts Bay Colony had authorised John Hull (not the first husband of Phipps' wife but another 'John Hull') and his chosen assistant Robert Sanderson to mint silver coins. It proved a brilliant move. Up to this point the colony had suffered from lack of ready money. There was no coinage to be had except for Spanish pieces of eight, and the colony was largely reduced to surviving as a barter economy, severely hampered when it came to buying anything from England, or anywhere else outside the colony for that matter. No doubt Cotton Mather would have compared the miracle of John Hull's operation to the feeding of the five thousand.

The mint had no silver of its own but operated on a 'while you wait' basis. Settlers could bring along their battered silver plates, their dented silver mugs, or bent silver spoons. Hull would assess whatever came in for its silver content, smelt it, and stamp out an appropriate number of coins.

Suddenly settlers were searching drawers and under beds for forgotten utensils, chains, buckles and buttons. People who had stolen goods to hide, smugglers, privateers and pirates for example, had a ready-made money-laundering service. From nowhere, New Englanders had enough, or nearly enough, ready money to get the local economy moving.

John Hull charged one shilling per twenty for his work, a level of reward which made him a rich man, reputedly the richest in the colony, and allowed him to accumulate shipping, trading and farming interests. It is said that when his daughter married, he gave as her dowry her own weight in pine tree shillings.[4.3]

It is also said, perhaps with even less authority, that when Charles II expressed his anger at the disregard for his exclusive right to mint coins, it was suggested that the image of a tree imprinted on pine tree shillings was in fact a mark of respect. It was in remembrance of his own famous escape to the Continent after the Battle of Worcester. It was then that he had been obliged to hide from Parliamentary pursuers in the branches of a tree: in fact an oak rather than a pine. This had happened in 1651, a year before Hull began his mint.

The law of unexpected consequences had a happy surprise for the Massachusetts community. The silver content of Hull's shillings was set at three-quarters that of an English shilling. The idea was that nobody would think it worth exporting or melting down the coins for their silver content. Perhaps this was the case. But in a world where traders were well used (and equipped) to valuing coins of any currency by the weight and purity of their precious metal content, this move also meant that Massachusetts had deliberately debased and devalued its own currency. Its imports became more expensive and its exports cheaper (to buy in foreign, more expensive currency). Inflation, the bedfellow of expansion, was induced and Boston took on the mantle of a bustling, prosperous, mercantile port.

And then the Restoration came along. In his enthusiasm for his new job, Charles might very well want to do something about the independence that the Massachusetts Puritans were enjoying. As a matter of prudence, and in the hope of otherwise being left alone, agents Simon Bradstreet (destined to become governor of the Massachusetts Bay Colony in 1679) and John Norton were sent to England to pledge the colony's loyalty to the new king.

Charles responded by saying he was ready to confirm the colony's charter. As in other parts of his kingdom, Massachusetts should now conduct its official business in the king's name. He also expected the colony to ease back on its strict religious stance by allowing use of the *Book of Common Prayer*, and by doing away with an insistence that church membership should be the criterion for the right to vote. And all Massachusetts colonists should be asked to pledge an oath of allegiance to the king.

The colony's general court, committed to maintaining its independence, was not impressed. It accepted some things might have to change, but it would make sure the process was not made easy. It agreed to use of revised letterheads so as to acknowledge the king but made no other immediate changes.

Nothing in New England would have pleased Charles more than the remittances he received. These needed to be protected at all costs. He needed to respond in some way to the rebuff but also to keep Massachusetts onside. He, or his advisers, hit by accident or design upon a plan that would bring the feisty New Englanders back into line without jeopardising the income they provided. Their claims of self-governance were an affront. He would set up enquiries into how the colonies were run. The findings were more than likely to give him enough to justify withdrawal or amendment of existing charters, and to impose his authority on New England by appointing his own administrators.

New England land rights were in a mess, and this gave Charles just the excuse to intervene that he was looking for.

Some settlers had obtained titles to their holdings via charter holders, some by royal grant. Others had made direct purchases from Native Americans. These titles had been 'registered' with municipal authorities that had no legal right to require registration or to maintain registries. Various charters, some royal, some not, some personal, some corporate, had been granted over many years. Often these paid little or no regard to previously or even contemporaneously granted land rights.

As pointed out earlier, land granted the two 'Virginia' companies in fact overlapped, both having claims to that between Charlottesville and Long Island. But that was not all. Grants had been made in the early 1600s to benefactors who had been unable to take them up with any success. The result was that new grants had superseded the old, although the old were not necessarily withdrawn or surrendered. Now that New England was enjoying some economic success, old claims were being resurrected by claimants, or claimants' heirs. The 'Gorges' claim was a prime example of what had been going on and of its lasting consequences. Sir Ferdinando Gorges, who never actually visited America but had at one time been appointed absentee Governor of New England, had a disputed claim to ownership of Maine dating back to 1620.

There was no shortage of 'governors' in colonial America and Gorges' title, granted in 1635 when he was 70 years old, was effectively no more than that: a title. By the time he was given it, his energy, health and money had run out and he was no more than an irritating curiosity to the settlers who lived in and ran New England. He had been a leading investor in the Virginia company 'of Plymouth' and later a successor company he created, the Council for New England. And in 1639 Charles I had confirmed his claim to land formally allotted to him by that company, land 'which is still called the County of Maine'. But Gorges' attempts at governing Maine through agents had been half-hearted and ineffectual and Maine settlers eventually agreed to throw in their lot with the colony of Massachusetts. This did not stop Gorges' heirs, and those of his friend and business partner John Mason, in their pursuit of an American inheritance.

There were other disputes involving Rhode Island, Connecticut and even Newfoundland. And then there was the little matter of the then very recent Atherton Company scandal and the subsequent refusal of shareholders to let matters rest (of which there is more later).

All this must have been music to Charles II's ears. In 1664, with Massachusetts showing no signs of abandoning its self-governing claims, commissioners Colonel Richards Nicolls, Sir Robert Carr, George Cartwright and Samuel Maverick were instructed 'to visit the several colonies of New England'. Here they were to 'examine and determine all complaints and appeals in all causes, as well military as criminal and civil, and proceed in all things for settling the peace and security of that country according to their discretions and such instructions as they receive from the King in that behalf'.[4.4]

Appointment of the commission was something of a fishing expedition. The New Englanders had had a good run at 'self-governing' status. They had tested their independence to the full and the 'old guard' at least had doggedly pursuit their Puritan dream. But the Restoration had marked a turning point. Charles was prepared to act cautiously, at first, but was determined to exercise greater oversight of his American colonies. He wanted control, he wanted religious freedom (which to him would have meant an end to Puritan dominance), he wanted to collect all the customs duties to which he believed himself entitled, and he wanted the New Englanders to observe the *Navigation Acts* and stop competing with English interests. In other words, he wanted subservience.

The commission was itself a means of control, with Nicolls, Carr, Cartwright and Maverick empowered to make judicial decisions that the New Englanders, and the Massachusetts Bay Colonists in particular, thought were theirs to make. But all was to be done diplomatically with emphasis placed on not upsetting the colonists (for now, at least). In the meantime, the commission was to collect information about the colonies and their governance.

Besides their publicly acknowledged instructions, the commissioners had been given 'secret instructions' which ordered them to assess the true state of the colonies and 'to reduce the people to obedience to the King's Government'. They were also 'to press the Governor to call a General Assembly, and to do their utmost to have members chosen who are most inclined to promote the King's service'.[4.5] And they were to gain control of Long Island, recently gifted to the Duke of York but at that moment in the hands of the Dutch.

The king wrote directly to the governor and council of the Massachusetts Bay Colony assuring them of his good intentions. He had, he said, sent commissioners 'to take a view of the good Government there' so that he could 'better judge what he is to do either for the better repairing of any thing that is amiss, or the better improving and encouragement of what is good'. The commissioners, he said, had been sent to dispel 'unreasonable jealousies and malicious calumnies' which had led some to suggest Massachusetts colonists 'do not submit to his Majesty's Government, but look upon themselves as independent upon us and our laws, and that the King has not confidence in their affection and obedience'.

He assured the colonists that he had no intention of violating or 'in the least degree infringing their charter or restraining the liberty of conscience thereby allowed'. He also wrote in similar terms to the Colony of Connecticut.

Charles' commissioners duly made their rounds of the colonies, taking evidence and reaching their conclusions. When it came to Massachusetts Bay, they had met something of a brick wall. The colony's governing General Court had protested that 'instead of being governed by rulers of our own choosing (which is the fundamental privilege of our patent) and by laws of our own, we are like to be subjected to the arbitrary power of strangers, proceeding, not by any established law, but by their own discretions'.[4.6]

Seeing this reaction, Charles summoned Massachusetts to send agents to London where questions raised by his commissioners could be discussed more fully. Massachusetts declined the 'invitation'. If this infuriated the king and his government, it did not show. It did not show because their attention was elsewhere. There was plague, a 'Great Fire', war with the Dutch and secret and other treaties to occupy their not-too-robust working days. Charles' initial resolve to bring the Massachusetts Bay Colony to heel had dissipated for now.

Chapter 5

Boston Bound

WHEN 18 (in 1669), William Phipps decided it was time to learn a trade. He had received no formal education and was probably unable to read or write. But he was not without ambition and realised that to go places he needed the start that a qualification or two would give him. His chosen trade was that of carpenter and shipwright. And he probably elected to serve his four-year apprenticeship with Clarke & Lake.

Cotton Mather was almost beside himself with joy at the choice. 'His first contrivance was to bind himself an apprentice unto a ship carpenter for four years: in which time he became master of the trade that once, in a vessel of more than fifty thousand tons, repaired the ruins of the earth: Noah's I mean'.[5.1]

No sooner had William mastered his trade, than he took himself off to Boston. Perhaps he went of his own accord to seek his fortune, perhaps he went at the behest of Clarke & Lake. He almost certainly made the trip in a company ship. It may have been the first time he had been to sea.

Woolwich had become relatively prosperous, but Phipps would have been astounded at what he found on arrival in Boston. It was now a thriving coastal port with a population of around 4,000. William would have been taken aback by the number. Working at Clarke & Lake he might have been one of fifty or so employees. But here, there were so many people, and not all wearing deerskins, canvas or leather work clothes or aprons. There were men in black coats and white stockings, tall black hats upon their heads. And women in starched white bonnets and tailored dresses, the like of which he had never seen.

And there were horses. So many horses pulling carts and laden waggons, even fine carriages. Some of the streets were cobbled and the houses were not log cabins but two-storey clapperboard constructions, with pitched and tiled roofs. There were even one or two brick-build houses.

The harbourside would have been busy, with workmen carting sacks and bales, rolling barrels to and from warehouses. There would have been others making nets and cordage, the beginnings of a ropemaking trade that was to become important for the growing town. In the harbour there were ships, the size of which would have impressed him no end – high-sided vessels fit for voyages to England and the Caribbean or beyond. Ships such as the *Dove*, a ketch making the round trip to Nevis and back, the *Society*, a ketch owned by John Hull, bound for Bristol, England, or perhaps one of the ships owned by the Gillams, a Boston family of seafarers and shipwrights.

The sound and smell of it all would have been intoxicating. The splashing of oars, the cracking of unfurled canvas and the calls of seabirds would have been accompanied by the aroma of rotting food, of horse manure, of fish, and of pitch to coat the hulls of ships, and of much more.

Boston, known to the Indians as Shawmut, had been given its colonial name by John Winthrop who, after first landing at Salem, had eventually led most of his fellow settlers there.[5.2]

William would have headed first to the 'north end' of the town that lay immediately behind its natural harbour. The North Square, where the Mathers oversaw the Second Church meeting house, was the centre of the district. It was here that Thomas Lake lived in a house assessed in the 1676 list of Boston taxpayers as worth £150, one of the highest values recorded. (He also had 'one cowe' but no horses, swine or sheep.)[5.3]

'The town pump was there, and one of the earliest marketplaces, and after the building of the church the residences of the most influential parishioners clustered about it or were built in the adjoining streets. The successive generations of Mathers all lived near the church, and men like (Elizur) Holyoke, the soap-boiler, father of the future Harvard president, plied their trades in the cottages round about,' according to a 1903 study.[5.4]

William Phipps must have spent his time in Boston living and working in this area. Confirmation comes from Cotton Mather who reported that in 1674, the 23-year-old heard Increase Mather preaching for the first time. It must have been an unnerving experience. Increase took his preaching seriously. He was a practised performer who rehearsed his lines and his delivery, which probably came from the Reverend Ian Paisley psalm book.

If Phipps found Mather's blood and thunder warnings disconcerting, he might have been even more worried by the discovery that he had come from a freewheeling country environment to a 'zero-tolerance' town. Puritans ran the place and they expected all to follow their moral code. Drunkenness, lewdness and blasphemy were not tolerated and there was no time for divergent religious views. A little more than ten years previously 'repeat offender' Quakers had been hanged for their beliefs and known Quakers arrested on sight and banished. Boston maintained a whipping post and hanging tree, and was not backward in use of either, neither of branding irons nor manacles. Ears were sometimes sliced off so that offenders might be recognised as non-conforming non-conformers. 'Godly' Bostonians witnessing such punishments must have shaken their heads and tutted at the foolishness of those being punished for offending Puritan laws.

William Phipps must have caught the eye of many as he made his way about the town. If Cotton Mather is to be believed, he was a big man, both tall and broad. 'For his exterior, he was one tall, beyond the common set of men, and thick as well as tall, and strong as well as thick: he was, in all respects, exceedingly robust, and able to conquer such difficulties of diet and of travel, as would have killed most men alive: nor did the fat, whereinto he grew very much in his later years, take away the vigour of his motions. He was well set, and he was therewithal of a very comely, though a very manly countenance; a countenance where any true skill in physiognomy would have read the characters of a generous mind.'[5.5]

Phipps certainly caught the eye of Widow Hull. A year after Phipps' arrival in Boston, in 1673 when William was 22, he married Mary Hull and presumably moved in with her. Her husband, John Hull had died that very year. He was not the ship-owning 'John Hull' but another who had died in his forties only a year or two after Mary and he had married. Mary must have been taken with William's country ways, his 'generous mind' and athletic build. Although not tutored, she knew he was bright. He was teaching himself to read and write, and perhaps Mary helped. It seems, though, that Phipps was never able to achieve fluency with the written word, despite Cotton Mather's attempts to suggest otherwise.

Mary seems to have been close in age to William. She was the daughter of Captain Roger Spencer, a mariner and landowner who had arrived in Boston sometime before 1669. Prior to that he had lived in Saco, eighty miles along the coast, north of Boston. There he had, in 1653, been given permission to build a sawmill (provided he did so within a year, and that 'all the townsmen shall have bordes 12d in a hundared cheaper than any stranger', and 'secondly that the townsmen shall be imployed in the worke before a stranger provided that they doo their worke so cheap as a stranger'.[5.6]

The captain's Saco business seems to have been something of a sawmill stone around his neck and was the subject of various transactions including mortgages and eventual sale. He had, in the words of Cotton Mather, 'suffered much damage in his estate, by some unkind and unjust actions, which he bore with such patience'.[5.7]

Whatever that 'damage' had been, it had not stopped Spencer marrying off his daughters, Lydia to Freegrace Norton and Mary to John Hull, 'a well-bred merchant'. A third daughter, Rebecca, married Dr David Bennet of Rowley who lived on in that town until 1719, by when he had reached the unlikely age of 103. Rebecca seems to have been his third wife.

Mary's father had moved in the same circles as the Lakes and the Mathers. She knew a thing or two about sawmills, ships and shipbuilding and perhaps helped with introductions also. As she showed in later life, she was quite a businesswoman in her own right and was confident enough to take responsibility for important decisions and actions.

John Hull left Mary an estate valued at £81,[5.8] not a lottery-winning fortune but a reasonable dowry. It seems to have been enough to allow her new husband to strike out on his own. 'He indented with several persons in Boston to build them a ship at Sheepscoat River,' says Cotton Mather. One of these merchants was Thomas Joles.

William took his saws, adzes, axes and hammers back to the Phipps/White homestead and on the banks of the Sheepscot River laid down the keel of his intended ship. Described as 'large', it would probably have been no more than sixty feet (eighteen metres) in length, still a hefty vessel for a first build. Phipps would have needed help, probably from his stepbrother John White and/or local friends including those he had worked with at Clarke & Lake.

Where possible he would have used ('free') local resources, cutting down straight-growing pines for masts and planking, perhaps other harder-wood species, such as white oak, for the keel and ribs of the ship. He might have bought planking from the Clarke & Lake sawmill or taken his own lumber for processing. If he had been thinking ahead be may already have had stocks of previously felled timber stored for drying. The son of a smith, he would certainly have had to buy in metal, preformed or later shaped by himself into nails, hoops and straps. His capital outlay would have also included the purchase of canvas and hemp lines, tar and pitch.

The process was laborious and testing, even for a young man of Phipps' size and strength. Having reading and writing skills on the shaky side of not too good cannot have helped. On the other hand, he knew how to measure and cut accurately.

After a year or so came the nail-biting launch. Phipps could then relax, his first ship lay riding at anchor, watertight and buoyant. All he had to do was to complete the fitting out and load his first cargo. What could possibly go wrong?

Chapter 6

King Philip's Revenge

WILLIAM PHIPPS' SHIPBUILDING career was short-lived. It came to an end one night in August 1676. It was then that 'King Philip's War' came to the Kennebec River and to Woolwich.

Relations between Puritan and other settlers and those people they sought to displace had been uncertain since the beginning. An attempted settlement on Roanoke Island towards the end of the fifteenth century had disappeared without trace, perhaps the would-be settlers were all killed by Indians, perhaps they were simply integrated into local groups. Those settlers who established Jamestown in Virginia in 1607 did so despite the unwelcoming and sometimes aggressively hostile local native Americans. On the other hand, the few Pilgrim Fathers who survived their first New England winter in 1620/21, did so only with the help of the local Indians. The unsurprising truth was that settlers and Indians had little understanding of each other's cultures and traditions. Happy enough to trade and accept occasional help from each other, there was a natural wariness between the two sides.

And yet the settlers kept coming and kept bringing their diseases and their belligerent ways with them. These people from beyond the seas insisted they knew better than the Indians in so many ways. Their religion, although only one among the many thousands in the world, was, they insisted, unquestionably the only true religion. Their ethics were the only acceptable code, and their laws were the only rightful laws. They believed in conformity and regimentation, not in freedom and self-expression.

It was all an annoyance to native inhabitants of this vast land, whose climate was so hard at times but whose resources were so rich that there was room for everybody. Indian culture was more free flowing than that of Europeans. Native Americans lived in loose-knit, extended-family groupings, united by common languages and customs. Tribal assemblies met together each year and accepted the authority of a sachem, a chief of chiefs.

Semi-nomadic, groups stayed put in summer, (the women) tending their crops and (the men) taking advantage of the easy fishing and hunting. Their villages were established in traditional sites and were sometimes fortified with palisades. In winter hunting parties travelled further afield, following the movements of their prey and living in temporary birch-bark shelters – 'wigwams'.

For sure there were hostilities between different tribes, who each held on firmly to their traditional territories. Some, such as the Iroquois and their particularly aggressive Mohican families, were warlike. Those that inhabited New England, Algonquin-speaking people, were hard-living but mostly, despite occasional misunderstandings, fights and even murders, seem to have been prepared to live and let live (to an extent, at least).

A good number were also prepared to allow themselves to be converted to Christianity. The religion had something of a resonance with them. Indians had their own creation myths; they, too, believed in spirits, and they loved a good story. Conversion of the 'heathen' Indians to Christianity had been one of the reasons given for allowing settlements in New England in the first place. And hard-working Puritan preachers soon got to work on the project. Notable among these was John Eliot who, born in Hertfordshire, England, in 1604, turned up in Boston some twenty-seven years later. He soon took up a ministry in Roxbury, preaching in its meeting house. (Roxbury was then a separate community next to Dorchester, where Richard, father of Increase, Mather was the resident minister. Both places have long since been subsumed into, and are now suburbs of, Boston).

Eliot reached out to the local Massachusett Indians, learnt their Algonquin dialect, and formed a particular friendship with the Nipmuc people and their leader Waban. The chief invited Eliot to preach at his home village of Nonantum, provided he agreed to help the Nipmuc gain rights through the New England courts to the land on which the village stood. A long-running legal battle followed.

Meanwhile, Eliot's work had somehow been noticed by Oliver Cromwell's Puritan government in England. And in 1649 it passed an *Act for the promoting and propagating the Gospel of Jesus Christ in New England*. This set up an English corporation charged with supporting missionary work with native American people ('The President and Society for the propagation of the Gospel in New England', what now would be called a charity).

It was enacted that a general collection be made in congregations 'in and through all the Counties, Cities, Towns and Parishes of England and Wales', when ministers were to 'exhort the people to a cheerful and liberal contribution, and are to give their best assistance to so pious a work'.[6.1]

By 1651, having signed off on his legal battle and with funds in hand from this society, Eliot together with the Nipmuc people set up the first Praying Town 'on a bend in the Charles River'.

The Nipmucs had lost the right to live at Nonantum but had secured (to some degree at least) other land along the Charles River. Eliot had obtained permission from the Massachusetts General Court to establish Natick, a town on 2,000 acres he had acquired from John Speen, a native American. 'Legal questions surrounding this land transfer endured for over a decade. Nonetheless, Natick residents quickly built homes, planted crops and orchards, fenced in livestock, and established a meeting house with a school run by a Massachusett schoolmaster named Monequassun.'[6.2] They also built a bridge across the river allowing land to be farmed on both sides.

Over the next twenty-three years the Natick model was followed by thirteen other such towns that together had a population of about 4,000 converts, a significant proportion of the surviving native population of New England.[6.3]

The idea was that Praying Towns were to be English settlements populated entirely by indigenous people committed to conversion. 'Eliot believed that in order to become a Christian, native people would have to embrace English gender roles and fashion; English-style farming and work habits; English systems of trade; and, of course, English habits of worship and faith,' says the Natick Historical Society.

In other words, no value at all was attributed to Indian traditions or customs. Among many other differences, Indian society was one in which women played a much more assertive role than their European counterparts. They generally dealt with property matters and were the people who elected their sachems, leadership roles from which they were not excluded.

Eliot continued his fortnightly preaching in Natick's meeting house but never lived in the town. Although he helped to establish the other Praying Towns his duties in Roxbury, where he was minister for almost sixty years, remained his priority.

Not all the Indians, probably most of those who agreed to live in Praying Towns, did so for religious reasons. Security of tenure was likely more important to them as well as the likelihood of being left in relative peace. Many of those who accepted English ways and strictures would have realised that things were only going one way, and it was not their way. It was better to sign up to change than to wait for it to be forced upon them.

Those Indians who stayed clear probably knew they were fighting a losing battle but fight they would. They felt simmering resentment about the way they had been pushed aside and how their lands had been taken from them and how they were used. One 1660 example had been particularly galling. Rhode Island, seventy miles or so south of Boston, had been an English colony since 1636 when its founder, Puritan pastor Roger Williams, had acquired land there. It had either been given or sold to him by the Narragansett people with whom he had lived. In 1643 Williams obtained an official charter from Oliver Cromwell's government and established a settlement that soon gained a reputation for religious tolerance and as a haven for Quakers and other persecuted groups. This amounted to what at the time would have passed as liberal and progressive thinking, although the Massachusetts Bay Colony would not have called it that. It was certainly party to excluding Rhode Island from the United Colonies of New England, an alliance formed in 1643 between the Massachusetts Bay, Plymouth, Connecticut and New Haven colonies.

The Rhode Island colony went its own way and passed anti-slavery laws in 1652, and in 1659 restricted the purchase of land from Indian groups. This did not stop a group of New England investors trying to acquire Narragansett land by devious means. They were led by one of the most upstanding of the Massachusetts Bay 'godly' settlers.

Major-General Humphrey Atherton had come to New England towards the end of the 'great migration' when aged about thirty. It seems probable that he arrived on the same ship as Richard (father of Increase) Mather. They both came from Lancashire and travelled to New England via Bristol, sailing on the *James*, part of a flotilla of five ships, three heading for Newfoundland. Like Mather, Atherton took up residence in Dorchester and had been working his way up the social, military and political ranks ever since.[6.4] Atherton's military commission, by 1660 the highest ranking in New England, was with the Military Company of Massachusetts, which he had joined at its inception. So, Atherton must have known and mixed in the same circles as Clarke and Lake. As superintendent of Indian affairs, a 1658 appointment, he must also have been well known by John Eliot. Atherton had served in various capacities in the General Court of Massachusetts, the Massachusetts Bay legislature, and was a magistrate. In his law-enforcement roles he was big on punishing Quakers and heretics. He was involved in the 1656 witchcraft trial, condemnation and hanging of Ann Higgins, and the 1660 hanging of Mary Dyer, a recalcitrant Quaker.

In 1659 Atherton, along with Connecticut governor John Winthrop (the younger), the son of Massachusetts Bay Colony founder John Winthrop, headed a consortium of investors intent on buying Indian land. This 'Atherton Company' first 'bought' some 6,000 acres of prime Narragansett Rhode Island land. They paid not in pumpkins but in gifts said to be worth £75. The seller was a cousin of a recently dead Narragansett chief who almost certainly had no more right to sell the land than Atherton had to buy it. The deed of transfer, which described the transaction as a gift in 'great love and affection', was said to have been drawn up in accordance with the laws of the United Colonies. It was not effective under Rhode Island law, that of the place where the land was sited, since this now required prior approval of transfers of Indian land by that colony's General Council. And approval was unlikely to have been given, especially when it became known that the 'love and affection' of the donor had been the consequence of a few days of enforced drinking. When the purchase was blocked, the Atherton investors came up with another equally unchristian wheeze.[6.5]

Narragansett warriors, acting on their own initiative, had raided a Mohegan camp during which some musket shots had found their way into a homestead in which 'Englishmen' were sleeping. The case was taken up by the Connecticut Grand Court, resulting in Governor Winthrop ordering the Narragansett to deliver up 'at least four' of those involved so that they could be sent to the West Indies as slaves. But there was a second choice. The Narragansett could pay a fine set at an unlikely high amount.

Atherton and co now stepped forward as potential saviours. Knowing how Native Americans would do almost anything to avoid being enslaved, the investors offered to pay the fine in return for a mortgage on Narragansett land. Preferring to borrow than to condemn their wayward warriors to a short life of misery followed by an almost certain untimely death, the Narragansett agreed.

The ink was barely dry on the mortgage document when the Atherton Company foreclosed on the mortgage, demanding ownership of the Narragansett land.

There was something of an uproar in Rhode Island which declared the transfers illegal and various court cases and appeals to London followed. Bribes were paid and petitions made for the extension of Connecticut territory, and therefore jurisdiction, to include the Narragansett land. It was not until 1688 that a Royal Commission ruled the Atherton claim illegal. Atherton did not live to hear the outcome. In 1661, while riding home across Boston Common, where fifteen months earlier Mary Dyer had been hanged, this stalwart of the 'godly' community fell off his horse and died.

The Atherton Company affair had both started and ended with corruption. The person appointed to head the commission investigating the rival claims was Edward Cranfield, governor of New Hampshire. In February 1683 he had written to those responsible for making the appointment: 'I do give you my faith that you two shall come into an equall part of every thing that tends to proffitt.' He went on to say that 'the Narragansett Countrey lyes betwixt severall claimours. Both partys have mony and 3000li or 4000li will not be felt in the disposeing those Land's'.[6.6]

Given Rhode Island's relatively liberal and supportive attitude towards Native Americans (partly, at least, because it wanted to maintain the colony's territory intact) it is somewhat ironic that the devastating 'King Philip's War' should have started and ended there.

King Philip, known to his kin as Metacom, had received the English name at his own request after stepping up to the role of sachem in 1662, not long after Atherton's attempt to get hold of Narragansett land. Metacom headed a confederation of Wampanoag groups, who, like the neighbouring Narragansetts, spoke an Algonquin dialect. His base of operations was at Mount Hope (where Bristol now stands) in Rhode Island. Led by Metacom, the group considered themselves trading partners with the settlers.

In his mid-thirties in 1675, Metacom was no hothead, but he was more than put out with the way things were moving and in particular by attempts by settlers and other Indian groups to acquire his land. Also disturbing was the growing use of slavery as a punishment meted out to Indians by the colonial courts in a legal system biased against them.

That Native Americans would never be treated as equals was obvious from the way they were often summoned to explain themselves, when hostages would often be required and when firearms, by then a necessity of life, were confiscated. Instead, they were played off against other Indian groups and against colonies comprised of Dutch or French settlers. Metacom had had enough. Forging alliances with other Algonquin-speaking groups, he declared war on the colonists.

'War' is hardly an accurate description of what went on. There were no pitched battles, only a series of raids, ambushes and skirmishes. The numbers involved were not huge, usually in the hundreds, sometimes many fewer. Yet the effect was devastating.

Metacom's first tactic was to raid isolated homesteads and settlements, killing the hated cattle and burning abandoned property. The Indians were more mobile and more elusive than the colonists. They infiltrated settlements at night and attacked at first light.

Atrocities were committed by both sides. Women and children were killed mercilessly. No quarter was given. There was terror and distrust. Worried about the 'enemy within', the Massachusetts Colony herded its 'Praying Indians' onto Boston's Deer Island where they were left to fend for themselves.

Initially the Indians were on top. The settlers had no answer to their hit-and-run approach, their cruelty, their stealth, their bravery and commitment. And the 'war' was moving up the coast. By February 1676 it was just a few miles from Boston. It was then that Indians destroyed Medfield, just twenty miles or so inland. They killed about twenty people and took many prisoners besides burning bridges that spanned the Charles River.

'One of them (legend names James the Printer, the Nipmuc who had helped print Eliot's Bibles at Harvard College) left a note "that the Indians that thou hast provoked to Wrath and Anger" would if necessary wage twenty more years of war, and noting that his people "had nothing to lose, whereas [settlers] had Houses, Barnes, and Corn," reports Daniel Mandell in *King Philip's War*. 'Four days later, a raiding party burned seven or eight buildings in Weymouth along the coast just south of Boston. Colonists throughout the region, even in Boston, feared that the merciless "savages" would suddenly appear at any moment and begin slaughtering "civilized" women and children.'[6.7]

In August the war came to Woolwich and the Kennebec River, where William Phipps was busy finishing off his first ship. Richard Hammond's Woolwich trading post was attacked and he was killed. The remaining fifteen members of Hammond's family were also killed or captured.

A group of the marauding Indians crossed the river to Arrowsic Island where they attacked the Clarke & Lake compound that contained its trading post, warehouse, sawmill and Lake's own house. Thomas Lake was staying there at the time. He managed to escape the attack but was hunted down and killed, possibly by a musket, knife or hatchet he had sold the Indians. He was sixty-one.

Lake's tombstone in Boston's Copp's Hill cemetery records that Hannah Hull's new husband, Samuel Sewall, wrote in his diary: 'We heard amazing news of sixty persons killed at Quinebeck, by barbarous Indians, of which were Capt. Lake, Mr Collicot, Mr Padeshell.' The plaque goes on to say that during the attack Lake fled the trading post, but was later captured and killed. His body was found several months later, 'still frozen'. In 1677 the remainder of his corpse was honourably buried at Copp's Hill. 'Some say that the lead shot from his body was melted and poured into the gravestone.'[6.8] 'By the end of the month, the English had almost completely abandoned the region northeast of Scarborough; many headed for Salem, where they had relatives or could easily find refuge. The settlers were reluctant to stand their ground against these attacks, at least in part because Boston had relatively little authority in Maine, and the United Colonies was ineffective in this part of the war because other colonies and well-connected English speculators continued to challenge the Puritan colony's claim to the region.'[6.9]

According to Cotton Mather, it was at this point that William Phipps sailed to the rescue. He had launched but 'hardly finished' the ship he was building, when the 'barbarous Indians on that river broke forth into an open and cruel war upon the English; and the miserable people, surprized by so sudden a storm of blood, had no refuge from the infidels but the ship now finishing in the harbour. Whereupon he left his intended lading behind him, and, instead thereof, carried with him his old neighbours and their families, free of all charges to Boston; so the first action that he did, after he was his own man, was to save his father's house, with the rest of the neighbourhood, from ruin; but the disappointment which befel him from the loss of his other lading, plunged his affairs into greater embarrassments with such as had employed him.'[6.10]

By the time of these events, King Philip's War was all but over.

The colonists had struck a major blow in December 1675 when they took a fortified Narragansett stronghold hidden in Rhode Island's 'Great Swamp', near what is now West Kingston. The Indians had previously mocked the militia for their hapless attempts to fight in the wetlands. But when they arrived this time, all was frozen and no boats or canoes were needed. The largest New England force mustered during the 'war', over 1,000 men, simply marched across the ice into the camp. At first the fighting was fierce but once the palisade had been breached the outcome was inevitable. Many of the Indian warriors decided it was time to leave. Their women and children were not so mobile and many died, burned alive when the settlers' force torched the village. Narragansetts tell that, in 1675, they 'allied themselves with King Philip and the Wampanoag Sachem, to support the Wampanoag Tribe's efforts to reclaim land in Massachusetts'. After 'the Great Swamp Massacre', many who survived 'retreated deep into the forest and swamp lands' that 'now makes up today's Reservation' and 'any who refused to be subjected to the authority of the United Colonies left the area or were hunted down and killed. Some were sold into slavery in the Caribbean, others migrated to upstate New York and many went to Brotherton, Wisconsin'.[6.11]

By August 1676 Metacom was dead. He had been tracked down and shot by John Alderman, a Wampanoag Praying Indian who was a member of a group of militia commanded by Captain Benjamin Church. Church's 'old Indian executioner' had told him that Metacom 'had been a very great man, and had made many a man afraid of him, but so big as he was, he would now chop his arse for him'. The man beheaded and quartered Metacom; Church hung each quarter in a different tree and gave a hand to Alderman, who later earned money by showing it around the colonies, supposedly preserved in a bucket of rum. 'When Plymouth authorities heard the news, they called for a day of thanksgiving on August 17; soon after the Reverend John Cotton finished his sermon, Church arrived with the sachem's head, which was paraded through the town and then put on a tall post for all of the colonists to view and revile.'[6.12]

The colonists had subdued the Indians, for the time being. They had done so by changing tactics; by targeting Indian food supplies, by recruiting the feared Mohawks as allies, and by allowing the distrusted Praying Indians to fight for them. They had not won. Their brutality in victory, their killing and enslavement of their native American adversaries, and their internment of Praying Indians, ensured lasting resentment. This bred continuing Indian 'wars' well into the next century.

Many of the Praying Indians confined to Deer Island did not survive, dying from starvation or exposure in the severe winter of 1675. Of those who did survive and return to Natick, many found their village and homes had been destroyed.[6.13]

Meanwhile, those Indian groups involved in the fighting, the Wampanoag and Narragansett Indians, but also the Nipmuc and Pocumtuck people, saw their numbers much depleted by deaths, desertions to other areas, and by enslavement.

The colonists suffered too. Many had died at the hands of the Indians, many others must have been wounded or traumatised, and yet more had seen their hard-worked-for homesteads and their animals and crops destroyed.

William Phipps had escaped with his property intact, but not his boatbuilding business. The area around Woolwich, further upstream and across the river at Arrowsic, had been abandoned. The settlers had left, gone to Boston or Salem or elsewhere, their fields abandoned to become overgrown and their homes, those that had not been burnt, left to rot. It was some years before they returned.

At least Phipps had a home to go to. He returned to Boston and to another twist of fate.

Chapter 7

Randolph Arrives

FERDINANDO GORGES (grandson of Sir Ferdinando Gorges) and Robert Mason (grandson of John Mason) had continued their claims to large tracts of land in Maine and New Hampshire. In 1671 and 1672 they presented new petitions and managed to have these claims examined by various government committees. They probably had only slim hopes of taking possession of the land in question, but they must have realised that their nuisance value alone warranted a reasonable payoff.

So, for example, in November 1671 Robert Mason suggested a deal in which he would sell his patent for New Hampshire in return for a permit to import into London '300 tuns of French wine' free of all customs, the 'said wine to be imported in three ships and no more'.[7.1]

Nothing came of this, but Mason did not give up. And in 1675 the pair were able to tell the Lords of Trade and Plantation that no less than the attorney general had declared their titles 'good and legal'. The committee referred the matter to lords chief justices Sir Richard Raynsford and Sir Francis North.

Mason somehow persuaded the Privy Council's Lords of Trade committee to demand that Massachusetts send agents to explain the colony's position. And perhaps mindful of the earlier reluctance of Massachusetts to despatch representatives to England, it was decided that a strong message should be sent, so indicating that refusal to comply was not advisable. This should come in the form of a letter from the king, delivered by special envoy.

Mason had seized on this opening. He had a relative who was in search of employment and willing to travel to New England. The man was a country gentleman from Kent, a little down on his luck, but somebody who had been a supplier of timber to the navy. That man was his cousin, by marriage, Edward Rudolph.

When Rudolph got the job, he must have immediately realised it was the opportunity he had always been seeking. It was an introduction to government service and a sure way to make money. Soon he had managed to get himself appointed not only as envoy, but somebody entrusted to write a report on the current economic and military strengths of the colonies. He became, in effect, a new one-man commission, charged with spending a month touring New England and reporting on its governance.

His conclusions would hardly have been pleasing to the leaders of the Massachusetts Bay Colony who, said Randolph, 'keep the country in subjection and slavery'. Having sought out dissident voices, he had convinced himself that the insistence of Massachusetts lawmakers on their right to independent government (and that the laws of England were not binding on them) was not a view shared by most colonists. He claimed most, if given the opportunity, would be more than willing to be loyal royal subjects.

Randolph may have been shocked by what he found and sincere in his views. In England they were largely taken as well founded and fitted well with the king's wish to assert his authority over the whole of New England. But Randolph's conclusions would have been less questionable (by the colonists in particular) had they not coincided so neatly with his own and his cousin Robert Mason's self-interests.

Randolph's report questioned the very legality of the Puritan dominance in Massachusetts and many of the laws and practices that resulted from this. The colony did not allow for appeal to English courts, it protected regicides, it minted its own currency, it executed people because of their religious beliefs, it insisted on its own form of oath of allegiance (which put the authority of the colony on an equal footing to that of the king), and it allowed flagrant disregard of England's *Navigation Acts*.

Intervention was needed, he said. And there should be customs officials appointed and sent from England to look out for the king's interests. He had a supervisory role in mind for himself.[7.2]

Massachusetts did send agents to England. There, they argued strongly against Randolph's conclusions. The colony's ruling elite had worried that its charter would be withdrawn, and all would be lost. And so, they were overjoyed when, after hearing from those agents, the Lords of Trade took a step back from such drastic action. The charter should stay in place but be supplemented by a further explanatory charter which introduced limited supervision, they suggested.

Massachusetts was so pleased with the result that its General Council reacted to Randolph's criticism in its time-honoured fashion. It did virtually nothing other than concede that now the king had made it clear that, after all, he did wish the *Navigation Acts* to apply to New England, Massachusetts would confirm this in its own law.

Meanwhile, in 1677, the lords chief justices Raynsford and North reported that they had heard evidence from the Massachusetts Bay Colony and from Gorges and Mason about the ownership and governance of Maine and New Hampshire. But 'it appeared that the said lands are in the possession of several persons not before the lords chief justices'. They could not, they said, decide who had valid titles without first hearing from tenants ('squatters', according to Mason) giving their side of the dispute. It was therefore recommended that everything should be decided by local courts. In other words, it was being left to Massachusetts to decide. This must have been bad news for Mason and Gorges. It was certainly very disappointing for Mason. The chief justices had decided that whoever turned out to own New Hampshire, Mason had no right to govern it.

When it came to Maine, Gorges had the right to govern by virtue of King Charles I's 1639 patent. This gave him the opportunity to claim a potentially very lucrative appointment. Unfortunately for Gorges (the grandson), it was soon disclosed that he had already given up and sold all his rights to Maine to the state of Massachusetts for £1,250.[7.3]

Everything seemed to be going well for Massachusetts. But in early 1678 its agents, Massachusetts magistrates William Stoughton and Peter Bulkeley, made what turned out to be a momentous mistake. Having obtained a copy of Randolph's unpublished report criticising their colony, the two offered to provide a line-by-line rebuttal. They may well have been able to point to Randolph's mistakes, misunderstandings and exaggerations, but they did not get the chance. Instead, they found themselves accused of underhand actions. How had they obtained a private government report whose conclusions might well put at risk those colonists who had provided views critical of their General Council?

Randolph weighed in with his own petition to the king, pointing out that Massachusetts had done next to nothing to put right the wrongs he had reported. It had not come up with a satisfactory oath of allegiance and it continued to reserve voting rights to those who belonged to a Puritan church.

Now the attorney general gave the Lords of Trade his opinion that the Massachusetts Bay Colony had failed so lamentably to administer its charter that the document could be considered void. The committee voted to advise the king to issue a writ of *quo warranto* against the colony, requiring it to justify its actions.

Shortly there was another blow for the colony. In that same year, by order of the king, Randolph was appointed collector and surveyor of customs for all New England. It was the start of a twenty-year career that saw Randolph accumulate a growing number of appointments, and enemies. It seems that whenever there was an opportunity to meddle in the affairs of New England, and Massachusetts in particular, Randolph took it.

An arrogant and imperious figure, he seemed to take delight in his own notoriety, basking in the hatred he generated. He was the king's man, and it was his personal mission to ensure the letter of the law was obeyed. In this he was efficient and tireless, especially in matters that coincided with his own self-interest. As a government official he could expect a percentage of all he 'discovered' and collected. This was an opportunity that he would not allow to pass. Once installed in his new Boston-based post, he set about boarding and seizing any vessel he suspected of breaching the *Navigation Acts* and avoiding the plantation tax. Lacking the sympathy of the local judiciary, he usually failed to translate these acts into successful prosecutions. But these rebuffs did not persuade him to stop trying.

Massachusetts had got away relatively lightly from the attention of the king. It had been obliged to accept appointment of Randolph and of an Anglican bishop and it had watched with trepidation as New Hampshire became a royal colony governed directly from England (in which Randolph involved himself). But things might have been worse. After the trauma of the last few years Massachusetts found itself left, barring Randolph's energetic presence, largely to its own devices.

King Charles was a busy man and he had other things to deal with. He was mainly busy pursuing his interests in horse racing, hunting, hawking, wrestling, boxing matches, womanising and socialising.[7.4]

What small time Charles had for actual work was now taken up with issues other than those concerning New England. The question of religion had again raised its head. First came the 'Popish Plot' which emerged from the imagination of Titus Oates in 1678, and a year later the 'Exclusion Crisis'. Ten years after becoming king of England, Charles had concluded a secret deal with Louis XIV of France (included in an undisclosed part of the 1670 Treaty of Dover). In return for an annual payoff, Charles agreed to convert to Roman Catholicism at some time in the future and to lead his subjects in the same direction. If needed, he would welcome French troops onto his shores to quell any rebellion.

If Charles' secret deal had been known, it would have been obvious that Oates' suggestion that Jesuits were out to kill the king and replace him with his openly Catholic brother was ludicrous. Charles chose not to mention his secret treaty and, ludicrous or not, Oates was believed. His claims led to the false conviction and unjust and often bloody execution of more than thirty people. It was only years later that Oates was exposed as a fantasist and fraudster. But for now, anti-Catholic feelings ran high.

The *Test Act* of 1673 had required all those wishing to hold public office to swear an oath to the king and the Church of England, and to reject Catholic principles. In 1678 a revision extended *Test Act* requirement to members of both houses of Parliament, the Lords and the Commons. Charles II's younger brother and heir to his throne, James, Duke of York, had declined to take any such oath. Following Oates' 'revelations', some parliamentarians wanted James excluded from succession to the English throne. Starting in 1679, three Bills were introduced that would have had this effect. None became law, not least because when enactment looked likely, King Charles used his royal prerogative to dissolve Parliament.

It was not until the early 1680s that things had calmed down and the goings-on in Massachusetts were back on the agenda.

Even in the early years of his tenure, Randolph would have known of, and perhaps have tussled with the much younger William Phipps. The would-be shipbuilder would not have known it at the time, but Randolph's Massachusetts interventions had already brought forward the dispute over the colony's charter that would much affect his later career. Their paths were destined to cross again.

Chapter 8

Captain Phipps Goes to Sea

KING PHILIP'S WAR cost New England dearly. It had caused death, trauma and destruction, homelessness and financial loss on both sides. Homes, villages, towns and crops had been destroyed, animals slaughtered, women and children, both settlers and native Americans, scalped and burned alive. Trusted trading relationships, friendships and families had been torn apart.

The attack on Woolwich had been devastating for Phipps personally. He had put his all into building his ship, a venture that would put him on the road to riches. But that August night had taken everything away. Instead of making money, he lost all he had invested and more. Among his debts was a judgement in favour of his client Thomas Joles, who convinced a court to award him £85. On hearing the verdict, Phipps exploded, ripping the paperwork from a lawyer's hands and hurling it into the fire, an act for which he was fined.[8.1]

Phipps had to find a way to start again.

Boston was a prosperous place and had not suffered direct attacks during the war, although its citizens had been engaged in the fighting and some had been killed. Praying Indians, thought likely to backslide into heathen ways ('barbarous', 'murderous', 'diabolical', 'savage' and 'pagan', were words used by Cotton Mather to describe Indians[8.2]) had been herded onto Boston's Deer Island and left to fend for themselves.

But war was not the only catastrophe to strike the town. In November 1676, it was woken in the night by the largest fire it had ever experienced. The blaze had been started accidentally by a boy. Having been 'called up to work very early in the morning', he fell asleep on the job. His candle continued to burn and proceeded to set his workplace on fire 'whereby many other houses were consumed, together with the meeting-house at that end of the said town'.[8.3] 'Whole streets were laid in ashes'. Among much else, some forty-six houses were burned to the ground, including that of Increase Mather along with his meeting house and a portion of his valuable library. But 'some mercy was observed mixed with judgment; for, if a great rain had not continued all the time (the roofs and walls of their ordinary buildings consisting of such combustible matter), that whole (north) end of the town had at that time been consumed'.[8.4]

Only a year later the town was visited with another calamity; smallpox raged through the community, Enoch Pond reported. 'Never before had Boston seen so dreadful a mortality.' It had been brought, 'as usual' by English ships, and caused an alarming number of deaths including those of leading citizens. The height of the outbreak came in September 1677, when on the last day of the month thirty people died. In that long winter the total death toll among Boston's 4,500 inhabitants was an estimated seven hundred. It could have been more.

To the Puritan preachers, and Increase Mather in particular, it seemed as if the town was being punished for its lack of piety. He pushed for and obtained a synod, a meeting of church leaders charged with deciding what evils had provoked the wrath of God, and what was to be done to put matters right.

Lack of empathy or sympathy with the lot of the Indians was not on the agenda, neither the choice of building materials in the town, the lack of adequate fire-fighting equipment, or the need to quarantine arriving ships with disease aboard. Nothing remotely concerned with practical issues was talked about. Instead, with the arrogance of conviction, these pastors and purists bemoaned 'a great and visible decay of the power of godliness', 'abounding pride', 'profaneness', 'sabbath-breaking', 'neglecting family government', 'indulgence of inordinate passions', 'intemperance', 'violations of honesty and truth', 'inordinate love of the world', 'want of public spirit', 'sins more directly against the gospel', and 'a manifest unwillingness to be reformed'. This last was surely a case of the pot calling the kettle black. The Puritans had steadfastly held on to their view of life against allcomers.

The outcome of this 'Reforming Synod' was a series of recommendations including public declaration of adherence to the 'Cambridge Platform', a 1648 statement largely repeating the views of Richard Mather and John Cotton (Increase Mather's father and father-in-law). It identified New England Puritanism as adhering to the 'congregational' principle, in which each church is governed by its own members '(no bishops).' But membership of each church was to be limited to those who had been baptised into the faith, in practice having persuaded the church elders that the applicant had undergone some sort of revelation: had, in fact, 'seen the light'. And, said the synod, these membership rules should be administered with 'greater strictness and faithfulness'.[8.5]

The synod and its recommendations have been seen as a victory of some kind for Increase Mather who was acknowledged as a leading theologian and intellectual. But it can also be seen as an admission that the intransigent rule of the Puritans was under threat from within. Cotton Mather, son of Increase, gave the game away somewhat: 'New England was not become, at this time, so degenerate a country but that there was yet preserved in it far more of serious religion, as well as of blameless morality, than was proportionally to be seen in any country upon the face of the earth. Nevertheless, the spirit of the world had begun so far to operate, that there was a visible decay of real and vital piety, and the power of godliness had sensibly suffered some abatements. Watchful, fruitful, prayerful Christians, and humble walkers with God, were not so many as they had been, among a people greatly multiplying, and the holy God might also say, "There are wicked men among my people.'"[8.6]

Many of those 'wicked men' he had in mind were no doubt the new breed of merchants taking over Boston's wharfs, jetties, shops and warehouses. Some had newly arrived from London or Bristol and on the lookout for business opportunities, others were second- and third-generation Bostonians who saw which way the wind was blowing. And the merchants knew that the colony needed them.

The Puritan leaders of Massachusetts had tried to keep the place insulated from England and the ungodly ways of 'foreigners' (non-Puritans), they had tried to impose church-based laws, and had tried to make their colony self-sufficient. But since the 1660 restoration of Charles II to the English throne, they had faced increasing threats to their independence. Their price and wage control laws had proved unhelpful to business ventures serving local markets. Early attempts at salt production, woollen garment manufacture (there had at one time been a law requiring all colonists to take up spinning in their spare time) and iron smelting, had all come to nothing.

New England was rich in resources, especially beaver (to start with anyway), fish and timber, and particularly those valuable straight pines that could be worked into spars, an essential but not too durable component of any sailing ship. Yet these commodities were only valuable if exported, which meant engaging with the outside world.

The drift of development was obvious. New England and the Massachusetts Bay Colony could not survive and fend off greedy predators, including nearby Dutch and French colonies, by settling for an economy based on self-sufficiency and bartering. Access to the latest and most efficient imports were required for comfort, health and development; manufactured goods that would better clothe the colonists, improve their farming, their lumberjacking and their building methods. Progress made in other countries, including those in medicine and firefighting, could not be ignored.[8.7]

It is easy to image these 'wicked men', wheeler-dealers who bought and sold shiploads of anything that would turn a profit, as the City bankers of their day. Thinking themselves clever beyond clever, smart beyond smart, they were more than willing to push laws to the limit. They did not seek church membership unless they thought it worthwhile financially, they pushed their prices as much as the market allowed. And they broke other laws. They probably cursed and lied, at least in private, they may have played cards and gambled, and even played football on Sunday mornings. No doubt professing themselves 'Christian', they also acknowledged another god: that of wealth. Unlike the Mathers, they knew they had not been preselected for sainthood, and they didn't care.

In this growing schism, a power struggle between church and commercial interests, William Phipps had a delicate path for his large frame to navigate. His future seemed to lie in shipping, perhaps shipbuilding or ship-owning, perhaps commerce; anything except shepherding. His wife was the widow of a merchant, the daughter of mariner and sawmill owner, and yet she was a devout member of Increase Mather's church.

Phipps must have taken the path of least resistance. In keeping with convention, he would have declared himself Christian and have attended church on Sundays, perhaps even, as Cotton Mather claims, sometimes reserving days for private fasting and praying. But he was a man of action not contemplation, and somebody who enjoyed good company. He was affable enough, having the confidence of a powerfully built man. But he had insecurity bred of knowing there was much he did not know, including how to read and write well, which he countered with a blustering and quick-tempered manner. He was certainly not afraid to use his strength rather than neatly honed arguments to persuade others to accept his point of view. Phipps, then in his mid-twenties, would likely have sought the shipyard and the craftsmen and mariners who breathed in sawdust and washed themselves in saltwater. These were rough and ready men like himself, down-to-earth and not afraid of hard work or the dangers of the sea.

It is not known for sure what Phipps did in the ten years or so following the end of King Philip's War, but it is likely he fell back on his training, perhaps finding himself employment working in a local shipyard. At some point he went to sea, probably signing on as a ship's carpenter. Such skills were prized on wooden ships which needed constant attention. Carpenters were responsible for repairs to planking, decks and equipment. They played an important role in careening, the frequent scraping from hulls of marine life and recoating with pitch. They felled trees for firewood and to make charcoal and its pitch byproduct, and to make replacement spars and yardarms. And accordingly, they were paid more than a common seaman. It was a time of expansion for Boston's shipbuilding and shipping interests. Before too long Phipps would have been experienced enough to benefit – to captain a ship of some size, perhaps one he owned or at least owned a share of.

Jamaica had been acquired by England in 1655 when Oliver Cromwell sent a substantial force to capture the West Indian island of Hispaniola. Having a more hard-nosed brand of Puritanism than his New England counterparts, Cromwell saw engagement with the rest of the world as an essential step in putting England back on its feet after years of civil war. The attempt on Hispaniola (an island that is now the home of modern-day Haiti and the Dominican Republic) was part of this 'Western Design'. The assault failed but the joint leaders of the invasion force, Admiral William Penn and General Robert Venables, had moved on and taken Jamaica as a handsome second prize.

Spain objected, saying that all the Americas and West Indies belonged to it. But despite, or perhaps because of, the great wealth Spain had extracted from its new world colonies, this bloated empire was not well placed to defend its possessions against allcomers. And so, in 1670, after a bout of privateering tussles, it signed up to a peace treaty between itself and England.

The Treaty of Madrid 'expunged' and 'buried in oblivion' all previous 'damages, losses and injuries' inflicted by either upon the other. It also allowed England, or rather 'the Most Serene King of Great Britain, his Heirs and Successors', to 'hold, keep, and enjoy for ever, with plenary right of Sovereignty, Dominion, Possession, and Propriety, all those Lands, Regions, Islands, Colonies, and places whatsoever, being situated in the West Indies, or in any part of America, which the said King of Great Britain and his Subjects do at present hold and possess'.[8.8] English and Spanish ships were to have free movement within the Caribbean but were each to limit trading to their own possessions.

This was a major concession and Charles II, that self-same 'serene king', must have thought his promise to revoke all letters of reprisal (the cloak of legality under which privateers operated) and to supress piracy, a small price to pay. England had, for the time being at least, secure title to its three most important new world colonies: New England, Jamaica and Barbados.

The latter is a small island about 2,000 kilometres, or 1,259 miles, east by south of Jamaica and 3,500 kilometres, or 2,200 miles, south-east of New England) on which fewer than a hundred English settlers had first set foot in 1627. They came as employees of the owner of the island, a City of London merchant. Barbados was a 'proprietary' colony. With the help of slaves, the settlers moved early on into sugar production. By 1670 it had long been the island's main industry and its 20,000 or so settlers were outnumbered by its more than 30,000 slaves.

Much larger, Jamaica was also a sugar-producing island, having in 1670 some 57 sugar works. But its 15,000 inhabitants, not counting slaves, had other interests too. Cocoa trees had been planted (although many had died) and indigo was grown. Some tobacco and cotton were produced, but not being as profitable as sugar or chocolate, these were less important.[8,9]

The 15,000 islanders also included an estimated 2,500 privateers, people whose livelihood had supposedly been destroyed by the Treaty of Madrid. These 'lusty men' were in effect marine mercenaries. The cost of maintaining a large navy was considered prohibitive, especially by Charles II who thought he had better use for his money. The supposed solution to the problem of defending such possessions as Jamaica was to issue commissions, letters of reprisal, to private shipowners willing to fit out their vessels to fight the enemy. These commissions specified who might be attacked and the reward for doing so – invariably a share of the value of the ships taken and whatever it was they happened to be carrying.

Privateers were allowed to rummage their prize for loose valuables including those in the personal possession of captives, but they were not allowed to 'break bulk'. Instead, they were supposed to take their prize to the nearest Admiralty court where everything would be shared out, with something to the owners, a chunk to the Crown, and the rest to the captain and crew. Crews on privateer ventures were usually employed, much like some solicitors today, on a 'no win, no fee' basis (or as it was then more usually phrased, 'no purchase, no pay').

In theory everybody won. England and its possessions were better protected, seamen stood the chance of making more money than they could dream of earning by other means, and money flowed back to the Crown, which was by law entitled to a share of the spoils. But the divide between privateering and piracy was thin.

Employment terms might have been 'no purchase, no pay', but crews were unwilling to consider the 'no pay' option. The longer any voyage continued without a prize being taken, the more pressure was heaped upon the captain to do something to ensure a decent payoff for his crew.

Commissions might be specific about the ships of which nation might be attacked, or they might simply refer to 'enemies'. Either way, desperate captains were likely to take a more liberal attitude than the law presumed towards what was and what was not a legitimate target (especially since ships often flew false flags). And once a prize had been taken there was always great temptation to keep everything that was aboard or at least not to surrender the most valuable items to the courts.

Some of those privateers made redundant by the Treaty of Madrid went elsewhere for their commissions: the governor of the French half of Hispaniola was particularly helpful in this respect. Others simply turned to piracy, while still others went off to Campeche to become logwood cutters.

The 'lusty' privateers were not the only seamen to lose out to Charles II's growing interest in the Americas. In the civil war years and those of Cromwell's protectorate, New England had been left largely to its own devices. And for a few years after his 1660 restoration to the English throne, Charles II had other pressing business to deal with, including mopping up after Cromwell's Anglo-Spanish War and dealing with increasingly bad-tempered relations with the Dutch. Charles' aggression included the 1664 capture of New Amsterdam (now New York) by an English expeditionary force, use of privateers against the Dutch, and finally, a declaration of the second Anglo-Dutch War in 1665.

By 1670, with all quiet for now on the home front, Charles again directed his gaze to New England. The Puritan settlers were his natural enemies. Many had fled England because they had found Charles I's rule so obnoxious to their beliefs. Left to themselves they had made matters worse by entrenching their Puritan beliefs within New England laws, by disregarding English law, and even minting their own coins, a royal prerogative.

Charles II might have found the New England Puritans distasteful, but not their money. He viewed New England as a useful source of revenue. Cromwell had, in 1651, brought in an *Act of Trade and Navigation*, the first of a stream of *Navigation Acts* bearing various official titles. Although billed as a measure to promote trade, this legislation was protectionist in nature, restricting the use of foreign ships for goods bound to or from England. Later *Navigation Acts*, included those of 1660, 1662/63, and 1673. The latter two, also known as the *Staple Act* (1663) and *Plantation Trade Act* (1673), were of particular significance to the New England shipping industry.

The 1663 law demanded that all imports originating outside England be carried on English ships. On arrival, their cargoes were to be unloaded, inspected, assessed and duty had to be paid. There were tighter, and more expensive requirements for 'enumerated' commodities which if bound for Europe must first be exported to England where duty must be paid. These enumerated commodities coincided with New England's most important exports, including cotton, tobacco, sugar, wool and indigo, all of which, said the law, could be sent only to England in English ships.

This legislation might have put a stop to any direct trade between the colonies and any European country other than England. But the New Englanders had a wheeze. Their ports were 'English' ports and their ships 'English' ships, or so they said. So, the practice developed of shipping 'enumerated' goods from one colonial port to another before sending them onward to overseas customers. This, said the New Englanders, fulfilled the requirement of the law.

But it frustrated the purpose of the law, which was to cut out competition between England and the colonies and also to garner duties for the English Treasury (aka Charles II). And it infuriated the English Parliament.

The 1673 *Navigation Act*, officially *'An Act for the incouragement of the Greeneland and Eastland Trades, and for the better secureing the Plantation Trade'*, was designed to stop this. It wrapped up anti-duty-dodging measures in a good deal of legalese about the 'very considerable and profitable' whale-fishing trade. But the important thing for American colonists was that it required a bond to be paid when 'enumerated' goods were first shipped; this by way of a guarantee that they would be taken to England where 'Rates and Dutyes' were to be paid or a penalty levied if they were not.

The goods covered were white sugar (taxed at five shillings per hundredweight), brown sugar (one shilling and six pence per hundredweight), tobacco (one penny per pound), cottonwool (one halfpenny per pound), indigo (two pence per pound), ginger (one shilling per hundredweight), and logwood (five pounds per hundredweight). 'For Fusticke and all other Dying-wood the hundred Weight containing one hundred and twelve pounds, six pence.'[8.10]

There were stiff penalties for shipment of 'enumerated' commodities without a bond or customs certificate, and for illicit shipping or unloading of such cargoes outside England. Alongside this, ports were required to record and report commercial ship movements, their cargoes, and bonds and duties paid. And 'for the better collection of the severall Rates and Dutyes aforesaid imposed by this Act, Bee it enacted and it is hereby further enacted by the authoritie aforesaid That this whole busines shall bee ordered and mannaged, and the severall Dutyes hereby imposed shall be caused to be leavyed by the Commissioners of the Customes in England, now and for the time being by and under the authoritie and directions of the Lord Treasurer of England or Commissioners of the Treasury for the Time, being.'

Collection of duties was being put on a more professional basis.

Many New Englanders were outraged by these laws. They were, after all, English men and women but they were being treated as second-class citizens. By 1673, they were enjoying the fruits of their merchants' and shipowners' successes in building up trade not just with England and other colonies but with Portugal, Spain, the Canary Islands and the Azores. These laws were an attempt to damage their export trade and made their imports more expensive.[8.11]

Bostonians argued that the new law was impractical. Ships of the time were not too manoeuvrable. They could sail before the wind, and across it, but hardly at all against the wind. They were obliged to go more or less where the wind blew them, and the art of navigation was as much to do with using prevailing wind patterns and ocean currents as it was with knowing exactly where the ship was at any given time.

This meant that sailing ships could rarely travel there and back to any given destination by the same route. If the outward leg was before the wind, then the return route had to be at least a two-leg affair, first one way across the wind, and then the other (on the other 'tack'). The whole voyage, there and back, was at least triangular.

As voyages were nearly always of necessity at least three-sided, it made commercial sense to deliver and receive goods (and make a profit) at each stop. So, from New England a ship might sail easily enough to England. But for the return voyage it would be obliged to swing south towards the West Indies, and from there north along the east coast of America.

The so-called *Navigation Acts* added expense and bureaucracy to the process and made some of New England's established trading routes illegal. Taken together, these laws were an open invitation to smuggle. Honesty, or lack of it, didn't come into it. In New Englanders' eyes they were an attack on a god-fearing, hardworking community who deserved reward for their fortitude, not punishment. No doubt the Mathers would have said as much.

William Phipps was a member of this community, one of them, and probably at one with them. He had a ship, and his livelihood was under attack. He knew the New England coast and in particular Maine's myriad rivers, creaks and hidden waterways. The near certainty is that he flew close to the wind when it came to compliance with England's unfair laws, so close that Charles might have considered him a criminal. But that was before he provided the king with enough silver to make him a trusted friend.

Chapter 9

An Idea is Formed

A LITTLE (or a lot of) smuggling might not have been all Phipps got up to when out of the sight of officialdom.

Whether or not this included stepping beyond custom, law, or expected standards, Phipps would certainly have been involved in shipping slaves, perhaps from Africa to the West Indies, and more likely between New England and the West Indies. Despite their professed 'Christianity', the New England Puritans were not slow to exploit their fellow non-churchified human beings to the fullest extent possible.

Puritans had arrived in New England with indentured servants, a form of indebtedness that made these people slaves by another name. And the settlers had taken captive native Americans for slaves, condemned others to slavery as punishment for crimes against New England laws and sold more than a few to the West Indies. Later they had imported African slaves for themselves. Phipps had slaves of his own and so did Cotton and Increase Mather.[9.1]

Phipps seems to have known Caribbean waters well and in his undoubted visits to Barbados, Bermuda and Jamaica he would have rubbed shoulders with privateers and pirates. He may well have been tempted by the seemingly easy pickings these fellow seamen enjoyed. They could take most vessels with no more than a show of strength and had relatively little to fear from the law. Few pirates were arrested at this time, still fewer were found by local juries to have a case to answer in England. And every few years there were amnesties available.

During this time there were illegal raids by Jamaica-based 'privateers' on Portobello and across the Panama isthmus and around Cape Horn to the South Seas. The lure was Spanish gold and silver, stolen from or mined in Spain's American possessions. For the past eighty years or so, Portobello (on the Caribbean side of the isthmus, opposite Panama City, on the Pacific side) had been the principal New World shipping point for treasures and more mundane goods coming from and going to mainland Spain. Gold from the Andes and stolen from the Incas, and silver from the mines of Potosi (in modern-day Bolivia), were carried overland by pack animals to Panama City. Silver was shipped up there from Lima. Meanwhile, treasures of the East (precious gems, jade, valuable ceramics, lacquer-ware, silks and exotic fabrics, all arriving in Mexico by way of the annual 'Manila Galleon'), were also sent on to Panama.

In the years that the Spanish treasure fleets were expected (once this had been an annual event but by the 1670s their arrivals were less frequent), all was taken by mule-train the sixty miles or so from Panama City to Portobello. Portobello was ideally situated for ease of access, had a deep harbour and strong walls, but it was far from ideal when it came to living conditions. The place was swampy, hot, damp and notoriously unhealthy. Because of this, the full-time population was never large, just a fraction of the size that it would be for the month of each treasure fleet visitation.

The fleets arriving from Spain went first to Cartagena, where they typically stayed for two months. News of their arrival would be dispatched throughout the main, allowing towns to send their tributes in gold, silver and other valuables either directly to Portobello, or to Portobello via Panama City, which maintained stables full of mules kept ready to carry the 'King's Treasure' overland to Portobello.

Each treasure fleet was comprised of a mixture of ships: merchantmen and high-sided royal galleons charged with carrying bullion and protecting the other ships. It was a risky business. Loss of men through scurvy or flux was expected, but there were also the attentions of predatory interlopers to negotiate, unmarked reefs to avoid and unexpected storms to weather. Phipps would have known and might even have been in the area when, in 1681, the *Nuestra Señora de Encarnación*, a carrack belonging to the Treasure Fleet, was caught in a storm near the mouth of the river Chagres and sank. It would have been carrying what in today's markets would be worth very many millions of any currency.

And Phipps would have known that what the sea takes, it sometimes gives up.[9.2]

New England settlers had eyed the Spanish gold and silver mines and wondered if such riches lay beneath their own soil. A few had been interested enough to prospect for precious metals. Virtually none were found, although there were brief periods of graphite mining ('black lead' to the colonists) and bog-iron smelting. The former started in the mid-1640s on land granted to the younger John Winthrop and had been partly financed by Thomas Lake.[9.3]

The latter was undertaken at the Saugus Iron Works on the Massachusetts river of that name, between 1646 and 1668. A second facility had been established at Concord but before the end of the century all the available bog-iron ore had been used up.[9.4]

Phipps had his own ideas about where to find underground, or rather submerged treasures. He was a man of the sea, and he reasoned that it was to the sea that he should look for riches. He knew that Spanish treasure ships had been lost in the Caribbean. He knew, more or less, the sea routes that these ships would have taken to make the most of tides, currents and winds and to avoid obvious dangers. He decided to become a treasure hunter, to seek out sunken Spanish treasure ships and to raise their riches to the surface. This probably started as a hobby, a part-time adjunct to his shipping and trading, but seems soon to have developed into much more.

An obvious place to start looking was Bermuda and thereabouts. Even then the island had something of the 'Bermuda Triangle' mystique about it. Bermuda had been discovered in 1505 by and named for Juan Bermudez. The Portuguese mariner had not taken possession of the island and it had remained uninhabited until just over one hundred years later. It was in 1609 that the *Sea Venture,* sent from England to resupply the Virginia Company's recently established Jamestown Colony, had been washed up there. Hit by a hurricane, the purpose-built ship had run for the island where it was able to reach shallow water before sinking. The passengers and crew, including Captain Christopher Newport and Admiral Sir George Somers, all survived and took possession of the island.

Known to Newport and Somers as the 'Isles of Devils', Bermuda proved more hospitable than either man knew Jamestown to be, and they were reluctant to leave. The Virginia Company subsequently sold its interest in Bermuda to the newly formed Somers Islands Company, which received its royal charter in 1615.

Bermuda had proved popular with colonists and prospered by growing and curing tobacco (once the art of curing had been learned from slaves). But the price of tobacco proved unstable and the king's penny a pound duty did not help. By the second half of the 1600s, Bermudians were on the lookout for other sources of income. One of these was 'fishing' for sunken treasure.

The island sits out in the Atlantic Ocean away from the American coast, almost 800 miles south-east of Boston and 2,000 miles north-east from Jamaica. In the age of sail, it was a useful waypoint for ships bound from the Caribbean to Europe.

Mariners found their way by 'fixing' their position by means of longitude and latitude, imaginary lines drawn on charts running from north to south and west to east. Much like a game of 'battleships', the intersection of two lines told them where they were. The problem was that while navigation equipment available in Phipps' time could give a reading at sea for latitude (the line from west to east), it could not provide a reading for longitude (the line for north to south). To overcome this, navigators used waypoints. They sailed to the known latitude of some island or other prominent feature (whose longitude had previously been deduced by precise, land-based astronomical observation – of the moons of Jupiter) and then turned left or right, according to their best guess at where the waypoint lay. They would then sail 'down the line' of latitude (due west or due east) until the waypoint was sighted. This gave them a good idea of where exactly they were.

Sailing from Cuba to Spain, treasure ships might have sought out Bermuda before turning right to head for Spain. The dangers in this are obvious, especially when an intended waypoint is surrounded by reefs. And it meant that in the years before and after the *Sea Venture* sank, dozens of homeward-bound European ships had been wrecked on Bermuda's reefs.[9.5]

By the early 1680s, Bermudian wreckers and their 'Bermuda Tub' diving bells were well known throughout the Caribbean, according to author Michael Jarvis (*Eye of All Trade: Bermuda, Bermudians, and the Maritime Atlantic World, 1680–1783*).

As a Boston-based seaman, Phipps would certainly have known Bermuda and Bermudian mariners from the times he stopped over when en route from Jamaica to Boston, or simply carrying, perhaps contraband, tobacco between Bermuda and Boston. And he would have come across such Bermudian treasure hunters as William Davis and Abraham Adderley (with whom he worked and who crop up again later). No doubt he talked to them about likely local wrecks as well as those further afield. His preferred method seems to have been to trade upon his affinity with other seafarers. He mixed with them, drank with them and talked with them, always seeking out snippets of information that would allow him to pinpoint the site of sunken treasure.

By 1682 he had gained a reputation as a successful wrecker, a reputation good enough to attract local investors, including one John Hull (presumably the Boston 'mint master' who was then in the last year of his life), to put up money for a treasure-hunting voyage to the Bahamas. This had 'little more success than what just served him a little to furnish him for a voyage to England', reported Cotton Matther.[9.6]

The 'little' that was furnished by the voyage may not have been that little because it was successful enough to feature in a court case in which Phipps, as commander of the *Resolution*, and his quartermasters were sued over deductions made from the shares of some of their crew. Phipps lost.[9.7]

It seems that a share in the voyage, of which Phipps, as commander, might well have been entitled to two or three shares, was worth £54 (almost two years' pay for a skilled workman in England).

Phipps had had a taste of success and, according to Mather, had by now 'informed himself that there was another Spanish wreck, wherein was lost a mighty treasure, hitherto undiscovered'. Whether or not this was true, he must have decided that with more backing he could do better. He needed finance on a larger scale, and he knew where to find it.

Chapter 10

It Had Been Done Before

PHIPPS WOULD HAVE known about two French fur trappers who had gone to England to get financial support for their business plan. They had succeeded and continued to succeed with the help of the Gillams, a Boston-based family of shipwrights and mariners. Their exploits provided a blueprint for his own plan of action.

The two fur trappers were Médard Chouart des Groseilliers and his brother-in-law Pierre-Esprit Radisson. They were inveterate adventurers, explorers and business associates and they hoped to capitalise on their tolerance of the cold and Radisson's knowledge of and rapport with the Iroquois (with whom he had lived for two years after being captured and then adopted).[10.1] They would do this by specialising in venturing into the coldest extremes of what is now Canada, in search of beaver.

Beaver fur, warm, light and waterproof, was in much demand in Europe where the pelts sold for impressive amounts. The further north these industrious rodents lived, the colder the climate and the thicker (and more valuable) their fur. It was removed from the skins and felted to make the ultimate in seventeenth-century headgear – hats made from the Gore-Tex of their day. At their peak of popularity, beaver hats would cost the equivalent of six months' wages for a skilled worker, Elle Andra-Warner reported in *Hudson's Bay Company Adventures*. 'Fathers passed their beaver hats down to their sons.' The beaver hat was so valuable that in 1659 Nantucket Island was purchased (from Puritan settler Thomas Mayhew) for £30 and two beaver hats, one for Mayhew and one for his wife.[10.2]

By the late 1650s des Groseilliers and Radisson were experienced travellers to the remoter parts of America and Canada, parts not yet settled but home to semi-nomadic Indian tribes including Iroquois and Crees, from whom they bought beaver pelts. In 1660, after spending winter in the frozen wilderness (and possibly coming close to reaching Hudson Bay), the pair had returned to Quebec with sixty-canoes-worth of pelts and an accompanying Indian escort.[10.3]

Trying to balance the needs of settlers (for security), the demands of Native Americans (for respect of their rights) and the French crown (for income), the governor of New France, Pierre de Voyer d'Argenson, exercised something of a heavy hand over Quebec. Des Groseilliers and Radisson had broken his rules. They were licensed to conduct a transport business, not a merchant enterprise. And they had started their trek before a permit had been issued and without waiting for a Jesuit missionary to join them. Voyer d'Argenson confiscated most of the adventurers' valuable haul and gaoled des Groseilliers. Expecting to be welcomed back as heroic travellers, the two fur trappers were understandably miffed. When des Groseilliers was released from prison, he went off to France to challenge Voyer d'Argenson's actions. He was largely unsuccessful, later returning to America.

By now it was 1664 and Charles II had given his brother, the Duke of York (later James II), substantial tracts of land in America, land which Charles did not own and much of which was under Dutch control. James passed on a good portion of his gift, that land between the Hudson and the Delaware rivers, to Lord John Berkeley and Sir George Carteret (in recognition of their loyal deeds during the English Civil War).

The recently restored Charles had also decided it was time that he asserted his authority over those parts of New England controlled by English settlers. As a starting point, he had ordered commissions of enquiry be set up. These were now underway. Four commissioners had been appointed (Colonel Richard Nicolls, Sir Robert Carr, Colonel George Cartwright and Samuel Maverick, he who later reported so unfavourably on 'three rivers, the East of Kennebeck, Shipscot and Pemaquid' where fishermen were said to 'share in their wives as they do in their boats').[10.4]

Sailing from England with an expeditionary force comprising four warships and around 300 troops, they stopped first in Boston. It was here that des Groseilliers and Radisson, in town searching for support for a further expedition, came across Commissioner Cartwright. The colonel was on the lookout for opportunities for his boss and benefactors, one of whom seems to have been Sir George Carteret.

The commission's next task was to force the Dutch settlement of New Amsterdam into surrender so that the Duke of York could actually take possession of his gifted American lands: something in fact achieved in September of that year when Commissioner Colonel Richard Nicolls, commander in chief of the expeditionary force, appointed his fellow commissioners Carr and Cartwright plus four New England worthies, including John Winthrop and Thomas Lake, to agree terms.[10.5]

New Amsterdam would duly become New York and Carteret would be free to pursue his new-world and money-making enthusiasms to the full, including cashing in on the healthy beaver trade that had been developed by the New Amsterdammers.[10.6]

Cartwright suggested des Groseilliers and Radisson travel to England and offered an introduction to Carteret. If only they would work for the English rather than the ungrateful French, he was sure there would be profits all round. It was an idea they were happy to accept. It took them a while, but in 1665 they turned up in England. There they were heard out by a suitably impressed Carteret and received a royal nod of approval. At this point Prince Rupert, the reckless royal hero of the Civil War, entered the scene.

Since leaving the English battlefields he had pursued a colourful military career, first as a privateer-cum-pirate, and then as a mercenary for hire. Rupert's fortunes had been rehabilitated by the restoration. His cousin Charles II showed his gratitude in various ways for the funding that Rupert's privateering escapades had brought him while living in exile. In 1666 Rupert was appointed joint commander of the fleet, entering something of a double act with George Monck, a royalist turned republican general turned key player in the restoration (a role which saw him made Duke of Albemarle).

Although Rupert and Carteret were said to have argued during Rupert's privateering days, they were now both Admiralty creatures and were clearly not on such bad terms that information about investment opportunities could not be shared. Soon both were putting money into the venture put forward by des Groseilliers and Radisson.[10.7]

In 1668, after further delays caused in part by the demands of the Anglo-Dutch War then in progress, two ships set out from Gravesend on the Thames for Hudson Bay. The *Eaglet*, which carried Radisson, was forced to turn back due to heavy weather. The other, the *Nonesuch*, with des Groseilliers aboard and captained by Zachariah Gillam, reached its destination.

The experiment was not hugely profitable but was successful enough to persuade its eighteen backers that they should press ahead. This they did, obtaining a 1670 royal charter giving the Governor and Company of Adventurers of England trading into Hudson Bay 'all those Seas Streightes Bayes Rivers Lakes Creekes and Soundes in whatsoever Latitude they shall bee that lie within the entrance of the Streightes commonly called Hudsons Streightes together with all the Landes and Terriroryes upon the Countryes Coastes and confynes of the Seas Bayes Lakes Rivers Creekes and Soundes aforesaid that are not already actually possessed by or granted to any of our Subjectes or possessed by the Subjectes of any other Christian Prince or State with the Fishing of all Sortes of Fish Whales Sturgions and all other Royall Fishes in the Seas Bays Islets and Rivers within the premisses and the Fish therein taken together with the Royalty of the Sea upon the Coastes with the Lymittes aforesaid and all Mynes Royall as well discovered as not discovered of Gold Silver Gemms and pretious Stones to bee found or discovered within the Territoryes Lymittes and Places aforesaid And that the said Land bee from henceforth reckoned and reputed as one of our Plantacions or Colonyes in America called Ruperts Land.'

They were to be 'absolute Lordes and Proprietors of the same Territory lymittes' with 'every of theire Rightes Members Jurisdiccions Perogatives Royaltyes and Appurtenances'. For this, and exclusive trading rights, they were to pay the crown 'two Elkes and two Black beavers' a year.[10.8]

The eighteen 'adventurers' (who had stumped up a total of £4,720 but had not in fact ventured as far as Hudson Bay themselves) included the company's governor Prince Rupert (£270), his deputy and also his secretary, Sir James Hayes (£270), Sir Philip Carteret, son of George (£270), and Christopher, second Duke of Albemarle (£300).[10.9] Also included was Radisson's father-in-law, Sir John Kirke, a soldier and sailor who had long-standing interests in and at one time claims to parts of Arcadia (the name applied to French colonies in Newfoundland and further south as far as the Kennebec River).

Of course, as was now usual, King Charles' charter included the gift of territory he did not at the time own or control. Both Native American and French settlers had competing claims. Although Hudson's Bay had been 'discovered' by professional explorer Henry Hudson in 1610, when seeking the fabled North West Passage, there was no escaping the fact that a French trading post was operating there in 1668. France and Britain continued to dispute ownership until 1714 when the Treaty of Utrecht conceded control to the British.

The early years of the Hudson's Bay Company saw its trading posts change hands several times. Personal allegiances were equally fickle. Des Groseilliers and Radisson were originally employees of the Hudson's Bay Company, then changed sides and attempted to establish a rival French company, and then changed sides again. Their long-time mercantile associates, the Gillams, equally unconcerned about the dictates of officialdom, shadowed their movements. This did not prevent the Hudson's Bay company later offering Radisson, des Groseilliers or Zachariah or his son Benjamin Gillam further employment.

Prince Rupert remained governor of the Hudson's Bay Company until his death in 1682. He had survived Zachariah Gillam by only a few weeks. At the time Gillam was employed by the Hudson's Bay Company as captain of its ship *The Prince Rupert.* A storm caused it to drag its anchor and to get caught in and crushed by the ice. The captain and his crew all drowned in the freezing bay waters.

Both Rupert and Gillam narrowly missed the opportunity to become involved in another American-inspired venture, that of William Phipps. He wanted to move his treasure hunting up a notch, and he wanted finance to do so. And following their example, he had a good idea where to find investors.

PART II

BLUSTER, BULLION AND BELLIGERENCE

'[Robinson Crusoe] is the true prototype of the British colonist. The whole Anglo-Saxon spirit is in Crusoe: the manly independence, the unconscious cruelty, the persistence, the slow yet efficient intelligence, the sexual apathy, the calculating taciturnity.'

James Joyce

'Though I was not a belligerent kid, I do not think I ever passed up a good opportunity to fight.'

Gene Tunney

Chapter 11

A Right Royal Welcome

AT SOME TIME in late 1682 or early 1683, Phipps turned up in London. He had made enough from his *Resolution* foray to pay for his trip, he had information about promising-looking wreck sites, and he had a track record of successful foraging to boast about. All he needed were a few wealthy investors to push his 'treasure-fishing' business to new heights.

If, as is probable, this was Phipps' first visit to London, he must have been astounded by what he found. Boston had been a revelation, but London was in another league. The number of people would have been overwhelming, several times more in one city than in the whole of New England. And, especially near the river, they lived cheek by jowl, a heaving mass of humanity. There was little of the 'New England' restraint to be found. Anything and everything could be bought or sold on the filth-strewn London streets, including those doing the selling. There was noise and stench. The hustle and bustle went on between and in the shadow of a mixture of hovels and fine buildings. Much of the City of London had been rebuilt in the seventeen years since the Great Fire of London. There were many fine new stone-built churches and residences. The building work continued.

The river would have impressed Phipps with more and larger ships than he had seen in one place before. Besides these, there were numerous smaller vessels plying to and fro, laden with goods, animals and people.

One thing that might not have registered too much with Phipps was the weather. It was cold, just like New England. Britain was in the midst of a 'little ice age' and the winters were bitter; 1683/84 were 'Frost Fair' years in which the Thames froze solid.

Among all this, Phipps had to find his way. He was not overwhelmed. Baker and Reid[11.1] suggest he had the benefit of introductions from his cousin, Constantine Phipps. The 26-year-old trainee barrister was only at the start of his career and may not have known too many people of the kind to whom William needed to pitch his plans. One he certainly did know was parliamentarian and fellow lawyer Sir Robert Sawyer. He was the grandfather of Catherine Sawyer, to whom Constantine was engaged to be married (the two wed in 1684).

Sawyer was a contemporary and friend of secretary to the Navy Samuel Pepys, whom he had first met at Cambridge University. Through this and his work prosecuting government business, Sawyer must have been well known among Admiralty circles. Whether or not Constantine helped William with introductions, it was to the likes of the Admiralty men who had funded the Hudson's Bay Company that William made approach.

Prince Rupert had died in November 1682, but his former secretary Sir James Hayes, investor in, and deputy-governor of, the Hudson's Bay Company was still active. Rupert's old opponent-turned-Admiralty-opposite-number George Monck had died way back in 1670, but his son, Christopher Monck, had taken his place as the Duke of Albemarle and as HBC investor.

It is easy to image Phipps hawking his 'project', perhaps turning up in Change Alley where the recently opened Jonathan's Coffee House attracted a growing clientele of mariners, Royal Society gentlemen scientists, would-be investors and stockjobbers. (Lloyd's Coffee House, which came to be the haunt of shippers and ship owners, and which developed into Lloyd's of London, was yet to open.)

He would also have visited, and probably waited in drafty corridors for many an hour at the Admiralty's Westminster offices. He may have brought an introductory letter from Constantine Phipps' future grandfather-in-law and current attorney general, Sir Robert Sawyer. And he certainly brought his charts.

Phipps struggled with the written word, but he would have been at home with charts of the areas he knew so well. He could 'read' their symbols and graphics, the shape and relative positions of islands, the pictorial representation of coastlines and the mountain ranges and other prominent features that lay behind them. He was a carpenter and knew how to measure. He was at home with working plans and diagrams, with numbers and tables. And he knew how to sail a ship.

Phipps found surprisingly receptive listeners in Anthony Cary, Viscount Falkland (the stepson of Sir James Hayes), Admiral Sir John Narborough (sometimes spelled Narbrough) and Vice-Admiral Sir Richard Haddock. These men were wealthy in their own right and on the lookout for investment opportunities.

Born in Somerset, Falkland had come into his Scottish title when only seven. There had been no significant fortune to go along with this, but his marriage to the wealthy Rebecca Lytton (only a year before his first meeting with Phipps) had put this right. Now 26, he was official treasurer to the Navy, a post he had purchased from Sir Edward Seymour (a cousin of the Duke of Somerset) for £15,000. It no doubt entitled him to a levy on the funds that passed through his hands.

Narborough, on the other hand, was a career naval officer. He had joined his first ship as a cabin boy but by the age of 26 had worked his way up to captain.

By 33 he was a knight and an admiral and had grown rich on the prize money he had accumulated. Since 1680 he had been a commissioner of the Admiralty.

Sir Richard Haddock was, like Narborough, currently a deskbound sailor, holding the position of controller of the Navy.

The three Admiralty men and Phipps seemingly got along well. They were all adventurers of sorts, men of action rather than contemplation. At home, the ruling classes looked down on Phipps because of his lowly beginnings and lack of education. To Narborough and Haddock, used to dealing and facing danger with rough-and-ready seamen, this did not register so strongly.

In truth they had a strong reason to listen to what Phipps had to say. It was that the New Englander was not the first to come along with a treasure-hunting proposal. At that very moment two Navy ships were on the point of sailing to the West Indies in search of wrecks, in fact one wreck in particular.

Two men on the make, Isaac Harmon and Sir Richard White, who seemed to act as his agent, had gone to the Admiralty claiming special knowledge of the whereabouts of the remains of a Spanish galleon sunk just over forty years before.

Harmon, a Dutchman, claimed he had shared a cell with the imprisoned pilot, a survivor of the shipwreck who had been held at least partly to blame for its sinking. The ship in question was the *Nuestra Senora La Pura y Limpia Concepcion* (*Our Lady of the Pure and Clean Conception*).

The name '*Concepcion*' would have immediately captured Narborough's attention. Something of a quixotic character, he had sailed in Caribbean waters and knew the story of the legendary shipwreck.

Built in 1620, the ship had been chartered by the Spanish authorities as one of two lead ships for its 1640 treasure fleet. The *Concepcion* and its convoy had arrived in Vera Cruz in the summer of that year where it stayed for a little more than a year. Its holds filled with the king's bounty, but without the benefit of a refit, it began its return voyage to Spain in July 1641. A stopover in Cuba put its final departure date back to September, and into the hurricane season.

By the end of the month the fleet was off the American coast, north of Florida and heading towards Bermuda. It was then that it was struck by a storm. According to the US National Hurricane Center, this resulted in the loss of eight ships 'many lost in the Bahama Channel'.[11.2] It was not a particularly unusual event. In September of the previous year some thirty-six vessels had been caught in a hurricane to the west of Cuba with four 'thrown on shore' and many sailors drowned. And in September 1642, 'men in twenty-two ships' sailing the Lesser Antilles were drowned.

The loss of life was tragic, but for Spain the loss of the silver and gold carried in its treasure fleet was financially devastating. Its economy was built on the premise of a steady flow of wealth from its American colonies, and much of the 1641 tranche of such treasures had been carried in the holds of the *Concepcion,* one of the king's ships lost because of the storm.[11.3]

The Spanish authorities and no doubt the eager Bermudian 'fishers' did make attempts to recover the *Concepcion's* treasure. Even the captain, one of those to survive the ship's sinking, had a go. But to succeed it was necessary to first find the wreck of the galleon, and nobody could trace any sign of it.

Part of the problem was that the *Concepcion* had not sunk immediately. The ship might have been separated from the scattered fleet, it might have been damaged, old and unseaworthy, but its captain believed it could make port. He headed towards Puerto Rico, around 1,000 miles away. The voyage meant sailing south-east, skirting along the northern edge of the Bahamas Bank, with its 3,000 strung-out and sparsely inhabited islands, shallow seas and jagged reefs (to sail directly back to Cuba or Hispaniola would have meant sailing through this treacherous stretch of water).

The ship was slow and unresponsive, the weather indifferent, and their charts less than precise. Bashed and beaten by the seas, blown off course by the winds, they were uncertain where exactly they were. They did not know it, but by the end of October they were almost level with the Turks and Caicos Islands. The captain thought they were somewhere else, the two official pilots, whose conclusions he was mandated to heed, thought they were even further away.

Hit by another storm, the *Concepcion* ploughed into a reef, lodging itself between unseen outcrops. It was a surreal scene, when the tide was high there was no sign of the forest of coral-encrusted columns that lurked just beneath the waves. Only the superstructure of the ship and its spars would have been visible: a half-sunken ghost ship, motionless in open seas with no land visible in any direction.

During the night the *Concepcion* shifted, but not in a good way. It was clearly slipping below the waves. There was panic among those aboard and a rush to take to the long boat. But it was obvious this would not be able to carry them all and arguments began. Next morning they started to make rafts.[11.4]

It was agreed they should abandon the ship and make for land. The nearest, said the pilots, was Anegada (these days counted as one of the British Virgin Isles). It was the supposed home of cannibals and in fact lay 400 miles away. It didn't really matter where it was because the rafts had little option but to allow themselves to be taken where the howling winds and unseen but demanding currents dictated. Those thirty-something souls who eventually took command of the long boat, the captain and some officers among them, had more options. But they ended up in more or less the same place anyway. After four days without food or drink they were washed up on the remote northern shores of

Hispaniola, near what became Puerto Plata. At that time, the north of Hispaniola was all but unpopulated and it was not until late November that the dishevelled and disorientated seamen made it to the city of Santo Domingo, having trudged barefoot through forests and across mountains to reach the south of the island.

There were many deaths among those who had taken to the rafts, but also a good many survivors, equally as uncertain where they were and where they had been as were their more privileged 'long boat' colleagues. But there were enough, and enough who later made their home in Hispaniola, Cuba or even Jamaica to keep the story of the *Concepcion* and the mystery of its whereabouts alive.

Nobody knew for certain where it had sunk but stories, told and retold, embroidered and embellished, centred on the 'Abrojos', the name ('meaning submerged rocks and reefs' in English) given to the reefs off the north coast of Hispaniola, between it and the Turks and Caicos Islands.

The trouble was, the 'Abrojos' are only one of three reef systems in the area. The other two, which encompass many square miles of little-used sea, were unmarked on most charts of the day.

Furthest west of the three reef systems, a little south of Turks and Caicos, are the shoals known as 'Mouchoir' or 'Handkercher' (the 'Abrojos', the area where White and Harmon seem to have believed the wreck lay). To the east of this, and a little south, is the Ambrosia Bank, which soon came to be known as 'Silver Bank'. And east and south again, is the Navidad Bank.

The Ambrosia Bank had two distinct parts, the North Riff and South Bank. It and the Navidad Bank, the third reef system, were in virtually open sea.[11.5]

Harmon's and White's 'information' may well have been made up or derived from a misunderstanding. The pilot of the *Concepcion*, if held responsible for its sinking, is more likely to have been executed than held in prison for thirty or more years. But if it really was him with whom Harmon shared a cell, then the pilot's 'crime' was that he hadn't known where he was anyway.

Whatever Harmon and White said, it was enough to convince admirals Narborough and Haddock that it was worth following up. They were due to send the 40-gun fourth-rated warship *Falcon* to take up station in Jamaica and it would be relatively inexpensive to add a smaller consort to the mission, with orders for both to check out the new 'information' they had been given. And they were able to convince the Navy Board and the king of the sense of this.

Charles was involved because he was by law entitled to a share of anything found in English waters. And if the wreck of the *Concepcion* was somewhere on or near the Bahamas Bank, that meant it was in English waters and the king could lay claim to his share, no questions asked.

The ship chosen to accompany the *Falcon* was the *Bonito*, (also sometimes spelled *Bonetta*), a sixty-one-foot single-masted vessel with fore and aft sails.

She was described in late October 1682 by John Shish, master shipwright at the Navy's Deptford yard, as 'a good sloop'. If 'a convenient vessel' for the planned voyage, 'she could be ready in a week's time', he said.[11.6]

Just over a month later, former pirate Bartholomew Sharp was appointed the *Bonito*'s commander. He was one of those brigands who had crossed the Darien (effectively the Isthmus of Panama) in 1680 to attack Spanish south seas towns and shipping. Leader of the group for two spells, he had eventually sailed home to England (in his stolen ship) around Cape Horn. Along the way Sharp had captured a 'Spanish manuscript of prodigious value'. This was a *Wagonner*, a book of charts covering 'all the ports, roads, harbours, bayes, sands, rocks and riseing of the land and instructions how to work a ship into any port or harbour between the latitude 17° 15" N and 57° S'.[11.7]

Charts had clearly moved on since the *Concepcion*'s day. In the 1680s they were regarded as top-secret national intelligence. Sharp was duly rewarded for his 'largesse' in providing a copy of his *Waggoner* to the Admiralty when, in 1682, he was found innocent of piracy, one of the Admiralty Court judges being Admiral Sir John Narborough. This is evidence of the dissention and rivalry within government, with one department agreeing to the Spanish ambassador's insistence on Sharp being prosecuted and the Navy demonstrating its independence in the matter.[11.8]

Narborough clearly knew Sharp and from the moment of his appointment had him down to sail in consort with the *Falcon*, whose captain was George Churchill. But then there was a delay, and he had second thoughts.

Perhaps he worried whether he could trust a former pirate, one who had 'bought' his escape from the rope, to keep secret the whereabouts of the *Concepcion*? And would he really have the strength of character to resist the temptation to help himself to some or all of any contents that could be dragged to the surface?

The delay was due to a collision, in February 1683, between the *Bonito* and another ship, the *St. Christopher*. Sharp reported the incident and blamed the master of the other ship, Nathaniel Clarke, and its pilot 'Mr. Powes of Deal'.[11.9] Whoever's fault this was, by early April Sharp was obliged to give up his command and Navy career officer Edward Stanley was appointed captain.[11.10]

The *Falcon* and *Bonito* eventually set sail and were in Jamaica by the early autumn of 1683. Phipps was not far behind them. By Christmas he was in Boston in command of his new ship, the *Golden Rose,* provided courtesy of the king, no less.

Chapter 12

A Rose by Any Other Name

SOMEHOW WILLIAM PHIPPS had talked his way into the loan of a ship. It was variously referred to as the *Rose*, the *Rose of Argier* or *Algiers,* and other variations on the theme. Cotton Mather called it the 'Algier-Rose, a frigot of eighteen guns and ninety-five men'.[12.1] It was the *Golden Rose*, a prize taken from Barbary corsairs in 1681 (as confirmed in minutes of the Lords of Trade).[12.2]

The Algiers-based pirates were a plague on English coastal villages and shipping, sometimes snatching people and carrying them off to be sold into slavery. The Navy had mounted campaigns against the corsairs and, in 1675, it had built the *Kingfisher*, a forty-six gun fourth-rated ship of the line. Adapted to resemble a commercial vessel, its job was to act as a decoy. The ploy worked and, in 1682, near Naples, the *Kingfisher* was set upon by seven pirate ships.

A twelve-hour naval battle ensued in which the corsairs flew a variety of false colours. *Kingfisher*'s captain, 21-year-old commander Morgan Kempthorne and seven of his crew were killed. But the corsairs suffered heavier losses and their ship, the *Golden Rose*, was captured.

James, Duke of York, later King James II, commissioned a painting of the action by Dutch artist Willem van de Velde. This depicts the *Golden Rose* not as a dhow but as a square-rigged three-masted warship of some power. But being a pirate vessel, it was probably less sturdily built than its adversary, lighter (and faster) than similar-looking naval vessels. It was certainly substantially outgunned by, and no match for the *Kingfisher*.[12.3]

The *Golden Rose* may have been a 'King's ship', as Cotton Mather proudly reported, but Phipps was not a commissioned captain. What Narborough and Haddock had engineered was an appointment of a very different nature. Churchill and Stanley were naval officers. Phipps was more in the nature of a privateer, somebody with a self-funded venture and a letter of marque allowing him and his backers (which may well have included Narborough and Haddock) to seek out sunken treasure and to keep a good proportion of anything found (after the king had had his share). That the ship to be used was a prize for which the Navy had no other immediate use was neither here nor there.

This was an arrangement very similar to that made with Captain William Kidd some years later. New York mariner Kidd was given a king's commission to hunt down pirates and to be rewarded from anything that he recovered. Unfortunately, Kidd found it difficult to capture pirate vessels and, under pressure from his crew, began attacking any ship that came within his sights. He turned pirate and was famously hanged for his troubles.

But this was the flaw in privateering arrangements. They were cheap for the king, who merely granted his permission. In theory they were cheap for the ship's owner or owners, who had no wages to pay since the crew were only on a promise of a share of prize money ('no purchase, no pay'). In theory there was no risk to anybody except the captain and crew who laid their lives on the line.

It often didn't turn out that way. Crews expected paying no matter what. And that sometimes meant turning pirate or running off with the ship. Once at sea, privateer vessels became a law unto themselves, mini republics in which the crew had a significant say.

Despite this, Narborough and Haddock saw various advantages in sending a second treasure-hunting mission so closely on the heels of Churchill and Stanley, and in setting it up as a private venture. It would double their chances of success but would be a cheaper version of the venture, and hence more likely to gain royal approval. They probably thought that Phipps had something to add by way of experience and persistence but would also bring them what is now called 'deniability'. If anything went wrong and England's current equilibrium with Spain was disturbed, it could all be blamed on a blundering New Englander.

And with Phipps around pursuing other wrecks, the hunt for the *Concepcion* might be less conspicuous and the secrets of the whereabouts of the treasure ship, if discovered, more easily kept secret. Because Phipps had not yet homed in on the *Concepcion* as his main target. There were, after all, plenty of other possibilities.

The Spanish newspaper *El Pais* has reported on research undertaken as part of the 'National Plan for the Protection of the Cultural Underwater Heritage of Spain'. It said that, using official state records, the study had identified 681 Spanish ships sunk in the Atlantic and Caribbean seas between the fifteenth and twentieth centuries. The vast majority were caused by storms. Most occurred off Cuba, and a good many in the American Atlantic and off Spanish Florida. There were just over sixty off Hispaniola and almost seventy off Panama.[12.4]

Phipps, it seems, was being set up as something of a 'fall guy'. He was being sent to deflect attention away from what Churchill and Stanley were up to, and to take the blame if anything went wrong.

Not only that – developments in the king's long-running attempts to bring the feisty 'self-governing' New Englanders into line also played a part.

It had been five years since England's attorney general, at the time Sir William Jones, had ruled that Massachusetts' various breaches of its charter were sufficiently serious to have the charter cancelled. Since then, and despite the unceasing efforts of collector of taxes Edward Randolph to point out governance failings, the colony had been able to fend off any proposed action.

But by 1682, Randolph had some reason to believe that the campaign mounted by himself and his cousin, New Hampshire 'owner' Robert Mason, was at last making some progress. It was true that it had been held that Mason had no right to govern New Hampshire. But the upshot had been the appointment, in 1682, of Edward Cranfield (he who had petitioned to have himself made head of an enquiry into the Atherton company) as lieutenant governor of the colony, a royal appointment.

Cranfield had at first formed an alliance with Randolph, whom he made his attorney general. Mason had been told to take his claims of ownership of New Hampshire land occupied by settlers to the New Hampshire courts. Now it seemed he had, under the regime of Cranfield and his attorney general, a real prospect of being able to pitch out the 'squatters' from 'his' land.

Better still, to placate the renewed interest of the Lords of Trade in their affairs, the General Court of Massachusetts had agreed at last to recognise Randolph's previously contested authority to search and seize vessels that he believed had contravened England's *Navigation Acts*.

Even better still, Randolph was called to England to participate in a Lords of Trade debate on whether to issue a writ of *quo warranto* against the colony, requiring it to justify the way it had conducted its affairs. It was decided that if the decision should go against the Massachusetts Bay Colony's General Council, as seemed almost certain, Randolph should deliver this writ in person.[12.5]

So, when Phipps was given the loan of his ship, he was also charged with taking Randolph back to Boston, where he could deliver the writ for which he had worked so long and hard. In September 1683 he wrote to the newly appointed secretary of war William Blathwayt (who had purchased his appointment from Matthew Locke) from the *Golden Rose* 'in the Downes' where it was awaiting 'articles to be signed by the Master and whole ships Company'. The already truculent crew were, he said, 'ill disposed to be engaged further than what already upon'. Meanwhile the colony's own agents had already sailed and would be back in Boston to convey the news 'in a little tyme'.[12.6]

Phipps, then, must by now have been fully aware, perhaps for the first time, of the political struggle between the ruling elite of Massachusetts, who favoured independence with no concession, and the English government's drive for subservience.

The New Englander was not a fool and he probably realised he was being used by both Narborough and Haddock as a diversion, a subterfuge such as those so often employed in naval exchanges (including that which resulted in the capture of the *Golden Rose*). He would have come to suspect that he was also being used to drive home a warning message to the Massachusetts General Council. He was a New Englander on king's business, and he had been tutored by admirals to maintain the dignity and protocol of the Navy. At his captain's dinner table, he had probably also been lectured by a feared English government official (Randolph) on the importance of law and order, and the reach of the king's authority.

Phipps seemed to have relished what he perceived to be his newfound political clout. He didn't object to being used to drive home a point, provided, of course, there was something in it for himself. This, after all, was the seventeenth century when favours delivered in property, position, or preferment were expected to be repaid in full. Phipps was determined to make sure that this would be so in his case.

Randolph was correct in his assumption that the Massachusetts Bay agents would arrive home before him. But he did make it back to Boston in time to present the colony's General Council with the king's writ issued 'by reason of some crimes and misdemeano's' of the corporation of the Massachusetts. The king promised that 'proprieties of all persons within that our colony shall be continued and preserved to them, so that no man shall receive any prejudice in his freehold or estate'. But he made an offer. If, 'before further prosecution had upon the said *quo warranto*', the General Council 'make a full submission and entire resignation to our pleasure, wee will then regulate their charter in such manner as shall be for our service and the good of that our colony, without any other alterations' other than those 'necessary for the better support of our government there'.[12.7]

This last veiled threat, that if Massachusetts accepted the writ without contest the king would 'regulate' but not abolish its charter, had been Randolph's suggestion. The General Court heard that Randolph was to await its response which he was to take back to England. If Randolph thought the General Council would cave in at this stage, he was sorely disappointed. Further defiance would surely result in cancellation of the Massachusetts Bay Colony's charter but there was, for the hard-liners, no alternative but to resist. After all, look what was happening in New Hampshire.

By early December Randolph had his answer. After fierce debate the General Council had decided it would instruct lawyers to answer the writ in court. For good measure it also challenged the lawfulness of the writ itself. Could a charter exercised in America be 'tryed in a Court in England' and 'by what authority [could] the sherriffs of London serve a writt on persons who never were inhabitants there?' Not only that, the writ was addressed to a number of individuals whereas the complaints to be answered in court were against a company. Finally, 'the writt was not served on the persons concerned untill the time of appearance was past'.[12.8]

Randolph scurried back to London with the response.

The seemingly defective legal paperwork had presumably been drawn up by Constantine Phipps' grandfather-in-law, Attorney General Sir Robert Sawyer. Reviewing what the Massachusetts General Council had said, Sir Robert had to agree they had a point when it came to when and to whom the writ had been served. But he came up with some sharp legal footwork of his own. It meant that in 1684 the English courts agreed, without hearing from the Massachusetts Bay Colony, that its charter should be withdrawn.

Meanwhile Phipps, anchored in Boston harbour found himself at the centre of the long-running argument over independence between old-school, hard-line settlers and the more moderate business-minded merchants. It had been rumbling on for years and now it was reaching a crescendo. Phipps was a New Englander but something of an outsider, looked down on or ignored by Boston's elite. But he had accepted the king's shilling and believed he would be expected to act accordingly.

His reaction was to do what he could to uphold the king's authority. He did this by insisting that other ships in the harbour acknowledge the superior status of the *Golden Rose*, a king's ship, by saluting it when passing. The expected way of doing this was by the dipping of colours, and perhaps topsails, if raised. Ships that ignored this protocol were treated to a shot across their bows, followed by a demand for ten shillings to cover the cost of the shot.

Phipps was a rumbustious man in charge of a rumbustious crew and they all clearly gained some amusement from their sabre-rattling antics, and from the riotous visits to local taverns that seemed to follow. What churchgoing Mary (Hull) Phipps thought of it all is not recorded but at this stage Phipps clearly did not think of himself as other than a servant of the king, a free-wheeling treasure hunter at one with his crew.

The truth was that he was not as trusted as he might have cared to think, nor as free from scrutiny. Among his crew were two government agents, John Knepp and Charles Salmon. They did not hide their instructions which they believed entitled them to respect, although the crew of the *Golden Rose* thought otherwise. The two government men had been charged with preventing theft and embezzlement of the king's share of any riches raised from the sea. They were also to report to Narborough and Haddock on the behaviour of the captain and crew, a part of their task pursued with particular enthusiasm by head spy John Knepp. With unrealistic expectations that naval discipline (and punishments) would be exercised by Phipps over his unpaid gang of ruffians, Knepp took a dim view of the way the ship was run. And while in Boston he protested even more against near riots caused by the hard-drinking, hard-cussing crew, sometimes supported by their not-too-gentle giant of a captain.

One such occasion led to confrontation between Phipps and Governor Simon Bradstreet. Phipps said he was on king's business and therefore a law unto himself. Bradstreet rejected the notion, but conceded Phipps was about the king's private business. The result was that just as Phipps had been unable to discipline his own 'no purchase, no pay' crew, Bradstreet found it unwise to punish Phipps.

Well used to stonewalling any attempt at royal intervention in their affairs, the colony's governor and council never did accept that the treasure hunter's authority came anywhere near to trumping their own. But when Phipps discovered that another vessel was about to embark on a mission like his own, he tried again. He went to Governor Bradstreet claiming his king's commission gave him exclusive rights to scour the Bahama Banks for treasure. This was obviously not the case, but Phipps was trying again to assert the king's authority. He received the same answer as before. His mission was private business, and no action would be taken.

Phipps promptly took advantage of the situation and made the claimed interloper, the *Good Intent*'s Captain Warren, a franchise partner. He thereby gained access to that ship's diving tubs and divers.[12.9] (Phipps later made a similar franchise, or 'consort', arrangement with at least one other boat.)

After ten bad-tempered weeks in Boston, Phipps set sail for Providence and the Bahama Banks. He left without Knepp. No doubt the target of jibes, threats and petty thefts, he was in fear for his life. It was reported to him that *Golden Rose* crew members had been heard talking about ways to get rid of him (permanently) and he had subsequently been wounded in a scuffle. Enough was enough and he decided to stay in Boston and collect information about the *Golden Rose* from visiting ships.

It must have been his reports home that caused Treasury and Admiralty officials to worry about Phipps' approach to his voyage. In February 1684 the Lords of Trade heard that the king had written to Joseph Dudley and William Stoughton, both known in London and destined to head the replacement Massachusetts government, 'ordering H.M.S. Rose, Captain William Phipps, to be seized if it appear that Phipps or his seamen have a design to defraud the King of the ship, with the plate and bullion thereon. This order to be kept secret'.[12.10]

The letter had accidentally raised the status of 'H.M.S Rose' to a 'Navy ship' and had obviously been written in ignorance of Phipps' own attempts at this.

Stoughton and Dudley subsequently replied with barely concealed glee that they had received the king's command and would 'keep them secret and execute them'. They added a rider that rather suggested the king should have gone to them first. 'We are sorry that the matter already bears so ill a face that one of the supervisors on the King's behalf has already deserted the business. We hope he will give you a true information, though we were never particularly advised of the cause of the breach.'[12.11]

But by then Phipps had taken his divers and his diving tubs and sailed off in search of treasure. He had, said Dudley and Stoughton, 'been some months upon the wreck' although they pledged to 'use our best endeavours to persuade his return from the wreck, and shall then do our utmost for the King's interest'.

Chapter 13

Laying the Groundwork

LEAVING BOSTON IN January 1684, Phipps spent the next two years scouring the Caribbean for the remains of treasure ships and generally making something of a nuisance of himself.

Finding wrecks was no easy business in Phipps' time. Even if there were survivors to provide the best guess of where their ship had gone down, the information gained this way was likely to be inaccurate or imprecise, or both. Intuition and conjecture, even good luck, were helpful to some. But generally, there was little other than the human eye to pinpoint wreck sites, which meant peering over the side of a boat into heaving water or brief free-diving visits to the depths.

Such constraints meant only ships that had sunk in relatively shallow water were likely to be found, and it was in such places that it was most profitable to look. The sea around Bermuda was a possibility but had been raked over many times by local wreckers and even by Phipps. The area around the Bahamas offered much more scope, with shallow surrounds of over 120,000 square kilometres (46,000 square miles). They extend about 1,600 kilometres (close to 1,000 miles) in length, from the Little Bahamas Bank in the north-west to the Navidad Bank in the south-east.

The Bahamas (owned by England) lie north of Cuba (then Spanish) and Hispaniola (part Spanish, part French). Jamaica, with its significant English community of seafaring ruffians, was and is south of these islands. In a direct line, the distance between the Bahamas and Jamaica is about 800 kilometres, roughly 500 miles. But any sea voyage would not be direct and would have been longer. However, there is a direct 'north west passage' from Jamaica to the Turks and Caicos Islands at the southern end of the Bahamas Bank. It is a voyage of around 650 kilometres, about 400 miles and, depending on the time of year, would probably have been a sail of two or three days.

It was to the Bahamas that Phipps headed, not in search of the *Concepcion* but to search other known wreck sites that had already been picked over by others. By the end of the year, he had moved on to Jamaica where he would have soon discovered that Churchill and Stanley (captains of the *Falcon* and the *Bonito*) had got there more than a year before. Their instincts (and orders) may have been to keep their treasure-hunting activities as secret and low key as possible, but it had not turned out that way.

Captain Churchill had managed to make a big splash when he had taken the *Falcon* into Jamaica. It was all over the seemingly innocuous request of a cooper to join his crew. Governor Sir Thomas Lynch, writing to the Lords of Trade and Plantations, called it an 'unlucky incident'.[13.1]

Coopers were valuable members of any crew, turning out barrels to store anything from apples or grains to water or wine. This particular cooper had previously been employed by local seaman Captain Francis Mingham of the *Francis.* He was, said Lynch, a 'virulent, base-natured fellow'. In fact, Mingham had form. Three years previously he had been caught smuggling brandy. An Admiralty Court presided over by Sir Henry Morgan no less, at that time Lieutenant Governor of Jamaica, had confiscated his ship. This was the usual punishment for such crimes but was one Mingham was not inclined to accept. In a two-year court battle fought out in England and Jamaica, Mingham at first lost, was found guilty of libel as well as smuggling, imprisoned and fined. But amazingly, and against all logic, he eventually won his case. His ship, the *Francis*, had been returned to him and it now lay anchored in Port Royal harbour.

Captain Churchill may have heard about Mingham and his litigious nature. He was no doubt pleased by the opportunity to employ an extra cooper to help make the 'Bermuda Tubs' needed by his divers but thought it wise to check that the man had indeed been released by Mingham.

The autocratic captain, a younger brother of the future Duke of Marlborough and himself destined to become an admiral, sent for Mingham. The cooper's former employer 'insolently replied that he would not come, but that he dined at such and such places, and that Churchill might come to him', explained Lynch. Deciding to employ the cooper anyway, Churchill sent for his clothes and tools. When these were refused, he ordered five more of Mingham's men pressed into his service. Words were exchanged ('ill words and affronts', said Lynch), and one of the abusers was dangled from a yardarm ready to be dunked in the harbour.

He was let down when William Flood, the mate of another ship, climbed aboard the *Falcon* to remonstrate at Churchill's high-handedness towards a local man. Flood was now hoisted up to the *Falcon*'s yardarm and 'three times ducked', according to a deposition filed by Mingham. His temper unquenched, Flood continued to berate the *Falcon*'s captain and 'received twenty lashes on his bare back' for his troubles. Physicians, said Mingham, 'declare him more likely to die than live'.

He went off to the governor to demand Churchill be arrested. Lynch's reply was to tell Mingham he should not be so rude to the king's captains, and that he deserved punishment for involving him in an argument with a captain over whom he had no authority. 'I told him also to go on board and give the captain good words, and that he should have his men back,' said Lynch. 'Instead of this, he sends his mate on board, who says that the Governor has ordered the men to be given up. The captain told him he lied, but that if Mingham had come for them himself he should have had them.'

The argument rumbled on. Mingham tried to seize the cooper. Churchill's men retaliated, the cooper was rescued, there were near riots and some seamen were arrested. 'All this while the mate was sick of a fever. He fell ill four days after the ducking and whipping; and this it was that made the people so riotous when I said that I could not punish persons whom they judged criminal. Yesterday the mate died,' said Lynch.

A coroner's jury later decided, after deliberating for seven hours and not without misgivings and outside persuasions, that Flood had died of natural causes.

The report sent by Lynch to the Lords of Trade described an island colony on the frontiers of English authority. It was a lawless place where an economy based on sugar production competed with one based on privateering and another centred on the importation and sale of slaves. The legislature generally favoured the planters but was split. At the centre of it all was 'that little, drunken, silly party of Sir Henry Morgan's' (as Lynch described it). Much of the argument was over the supply and price of slaves. The plantation owners required muscle power to cultivate, cut, crush and boil their sugar cane and horses being not too good at planting or wielding machetes, and the planters themselves being unwilling to break their own backs, they had decided the only source of this was slave labour.[13.2] Slaves were available from the Royal African Company. This had been set up in 1660 up by Charles and James Stuart, with shareholders that included Prince Rupert, Samuel Pepys, and the philosopher and sometime chairman of the Board for Trade and Plantation, John Locke. Without any sense of injustice, let alone shame, it forced many thousands of West Africans to board its ships each year. Taken from their homes they were transported in dark, damp, filthy holds to a new life of hard labour and depredation. Many of these unfortunate souls, or at least those 'fortunate enough' to survive an Atlantic crossing, found themselves stepping unsteadily from putrid ships onto Jamaican wharves, destined to be sold to the highest bidder.

As far as the Royal African Company was concerned, those bidders might just as well be Spanish as English. Satisfying demand for slaves from Spanish colonies was good business. It boosted sales and kept the local price of slaves higher than would otherwise have been the case. It was also illegal, to the extent that it was contrary to international agreement; not that the Royal African Company cared too much about that.

Under the 1670 Treaty of Madrid, Spain had agreed not to continue to contest English sovereignty over Jamaica and other Caribbean islands already in England's possession. England, for its part, would suppress piracy and neither country would allow trade between their own and the other's Caribbean possessions.

England had failed to live up to its part of the bargain. English 'privateers' continued to range the Caribbean claiming their bought commissions gave them legitimacy. And trading between the islands continued, especially in human beings needed to work plantations.

Back in 1680 the Jamaican planters had complained to the Lords of Trade about the Royal African Company not supplying the island with sufficient slaves 'at moderate rates'. The Royal African Company in turn complained that the planters owed it £60,000 for the supply of slaves and that it needed more than the £16 or £17 per slave that the planters were willing to pay. It had costs to meet, it said. The Lords of Trade heard that 'the negroes cost them at first price £5, and £4,15 shillings the freight, besides the loss of 25 per cent by the usual mortality, and a charge of £20,000 a year for maintaining of ports'.[13.3] The upshot was that the Lords of Trade 'recommended' that company 'send 3,000 merchantable negroes to Jamaica annually (provided that they have good payment of their debts there), and sell them at £18 a head, the sum to be paid there at six months' forbearance upon good security'.

Two years later the Jamaican planters again asked for help from the Lords of Trade. In response the committee decided the Royal African Company should 'be ordered to furnish Jamaica with five thousand negroes for the first year from the date of the Order, and with three thousand every subsequent year'.[13.4]

But the argument continued. Morgan's party had 'whispered' that Lynch had been bribed to favour the Royal African Company over local planters. He and Morgan were at daggers drawn.

Lynch, who had recently sacked Morgan, was trying to justify his actions. 'In his drink Sir Henry reflects on the Government, swears, damns, and curses most extravagantly,' he told the Lords of Trade. 'Had you full knowledge of his behaviour while Lieutenant-Governor, of his excesses, passions, and incapacity, you would marvel rather how he ever came to be employed than why he is now turned out,' said Lynch.[13.5]

Despite all this, Churchill had apparently been charmed by the old(ish) rogue. When the jury of the inquest into the cause of Flood's death had at first been 'inclined' to rule it murder, Captain Churchill had been 'provoked' to curse and rail at dissenters', said Lynch. 'This suited Sir Henry Morgan and the club, who took Churchill's part against the jury, and made him one of their company. They had this great opportunity to inflame and misinform him.'

Possibly because of Lynch's report into Churchill's role in this 'unlucky incident', he was soon after replaced as captain of the *Falcon*. Stepping in was Charles Talbot, a seasoned sailor whose previous commands included the *Mary Rose*.

It was into this fermenting hotbed of rivalry and competing interests that William Phipps blundered in late 1684. His actions had Acting Governor Hender Molesworth (the tormented, harassed, flustered and sick Sir Thomas Lynch having died) writing to London, complaining about Phipps' behaviour. 'This afternoon the Spanish factor with one of his captains came to me with great complaints that they had been affronted by some unknown people, and could not pass the streets in peace. But their chief complaint is against Captain Phipps of H.M.S. Rose who is said, upon some mistaken punctilio of the sea, to have fired a shot at one of the Spaniards, who had on a festival day put his pendant under his ram, and made him take it in. Captain Phipps meeting the Spanish captain in the street, with a rabble at his heels, told him that if he did not pay him for his shot, he would take his sword from him. The Spaniard was unwilling either to give up his sword or to pay the money, and the rabble was ready to have laid hands on him if a gentleman passing by had not taken ten shillings from his pocket and paid it for him. I am told that this is not Phipps' first affront to the Spanish captain, but that he constantly seeks occasion for it, being egged on by ill-wishers to the trade.'

Unknowingly Phipps had got himself embroiled in another politically charged difficulty. Molesworth, besides being acting governor was an agent of the Royal African Company and had a vested interest in maintaining good relations with Spanish traders. He was not amused by Phipps' antics and told the Lords of Trade: 'I ordered Captain Phipps to come to me and explain his conduct, but as he is on the point of sailing I doubt whether he will do so, or, indeed, whether he thinks himself bound to obey. Valuing himself on his independence and his private instructions, he may run into further mistakes and not think himself accountable to this Government. This will show you how liable we are to be affronted by capricious captains. When privately animated by enemies to the Government they are ready to raise a faction against the authorities of the place, and, as it were, to use the King's name against himself. This man never had better than a carpenter's education, and never before pretended to the title of captain; but now he assumes it, though he cannot yet show a commission for it, and takes more to himself than any other of the King's captains.'[13.6]

The response of the committee to whom Molesworth complained was to decide that 'the matter [was] to be brought up when Captain Phipps returns to England'. There is no record that it ever was.[13.7]

Molesworth, however, soon admitted that the damage had not been too great. 'Once more there is a Spaniard among us, notwithstanding him who was lately maliciously frightened away, so that if the people keep quiet and negroes are to be had we have an opportunity of redeeming our credit,' he reported to secretary to the Lords of Trade, auditor-general of plantations revenues, and secretary for war, William Blathwayt.[13.8]

Phipps was certainly determined to make waves wherever he swaggered. He did not keep his intentions secret nor his growing number of enemies guessing. Perhaps it was a strategy; a ploy inviting those with information about sunken treasures to make themselves known. Some, perhaps admirers among those 'ill-wishers to the trade', would have given him information, especially about the activities of Churchill, Talbot and Stanley.

Whether Phipps was able to meet these captains while in Jamaica is uncertain. Besides their supposedly discreet treasure-hunting, they were kept busy by Lynch and later Molesworth. The *Bonito* in particular was sent scurrying here, there and everywhere.

In September 1684 Stanley was sent off to Cuba to collect the crew of a sloop that had been taken while attempting to capture the pirate Juan Corso. Stanley carried with him a letter with implied threats and also the sloop's commander Derick Cornelison, who had somehow escaped imprisonment.[13.9] 'Foul weather' forced Stanley into a bay where a boat he sent ashore was captured. But the doughty captain 'rescued four of our turtlers' sloops from a French privateer'. He was unable to deliver Molesworth's letter.

In early 1685 Stanley was off again chasing the pirate Joseph Bannister and later in the year he was cruising the northern side of Jamaica 'until the time when he is to seek for the wrecks'.[13.10]

Between all this there had been some time for treasure-hunting. Churchill and Stanley had brought the informers Isaac Harmon and Sir Richard White along with them. Soon after arrival in Jamaica, Churchill had taken them off to search for the *Concepcion* wreck site. Despite the assurances given by Harmon and White at the outset, they were unable to pinpoint the location.

And then another informer turned up. In January 1685 Thomas Smith signed a sworn deposition to the effect that when sailing along the north-east coast of Hispaniola, he had passed a reef where he saw 'several ingots of silver and one of gold, and within forty feet of it the hull of a ship wedged in upright'. At that point the wind had freshened and the ship was forced to bear away, but Smith was confident he could find the place again.[13.11]

The reef identified by Smith was not marked on any chart that Molesworth knew of, but Stanley confirmed he had seen it 'on a private map, and that his own pilot knew it as well'. An agreement was made with Smith 'who would not take less than a fifth share' of which half was to go to Harmon and Sir Richard White. Reported Molesworth: 'The man was so confident that he would have agreed to be hanged if he did not show them the wreck, provided they brought him to the reef. But I have bound him only in a penalty to serve the King seven years in his ships of war without pay, and to submit to such corporal punishment as I shall think fit (which I have threatened to him to be very terrible and severe) if he failed to answer expectations … I did this to fright him from prosecuting the thing further, in case he has sworn to a falsity. But on the contrary, he pressed hard for some encouragement to the seamen to prevent mutinies, promising them some of his own share. I therefore gave them assurance under my hand that, if the design was successful, they should each have £100 for their extraordinary service, beyond what the King might give them.'

Stanley was sent off with Smith to investigate. At least, if the search should fail, 'there will be no expense to the King'.[13.12]

By May, Stanley was back in Jamaica 'without further success'. But he was more confident than ever that he could find the wreck at the next attempt. He had only failed, he said, 'through bad weather and want of provisions'. He said he had twice been beaten off by a north wind and was obliged to put into Porto Rico for stores before finding the reef he had been searching for. 'But the bank being of great length, the weather dark and hazy, and no observations being possible by sun or stars, he was forced by bad weather to bear up for this port,' reported Molesworth. 'He is now very confident that the rocks on which the wreck was sunk are on this bank, and that all previous searchers have gone to the wrong bank. His calculations, compared with other information, make me entertain much fairer hopes than ever before of the venture. As soon therefore as the weather breaks up, and Stanley can provide himself with an astrolabe to take an exact observation, I shall send him off again and a sloop with him … He is so confident of finding it, weather permitting, that he told me he would forfeit all the wages due to him (about £300) if he did not. He would have preferred the month of September, but as we hear of two other vessels bound on the same design, one of them, with a Spaniard aboard who was cast away in the wreck, it is necessary to lose no time. We have the advantage of knowing the latitude certainly better than any others. I am anxious to send him off at once also because Smith and the pilot are so impatient that they may leave us and apply to others.'[13.13]

How long it took Stanley to find an astrolabe is unknown, but it was not until November, well into the hurricane season, that Molesworth reported to the Lords of Trade on the latest attempt to find the *Concepcion*: 'Stanley is returned, having been several times in great danger, beating upon the rocks many times but failing to find the rock that they looked for. The peril was such as to discourage them from further attempts. Smith still sticks positively to his first statement. Stanley thinks he must either have seen the wreck or the Spanish directions, for his relation corresponds exactly with it. You shall have his journal by next ship.'[13.14]

So, the hunt was over and Stanley was sent off in the *Bonito* to Cuba to collect Captain Chandler and thirty or forty other prisoners who, said Molesworth, had been unjustly arrested as no more than 'a parcel of thieves and robbers'.[13.15]

Phipps may have missed out on meeting Churchill, Talbot or Stanley when in Jamaica, but he almost certainly met the wheeler and dealer Sir Richard White, aka Don Ricardo White (or Don Ricardo de Vite). The son of one-time Mayor of Limerick, Sir Dominick White, and brother of James-Stuart-friend-and-advisor Ignatius White, Don Ricardo traded on his connections with Spain, for whom he was reputed to spy. He was up for any deal and as Molesworth had told the Lords of Trade, he and Harmon were impatient for success and 'may leave us and apply to others'.

Historian Peter Earle reported (in his book *The Treasure of the* Concepcion) that the Spanish ambassador Don Pedro Ronquillo, Marquis of Burgamemo, had subsequently written to King James II on White's behalf. In his letter he repeated White's claim that he had sent his brothers the exact location of the *Concepcion*. These details had been contained in a letter he had entrusted to Phipps to take to London and, he claimed, Phipps must have opened the letter. Two witnesses, said Ronquillo, had testified that Phipps had admitted that he would not have known where the wreck lay had it not been for White.[13.16]

Earle dismissed White's claim, saying 'he never missed a chance to make some money'. And some money he did make because he was later paid a 'royal bounty' of £1,000 by a credulous James II. But perhaps more to the point, his claims admitted that he had had contact with Phipps. By design or loose talk he had no doubt added to Phipps' growing fund of knowledge about the whereabouts of the *Concepcion* wreck. But Phipps left Jamaica before Stanley had given up the chase. Because by June 1685 Phipps was in Bermuda on his way back to England where he had sailed into yet more political upheaval. Richard Cony (or Coney) was a London-appointed governor (the first after the company owning the colony had been dissolved) who had been in place barely two years and was facing widespread unrest. Complaints ranged from the ownership of children born into slavery to customs duties and land ownership. And Cony sent frenzied letters home complaining he was being thwarted at every turn.[13.17]

Leading the opposition was one Henry Bysshe, described by Cony as a 'great incendiary'. He had been imprisoned but continued his campaign from his cell from where he had plotted to have the governor sent to England aboard the *Golden Rose*. Despite a warning from Bysshe not to meddle in the island's affairs, Phipps sailed home with not Cony but Bysshe. He also carried Sarah Oxford to England with instructions to deliver her to the custody of the Earl of Sunderland. Oxford, it was claimed, was a 'principal abettor of Henry Bysshe' but Phipps was warned not to disclose the warrant against her 'till you are in the river as high as Gravesend'.

On arrival In England, the feisty Bysshe had Phipps arrested. 'I am now in custody in the bailiff's hand in the liberties of the Tower; whereby I am kept from the King's business,' Phipps said in an appeal to the Lords of Trade, written from the Nagg's Head on little Tower Hill. He was released the following day.[13.18]

Phipps had arrived home to a changed world. The 'merry monarch' had been too merry for too long. In February 1685 he had succumbed to illnesses unknown (although it would be surprising if it were not linked to over-indulgence in some way). The king had died and his brother James had ascended to the throne. The tectonic plates of society, government, patronage and preferment had shifted.

Chapter 14

Albemarle Steps In

IN PLEADING WRONGFUL arrest, Phipps wrote not to Narborough, not to his cousin, the lawyer Constantine Phipps, nor to Constantine's grandfather-in-law, Attorney General Sir Robert Sawyer, not to the secretary to the Lords of Trade William Blathwayt, but to Secretary of State the Earl of Sunderland. It was to Sunderland to whom Cony had been pouring out his troubles, and Phipps must have known as much. His list of useful contacts was growing.

It was Blathwayt who responded: 'The King, on reading Captain Phips' letter, orders that bail be given on his behalf for so much as relates to Captain Phips' transportation of the prisoner.'[14.1] It was a slightly dusty reply, requiring bail to be granted only so far as matters relating to 'Captain Phips' transportation of the prisoner' were concerned. But this was a careful reply from a man who had once conveyed an order for Phipps' arrest in Boston, and whose Lords of Trade committee had only a few months before promised to call the captain to account concerning Molesworth's complaints about him.

Perhaps it was that Phipps had proved himself honest by actually returning the *Golden Rose* to the king. Perhaps it was Phipps' support for Governor Cony that had rehabilitated his reputation with the Lords of Trade. Phipps had already provided a sworn statement that 'when Governor Cony announced his power to choose a Council, many of the Council said that they had as much power as he, and would not submit to the King's Commission. This was by the advice of Henry Bysshe, who was imprisoned for conspiracy to seize the Government and Governor. It was reported in the Island that the people intended to set up a free Government and take to piracy.'

Owing to Bysshe's preaching, said Phipps, it was regarded as treason to repair Bermuda's fortifications, meaning 'the Governor could not find men to put the Island in a state of defence, so that the Island lay open to the enemy'. While in the island two months, Phipps said he 'never saw the governor in drink nor inclined thereto', and he 'would judge him a person well qualified for his place'.[14.2]

According to Phipps-apologist Cotton Mather, Phipps faced down two attempted mutinies while captain of the *Golden Rose*. On the first occasion he was said to have seen off armed crew members with no more than an ox-bone to defend himself (and batter the would-be mutineers). On the second, he outwitted a planned rebellion cooked up by a shore party. Alerted by his loyal ship's carpenter, Phipps was waiting with cannons charged and aimed at the gangplank when the group made to come back aboard.[14.3] These stories are likely to be as accurate as other Mather fantasies that made Phipps out to be a gentle giant only willing to use his strength when sorely tested but otherwise congenial to a fault. They are based on a misunderstanding of the nature of privateering.

'No purchase, no pay' crews did not consider themselves bound to a ship by their articles. It was the practice on privateer vessels for crew members to leave or to change ships whenever they chose. And many decisions, including who should captain the ship, were made by common vote.

Bartholomew Sharp, who almost captained the *Bonito* to Jamaica, experienced just such 'crew-power' when cruising the south seas. The pirate-author William Dampier wrote about it. Sharp had been voted in as captain of the group that had crossed the Isthmus of Panama but then had been voted out again. But his replacement had been killed and many of the 'meaner sort' in the crew 'began to be as earnest for choosing Captain Sharp again into the Vacancy, as before they had been as forward as any to turn him out', said Dampier. 'And on the other side, the abler and more experienced Men [Dampier counted himself among their number], being altogether dissatisfied with Sharp's former Conduct, would by no means consent to have him chosen'. The crew had a vote. Sharp was reinstated. There were no more arguments, no fighting and no bloodshed. Those who had voted against Sharp simply left for home.[14.4]

True, Sharp and his ruffian crewmates had no owners to answer to, but once out of sight of land, privateer crews usually acted as owners anyway and often demanded revisions to their terms of employment, giving them bigger shares of any spoils.

If anything, the 'mutinies' reported by Mather show Phipps as the bully, going against custom and forcing his crew to stay on against their will, rather than the other way around. But they likely did not happen, at least not in the way Mather described. Perhaps it was Phipps himself who talked up the 'mutiny' and the crew's desire to run away with the ship, so as to demonstrate his credentials as somebody who stayed loyal to his sponsors. He might easily have told Mather that the crew 'never had anything against him, except only his unwillingness to go away with the King's ship' to the south seas.

Mather's assertion that Phipps' crew was 'growing weary of their unsuccessful enterprize', with the implication that he was not raking in the fortune he had promised, is also likely to be somewhat far from the truth.

Based on a search of secretary to the Navy Samuel Pepys' papers, historian Robert George put the king's share of Phipps' 1685 haul at £470, 19 shillings and 8½ pence.[14.5] This was in 1933 and nobody has questioned the figure since. But this is not the whole story. If the king's tenth share was £470, total receipts of the voyage were close to £5,000, a tidy sum in 1685. They might have been more, because the Treasury became very interested in tracking down a silver ingot that might have gone missing. First it ordered Haddock and Narborough to provide a copy of the instructions given by Charles II to Phipps 'when he went in 1683 in the *Golden Rose* upon a private undertaking for recovery of plate, bullion etc. wrecked upon the islands and shoals of Bahama near the Gulf of Florida'.[14.6]

Next it summoned Phipps to a meeting in Rochester 'concerning your performance of the instructions given you in your late undertaking at the islands of Bahama'. Joseph Hornby, who with Nathaniel Hornby acted as a banker to the government (and was frequently paid £300 for 'secret services') was also ordered to attend. The Hornbys were apparently in possession of an ingot of silver weighing ninety-three pounds, three ounces belonging to Phipps.[14.7] It was a hefty lump of valuable metal.

The Hornbys were later told 'to deliver to the officers of the Mint the pig of silver which you received of Capt. William Phipps. It is to be there coined for his Majesty's use'.[14.8]

There was enough recovered for it be worth the while of Boston merchant Robert Bronson to chase Phipps for £200 (a crew member's share, he said) due to him for the loan of a servant to the *Golden Rose*. He was still pursuing the claimed debt in 1691.[14.9]

And Phipps provided more than money. His services included taking Randolph to Boston and bringing home Bysshe and Oxford (and a French privateer arrested by Cony) from Bermuda. It might be added that key members of the *Golden Rose* crew had done well enough from the voyage to sign on again with Phipps for a further cruise; they included William Covell and Francis Rogers. (After the claimed mutiny Phipps had put into Jamaica where he said the malcontents were paid off and some new crew members taken on.)

Sitting in the Nagg's Head Phipps must have reflected on his position. He had a track record for recovering treasure, he now had more information about the wreck that Stanley and Churchill had been searching for, and he knew it to be that of a treasure ship and he had a good idea of its whereabouts. He also had the nucleus of a crew. But he had no ship. The *Golden Rose* had been returned to the custody of the Navy. Samuel Pepys was already assessing the cost of a needed refit (£700, he thought[14.10]). In short, Phipps knew he needed backers if he was to cash in on his intelligence-gathering by mounting a new treasure hunt. And as the new king had much else on his mind and was disinclined to become involved, he needed private investors with deep pockets.

Phipps first port of call in his search for new financial backers was a visit to his previous benefactors, Narborough and Haddock and the Admiralty clique that included Falkland, and Hayes. At some point he was introduced to Christopher Monck, Duke of Albemarle, son of general and admiral George Monck, who had worked so closely with Hayes' old boss Prince Rupert.

Narborough and Haddock had followed reports from Jamaica and Albemarle, as one of the Lords of Trade, would also have seen Molesworth's letters home, including those mentioning Thomas Smith, the seaman who had claimed to have seen the wreck. Between them, the three would have known all that was then to know about the *Concepcion*.

Phipps' sales pitch, as repeated by Cotton Mather, claimed he had 'fished out of a very old Spaniard (or Portuguese) a little advice about the true spot where lay the wreck, that it was upon a reef of shoals, a few leagues to the northward of Port de la Plata [*sic*], upon Hispaniola, a port so called, it seems, from the landing of some of the shipwrecked company, with a boat full of plate'.[14.11]

Puerto de la Plata (in the modern-day Dominican Republic) was, and is, indeed on the north coast of Hispaniola and it was hereabouts that survivors of the *Concepcion* hauled their makeshift rafts ashore. But it is highly unlikely that any local, young or old, had any new information about the 'true spot' where the *Concepcion* lay. If they had, they would surely have visited the site themselves or sold the information long before. It is much more likely that having identified Puerto de la Plata as the place where most survivors of the sinking had been washed up, Phipps used his knowledge of local currents and prevailing winds to work out what their course from wreck to shore must have been (much as Stanley must also have done). Both Phipps and Stanley ruled out the Abrojos as the starting point for their search. They instead identified the Ambrosia Bank, to the north-east of Puerto de la Plata, as the most likely candidate for the wreck site. But whereas Stanley favoured the 'South Bank' of the reef, Phipps was confident the 'North Riff' was the place to look.

He might have gone there when still in possession of the *Golden Rose*, but his lease had been running out and anyway his ship was too large to attempt any 'fishing' on the Ambrosia Bank. This is and was an open water reef system which, apart from one or two coral outcrops that stand above the waves at low water, is only detectable by disturbances on the surface of the sea. 'Boilers' swirl around the deadly columns lurking just below the surface, giving an easily missed warning of their presence.

Phipps would have known that Stanley had found it impossible to prevent his much shallower draft *Bonito* from 'beating upon the rocks many times'. The danger was so great that the expert sailor had decided to give up the hunt.

Like Stanley, Phipps was a pragmatist. But when it came to treasure-hunting his pragmatism was trumped by conviction, an almost religious belief, unfounded in evidence, that he would somehow come up with the goods. All he needed was suitable backing and not one, but two ships, with one small enough and nimble enough to brave the North Riff of the Ambrosia Bank.

As it turned out he had found in Albemarle somebody who was equally enthusiastic about the project. Albemarle's father, the general and admiral George Monck, came from an aristocratic but not rich family. It was said to have numbered Plantagenets among its forebears. As a stiff and forbidding military man he no doubt struck terror into the hearts of his enemies, but his manner concealed a romantic streak within his own. He had taken for his wife a blacksmith's daughter and seamstress who had been married before and may still have been married when she and Monck signed their marriage contract. This was not too long before the birth, in 1653, of Christopher, their only and cherished child.

George and his wife, Anne Radford, née Clarges, remained married until the old general's death at the start of 1670 (shortly followed by that of Anne). The couple had spent the intervening years accumulating great wealth and position and preparing their son for greatness. By 13 Christopher had achieved the rank of colonel in the army and been elected a Member of Parliament.

George managed to stay alive long enough to arrange and oversee his then 16-year-old son's marriage to the heiress Elizabeth Cavendish, who came with a dowry of £20,000. Christopher's fortunes were massively increased by his inheritance. He was soon being talked about as the fourth richest man in England. He and his pretty 'wild child' bride were rich, carefree and out of control. Christopher hung out with a court 'rat pack' that included the Duke of Monmouth and other 'gallants'. His like-minded Betty also partied and spent money without thinking.[14.12]

When Albemarle met Phipps, he was beginning to feel the cost of his hellraising. He had maintained his popularity at court largely through largesse. King Charles had benefited greatly, using Albemarle as an unpaid private catering concern for the entertainment of dignitaries and other guests. But now the money was running out and houses were being sold to top up cash resources. The health of the duke and duchess was also suffering. Christopher was drinking himself to death and his mentally fragile wife was laying the foundations for her 'mad duchess' sobriquet.

James' accession to the throne meant the writing was on the mansion wall in other ways too. Albemarle had been sidelined in suppression of the attempt by his old party-partner Monmouth to depose the king. Holding senior army positions he should have been at the forefront of the action. He was not and never would be again, since he resigned his commands in protest. The duke may have congratulated himself on his own resourcefulness.

In 1685 Sir Philip Howard had been appointed governor of Jamaica, where he owned a plantation. But the debt-ridden parliamentarian and soldier, who had served under both George and Christopher Monck, had been prevented leaving to take up this appointment by his creditors. Things might have been sorted out but before they could be, the governor had inconveniently died.[14.13]

The gesture was not in vain since Albemarle must have concluded that a period out of the country, and away from James II and his own creditors would suit him just fine. And so he had lobbied for and obtained the office that Howard was unable to take up.

As a seasoned courtier Albemarle would have had no difficulty persuading the king that he wished to move his household to Jamaica as an act of penance that would restore his good name. James graciously agreed and in May 1686 the Lords of Trade were informed that Albemarle had been appointed governor of Jamaica.[14.14]

Of course, few thought Albemarle would actually go to Jamaica. He would surely use the appointment to make a little money, perhaps by farming it out to an agent. But the duke had other ideas. When he met Phipps in 1686, the last pieces of his exit strategy fell into place.

Chapter 15

A Company is Formed

ALBEMARLE DID NOT leave to take up his governorship immediately. He had much to arrange, including the formation of a joint-stock company to finance Phipps' new treasure hunt. In fact, Albemarle did not set sail to take over from acting governor of Jamaica Hender Molesworth until October 1687, a little after Phipps' triumphant return to England. He had spent the intervening period accumulating further privileges and patents for himself, selling his favourite manor houses Dalby and Broughton to the 'hanging judge' (by now Lord Chancellor) Jeffreys, and amending his will. The last had been an unwilling act undertaken after much haranguing by the duchess. Although Albemarle was only in his early thirties, his wife appears to have been alarmed by his heavy drinking and jaundiced, portly appearance and had become fixated on obtaining better terms for herself and her nominees.

The duke and duchess eventually sailed from Portsmouth aboard the *Assistance*, taking with them 500 tons of goods and 100 servants, many of whom were packed into the duke's private yacht which sailed in consort. They also took along Dr Hans Sloane (of Sloane Square fame). As personal physician to the couple, the good doctor, whose massive collection of curios later formed the basis on which the British Museum was formed, had his hands more than full.[15.1]

England was a much different place in the seventeenth century. There were far fewer people around. The population of near five million was roughly a twelfth of today's figure, the economy was based largely on agriculture, and travel was possible only on foot, horse or horse-drawn cart or carriage, or by oar or sail-powered boat. Other than a few furnaces and mines, there was virtually no heavy industry. Medicine was basic. The place was much quieter and very much smellier. People lived nearer the earth, often sharing their buildings with domestic animals, vermin and insects. They lacked the means to indulge too often in the luxury of bathing. Men, women and children, even those 'of quality', rarely changed their unwashed clothes.

What manufacturing there was, was undertaken by craftsmen: guild members such as the gunsmiths of Bristol, skilled immigrants such as Huguenot silk weavers, or those who had grown up and been tutored in traditional country and other skills such as button- and chair-making, potting, weaving or lacemaking. Potters, papermakers, carpenters and cabinetmakers, bucklemakers, wool spinners and weavers, bakers, smiths, wheelwrights, coopers, silversmiths and pewterers and many more trades were conducted as cottage industries. There was little need for substantial financial backing to set up in such home industries and where it was needed local landowners or merchants were on hand to help (for a price).

But things were changing. Mankind was gaining a better understanding of the world in which it found itself. In England, natural philosophers, men such as Issac Newton, Robert Hooke, Edmund Halley, Christopher Wren and Robert Boyle, met at the Royal Society where they rubbed shoulders with politicians, courtiers and government servants (such as Christopher Monck, Sir James Hayes, Samuel Pepys and Prince Rupert). There they heard about and discussed latest scientific developments and reported on their own experiments and findings (Newton had many interests including mathematics and alchemy, Halley magnetic variation, diving bells and astronomy, Hooke lenses and the microscopic world, Wren astronomy, and Boyle air pumps).

Prior to his death in 1682, the energetic Prince Rupert was far from being a passive observer. Despite having once attacked Windsor Castle he was by 1668 its 'constable', or governor. He liked the job because it gave him access to the hunting in Windsor's forest and provided him apartments, some of which he converted into workshops for experiments into explosives and ordnance.

The year 1680 'seems to have been remarkable for new projects in England, which were patronized by Prince Rupert, Duke of Cumberland, more especially such as related to mechanics,' reported Scottish economist Adam Anderson in his history of commerce: 'We have a yellow metal, much resembling gold, which, in our days, is still named Prince's Metal, as taking its name from him: and a water-mill was thereupon erected on Hackney river for casting of cannon of that metal; it is known at this day by the name of Temple Mill … Another project was, for a floating machine, worked by horses, for the towing of great ships against wind and tide. A third was, a machine for the raising of ballast; though found insufficient even before Prince Rupert's death. A fourth was, a diving machine or engine.'[15.2]

The world was getting more complicated. New and improved manufacturing processes were being devised, new solutions to old problems proposed. Economic exploitation of these discoveries required more than skilled homeworkers; it needed financial investment. New forms of commercial enterprise were required, structures that allowed for better management and access to finance. Joint-stock companies were about to have their day.

Corporations, including companies, had long been a feature of English society. But they were used sparingly to organise civic communities, such as the City of

London and the Massachusetts Bay Colony, or commercial enterprises of national importance, such as the East India Company, the Levant Company and the Hudson's Bay Company. Such were created by royal charter or act of Parliament.

Now this same basic structure, that of a company owned by investors and run by directors, was being adapted to cope with the needs of new businesses. So far as the laws of the day were concerned these were private enterprises; they were not regulated, there was no constraint on the money that could be raised, nor its use, no rules governing the buying and selling of shares nor any protection for shareholders. How these companies were organised and run was entirely down to their individually drafted prospectuses, in effect contracts drawn up by their initiators: the 'projectors'. Such men usually stood to do very well out of the company whether it prospered or not.

According to one study[15.3] there was a succession of companies formed about this time whose stated aims included white paper manufacture, linen manufacture, copper mining, hollow sword blade manufacture, pearl fishing in Cumbria, tapestry making, lead smelting ('with pit coal'), lutestring making, the digging of mines and production of saltpetre.

One of these companies was Albemarle's Gentlemen Adventurers. It was not so much that Albemarle needed to raise capital – he already had friends lined up to invest – but the use of a joint-stock company rather than a partnership made it easier to define in advance how much each investor would contribute and the share of profits to which they would be entitled. The list of Gentlemen Adventurers shareholders was short but included some familiar names. Together they had agreed to back Phipps on a return trip to the Bahama Banks.

Chapter 16

What Phipps Did Best

FLUSH WITH FINANCE, the adventurers set about equipping Phipps for his coming search. The company had raised £3,200 in capital. (Narborough biographer Florence Dyer[16.1] put it at £2,400, although others have come up with slightly different figures. Author Cyrus Karraker estimated the company's capital costs at nearer to £4,000[16.2] but Peter Earle, author of *The Treasure of the Concepcion*, said the total outlay, was £3,210.)[16.3] Albemarle put in the largest amount, £800. Six other investors contributed £400 each. They were Sir John Narborough, Viscount Falkland, Sir James Hayes and Sir Richard Haddock, Francis Nicholson and lawyer Isaac Foxcroft.

The last two may have been introduced to the group by Sir James Hayes. A few years later they were certainly involved with him in leasing property[16.4] (both Foxcroft and Nicholson were also involved in a court case concerning a property in St Giles in the Fields owned by Foxcroft on which fourteen houses had been built[16.5]). Foxcroft was a lawyer who had been admitted to the Inner Temple in May 1666, and dismissed as reader of Clifford's Inn in 1675.[16.6] Nicholson later became guardian of his two sons, Henry and Isaac Foxcroft[16.7].

The Adventurers used the money to buy two ships, the *Bridgewater*, a vessel of 200 tons and 23 guns, and the much smaller *Henry*. The latter was owned by merchant John Smith who, on overhearing what the ship was wanted for, offered to sell it for a £230 credit against a share in the company. Acceptance of this deal was something that Albemarle may have later regretted. Money was also invested in some trading goods that Phipps was to carry in his holds, an insurance against total loss. If he was unsuccessful in his search for treasure, he could sell the goods and still cover his costs.

In the meantime, the *Bridgewater* was renamed the *James and Mary* in honour of the present incumbent of the English throne and his second wife, Mary of Modena. By a happy coincidence 'James' and 'Mary' were also the names of Phipps' own parents.[16.8]

Albemarle was relying on a promise from James II for his right to fish the wreck of the *Concepcion*. On the advice of Narborough and lawyer Isaac Foxcroft, he now asked for this to be confirmed under Privy Seal 'in a legal manner', using 'proper words of grant' so that the king's intentions might not be frustrated.[16.9] In other words Narborough and Foxcroft did not put total faith in the king's word. James did not object and the Adventurers duly received their signed and sealed warrant.

By September 1686 all was in place and Phipps sailed for the West Indies. He had been in England a little over a year. Nobody was sure that he would be any more successful than previous searchers for the wreck of the *Concepcion.* By the standards of what had gone before his voyage turned out to be something of a smash and grab raid.

Phipps' first port of call was Barbados, which he reached in November. After a brief stay, he moved on to Hispaniola, rendezvousing with the *Henry* in Puerto de la Plata. Here, according to Cotton Mather, Phipps 'made a stout canoo of a stately cotton-tree, so large as to carry eight or ten oars, for the making of which periaga (as they call it) he did, with the same industry that he did every thing else, imploy his own hand and adse, and endure no little hardship, lying abroad in the woods many nights together'.[16.10] He also engaged in some trading and reprovisioned his ship.

In January the *Henry* was sent off to the Ambrosia Bank to start the hunt for the wreck along its North Riff. Anchored a safe distance away, the *Henry*'s Captain Rogers, and *James and Mary's* mate William Covell had taken to boat and canoe to survey the north side of the riff, then the south. The water was clear but nothing of the wreck could be seen.

On the second or third day of this, they were on the point of returning to the *Henry* when, by chance, one of their divers took a fancy to the look of a feather-shaped coral visible below the surface and decided to fetch it as a souvenir. Plunging into the water he found himself looking at a cannon lying on the bottom. Soon he noticed much more.

Where others had laboured to locate the by now almost mythical *Concepcion*, Rogers and Covell had found the wreck in a matter of days. It was lying in forty to fifty feet of water, an accessible depth.[16.11] And for the next few days the divers worked to bring up cannon, plate, pieces of eight and ingots of silver.

Phipps was oblivious to the find when the *Henry* made it back to Puerto de la Plata. Rogers strung out the suspense by first pretending his search had drawn a blank. Both ships, the *Henry* and the *James and Mary*, returned to the Ambrosia Bank in a matter of days. The *James and Mary* arrived first and anchored more than a mile away, possibly three or four. This was probably a precaution against giving away the exact position of the wreck, but it was also an indication of the respect with which Phipps regarded the dangers of the reef. The *Henry* arrived a day or so later and, having a shallower draft than its consort, was able to manoeuvre itself closer to, but still not over, the reef.

Shortly two other craft arrived, a nimble Bermudian sloop captained by William Davis and a shallop, little more than a longboat, captained by the Jamaican Abraham Adderley. Both had worked with Phipps on his previous voyage to the Bahama Banks and their arrival may have been prearranged. Whether so or not, the two newcomers were soon signed on as helpers with a promise of a share of any treasure they brought up. Their involvement was probably crucial to the success of the venture.

Specialist divers were needed for the salvage work that was about to begin; nothing could be brought to the surface without them. Phipps had only three or four among his crew, but Davis and Adderley had more, men they knew and trusted. They were probably slaves, but slaves who had some clout due to their much-prized diving skills.

Divers of the time had little equipment, no masks, helmets, snorkels or flippers. They were usually born to the occupation, such as the native divers who worked the pearl banks off the Caribbean coast of Colombia near Riohacha. Those involved gradually built up their lung capacity until they were able to stay underwater for surprising lengths of time. They were in great demand.[16.12]

Diving bells had been known about for centuries and were used by Caribbean wreck fishers. The local version was the 'Bermuda Tub', essentially an upturned open-ended barrel. When lowered into the water, weights attached to the lower open end of the barrel overcame the natural buoyancy of the air inside and kept the barrel upright and the air trapped at the sealed top end.

'By the early 1680s, Bermudian wreckers and their "Bermudas Tub" diving bells were well known throughout the Caribbean,' reported Michael Jarvis in his *Eye of All Trade: Bermuda, Bermudians, and the Maritime Atlantic World, 1680–1783*.[16.13] Use of such tubs was certainly well known in Boston where, as early as 1642, an Edward Bendall had used one in clearing the harbour of the wreck of the *Mary Rose*. This, said Governor John Winthrop, 'had been blown up and sunk with all her ordnance, ballast, much lead'. She was brought to shore 'by the industry of Bendall who made two great tubs, bigger than a butt, very tight, and open at one end, upon which were hanged so many weights as would sink it to the ground (600wt). It was let down, the diver sitting in it, a cord in his hand to give notice when they should draw him up, and another cord to show when they should remove it from place to place, so he could continue in his tub near half an hour, and fasten ropes to the ordnance, and put the lead, etc., into another tub.'[16.14]

Davis and Adderley brought tubs with them. Not only that, their vessels were small enough to be able to take the divers very close to, perhaps almost directly over, the wreck. Because to be of any use, tubs had to be suspended immediately above the diving site

Almost from the moment Phipps and his augmented team started working the wreck there could have been little doubt about what they had found. The *Concepcion* itself had all but disintegrated, its remains rotted or petrified in coral, but silver and gold was brought up daily. Soon the finds were being measured in weight rather than numbers of coins or bars.

The treasure hunters continued the work for just over two months. It was not easy. There was always the risk of storm and being dashed against the vicious reefs that surrounded their anchorage. Nearly everything recovered was encrusted with coral – congealed lumps of jagged-edged metal that might be silver or nothing of any value. The divers could work only so many hours each day, raking, scraping, pulling away at what remained of the ship, filling baskets with their finds and attaching lines and slings for those above to haul up.

The divers suffered fatigue and illness. Phipps responded by calling rest days but could do little to ease the need for physical exertion. Use of the tubs proved difficult. Those manning the small boats, the only vessels that dared go near the wreck, found it a dangerous proposition to hold station in the swirling waters, floating amidst the threatening 'boilers'. Nor were they comfortable with the restrictions to their manoeuvrability caused by dangling heavy barrels from their sides.

Besides all this, Phipps must have worried about the ever-present possibility that a hostile privateer might sail down upon them and snatch their prize. The loyalty of Phipps' own crew was not necessarily assured. This time they were on a wage rather than a share of profits. He must have wondered where the balance lay between loyalty and greed? Who would be first to suggest they run off with the ship and its mightily valuable cargo? And there was the state of repair and provisioning of the *James and Mary* and *Henry* to think about. Wooden ships required constant attention, and his had had little since the turn of the year.

In mid-April Phipps decided to head for home. He promised his crew a cut of what had been recovered, avoided (narrowly) ending up on the nearby Handkercher reef, and set a course for England. By some miracle he avoided crossing paths with other shipping, barring one friendly vessel. The danger posed by French privateers in the Channel was somehow sidestepped and by early June the *James and Mary* was anchored off the Downs.

It had taken Phipps a voyage of less than a year to bring home his treasure. He was either extremely lucky, or extremely shrewd. He was probably both. He might not be able to read or write too well, but he was clearly an accomplished seaman, and he knew the Caribbean well. He had used his knowledge and skills to narrow down the search area.

He must also have been a man of considerable charisma who had captured the attention of kings, governors, admirals and politicians. When he bothered to turn his mind to it, he could charm his way out of a paper bag. He had turned his mind to it, and in his open and boisterous way he had persuaded many people, some unknowingly, to add to his fund of knowledge about the whereabouts of the *Concepcion*. His jaunt about the Caribbean in the *Golden Rose* had not been the waste of time his detractors had thought.

Phipps soon sailed around the North Foreshore into the Thames Estuary. When he anchored at Gravesend, he was within a stone's throw of the grave of Pocahontas, the Indian 'princess' whom the adventurer Captain John Smith credited with saving his life and the future of the struggling Jamestown colony. She had, he said, saved him from execution by clubbing by placing her head upon his, to receive the blow herself. Despite being held hostage by the English for a while, Pocahontas married not Smith but planter John Rolfe (who had survived the *Sea Venture*'s unscheduled stop in Bermuda), when she was 13 or 14, and he twenty-eight. She had acted as an ambassador for the colony and had come to England with her husband on some kind of promotional trip. In 1617, when about to return home, she contracted smallpox and died in Gravesend where she was buried.[16.15] While in England Pocahontas and her entourage had caused something of a sensation. And so, now, did Phipps. His ship was soon hurried to Deptford where its contents could be better protected, examined and valued, and the king's tenth secured. Albemarle and his Gentlemen Adventurers were on hand to congratulate all, and pamphlets and newssheets broadcast the news.

A 'Relation … taken from a Gentleman who was on Board the … Ship the whole Voyage,' told the full story. 'Not the least Plank or Hull' of the *Concepcion* could be seen', 'the Ship being broak to pieces on the Rock, the parts were either driven away with the violence of the Waves, or consum'd by the Worms which in those Seas will Eat through the thickest Plank in some years time', said the report. 'And 'tis further remarkable, that the Silver had so long remain'd under Water, as to petrify a congeal'd Substance into White Coral-Trees growing thereon, some with mighty spreading Branches, even to a great height.'

But 'having taken up as much [treasure] as they could well find', Phipps left the wreck in May 'and with some stress of Weather made sight of *Cilly Island* the third of *June* following, and is now Happily arriv'd in the River of *Thames* on this side *Gravesend,* with such a Treasure as to the Honour as well as Profit of the, Nation no Ship ever perform'd the like … His Grace the Duke of *Alb—* upon the receipt of this News, accompanied with Sir *James Hayes*, &c. went down the River, to bid the Captain Welcome who coming on board, found all things so mightily to his Satisfaction, that his Grace Generously oblig'd every Man and Boy of the Ships Crew to Drink his Health; but left order that none go ashore till she is Unladen of her Cargo, being actually 26 Tons, and 700 lb weight of Silver, fifteen Tons thereof being Pieces of Eight, two Bars or Ingots of Gold 17 lb. weight, six Brass Cannon of thirty hundred weight each, being as serviceable as at first, which amount in the whole to above 200000 lb. besides all the Charges. She now rides on this side *Gravesend*, and is well Guarded, no persons being suffered to go aboard her, nor come ashore, without special Order. It is observable, that in this whole Voyage, the Captain hath lost neither Man nor Boy, although they were in so great hazard.'[16.16]

The treasure was enormous. Estimates of its 1687 worth range between just over £200,000 to £350,000, figures which today have a buying power of between £39m and £69m. Crew members (Albemarle had endorsed Phipps' decision to offer them a share of the treasure) shared the equivalent of at least £1.6m, the king took a cut worth at least £4m. Phipps went home with a reward worth at least £2m in today's money, and the individual shareholders each received dividends worth around £4m. Albemarle took double that. It is said that he smelted his share of the silver in his own garden.[16.17] Missing from the list of investors was Sir Richard Haddock. He had inexplicably lost his nerve or become bored with the venture and sold out his interest shortly before Phipps' return.

By the end of the month Phipps had been invited to Windsor where Albemarle presented him to King James. It was ordered that two medals be struck to commemorate his achievements, although his head was not one of those that was to appear on either medal.

In July 1687, *The London Gazette*, issue 2256, carried news of the audience. Amid reports of three men robbing a coach near Brecknan, taking away three silver plates, a sugar box and a pepper pot, and of establishment of a post office in Jamaica (postmaster James Wale), it was noted that on 28 June, Captain William Phipps had been presented to the king: 'His Majesty received him very graciously, and was pleased to Confer upon him the Honour of Knighthood.' Rewarded for his 'Loyalty and good Services in a late Expedition, Having brought home a very considerable Treasure which was taken out of the Sea, after it had lain there 44 years', Phipps was now Sir William Phipps.

He, his investors and his crew were not the only ones to benefit. The first crown-appointed governor of Bermuda, Royal Naval officer Sir Robert Robinson, had arrived in July. He was not happy with the lawless state of the island whose people, he said, 'are utterly undone if they are tied down to a single ship, and not free like other Colonies. They have spoiled two crops (of tobacco) already, and smuggled them out of the island'.

He told William Blathwayt, 'there is no lawyer here, "and them blind ones that there is" will never carry on anything to the King's interest. Therefore an able lawyer must be sent over to secure the King's negroes and lands that are withheld from him, for the people are all for a trial at law, in both cases'.

1 (*right*): William Phipps hauling treasure from the wreck of the *Concepcion* onto his ship. 'By the standards of what had gone before, his voyage turned out to be something of a smash and grab raid.'

2 (*below*): Fort William Henry, built by Phipps in 1693, was destroyed in King William's War but rebuilt in 1908, when an opening ceremony took place. The original fort, boasted Phipps, was 'strong enough to resist all the Indians in America'.

3 (*left*): Sir William Phipps shortly after receiving his knighthood. Phipps' clothing is not elaborate but neither does it have the plainness favoured by Puritans, nor the clerical look adopted by some of his contemporaries. He has a firm chin and a defiant look in his eyes.

4 (*right*): Sir William Phipps, first royal governor of the Province of Massachusetts Bay. 'He is perched on the edge of his chair as if ready to leap up at any moment.'

5: General, admiral, and Hudson's Bay investor, Prince Rupert of the Rhine produced a steady stream of inventions from his workshops within Windsor Castle.

Indians attacking a Garrison House

FROM AN OLD WOOD ENGRAVING

6 (*above*): King Philip's War between settlers and Native Americans amounted to a series of raids, ambushes and skirmishes. The Indians' first tactic was to attack isolated homesteads and settlements, killing the hated cattle and burning abandoned property.

7 (*below*): Damp and steaming villagers, even more jumpy than usual, given the supposed presence of witches, packed into the Salem Village meeting house. Here they witnessed the screaming, flinching, convulsing and fainting of the 'afflicted' victims.

8 (*right*): Puritan cleric Increase Mather took his preaching seriously. He was a practised performer who rehearsed his lines and his delivery, which probably came from the Reverend Ian Paisley psalm book.

9 (*left*): ''Tis well known, that the Devils make a Compact with some Witches,' said Cotton Mather, son of Increase. 'Such Witches have been among our selves.'

10 (*above*): Arrival of the Winthrop Fleet marked the start of a second phase of immigration to New England. It consisted of eleven ships and brought more than 1,000 settlers, families, their possessions and livestock, and their own charter for a Massachusetts Bay Colony.

11 (*left*): The hysteria which led to the Salem witch trials emanated from the home of Samuel Parris, a merchant-turned-preacher who had only been ordained as Salem Village minister in November 1689. The first of those 'afflicted' were his own daughter and his 10-year-old niece. And the 'witch' they accused of causing their fits was the Parris's household slave, Tituba.

12: Edmund Halley kept the Royal Society informed of his diving bell achievements, including its design, its construction, a personal test-dive in the Thames, and his involvement in the attempted recovery of 'elephants' teeth' from the wreck of the *Guynie*, sunk off Chichester.

13 (*left*): As the local Wabanaki people became less noticeable, the English settlers advanced, shaping the countryside to their own tastes and needs. Trees were felled for burning and building, more clearings were made in the forest for agriculture, plots were fenced and new homesteads built.

14 (*right*): Judge, politician, businessman and diarist Samuel Sewall went to the Salem meeting house in April 1692 where accused 'witches' were being examined. 'Twas awfull to see how the afflicted persons were agitated,' he said.

15: The Puritan connection with New England had started with the ‘Pilgrim Fathers’. Sailing on the *Mayflower*, members of a congregation that had first fled to the Netherlands, decided to try their luck in New England. In 1620 they arrived, somewhat unexpectedly to the north of their intended destination, in a bay they were to name Plymouth.

16 (*above*): *The* Mayflower *at Sea*. Many of the settlers had arrived 'weak and feeble through the length of the navigation, the leakiness of the ship, and want of many other necessaries such undertakings required'.

17 (*above*): The truth was that the Pilgrim Fathers did not bring salvation with them but death. The native population had no resistance to plague or pox, nor even to the common cold.

18 (*above*): Tituba Indian, accused of witchcraft, was harassed by the magistrates into saying that she had been pursued by spectres, two of which resembled Sarah Good and Sarah Osborn.

19 (*right*): The Old Stock Exchange in Amsterdam. 'Everything "Dutch" was now in vogue, including Dutch ideas on finance, investment and share trading. Among the examples now acted upon in England was that of the world's first functioning stock exchange.'

20 (*left*): Not all 'pine tree shillings' carried the image of a pine tree, although many did. All carried the date 1652, the year in which the colony had first authorised production of its own coinage.

21 (*above*): The young preacher John Eliot reached out to the local Massachusett Indians, learnt their Algonquin dialect, and formed a particular friendship with the Nipmuc people and their leader Waban.

22 (*above*): William of Orange had solicited an invitation to step in on behalf of the English people. He and his army arrived in November 1688, ferried to Brixham, in Devon, by a fleet of over 400 ships.

23 (*above*): The early years of the Hudson's Bay Company saw its trading posts change hands several times. Personal allegiances were equally fickle. Des Groseilliers and Radisson were originally employees of the Hudson's Bay Company, then changed sides and attempted to establish a rival French company, and then changed sides again.

24 (*right*): Sir George Carteret named his gifted American holdings 'New Jersey' in recognition of his family connections to the channel island, Jersey.

25: George Burroughs, who had once been Salem Village minister, had barely been back in the nine years since leaving. But his spectre had been seen by various 'afflicted' villagers, which was enough for him to be arrested, tried and hanged.

26 (*above left*): Simon Bradstreet, almost fifty years older than Phipps, had clashed with the future governor when captain of the *Golden Rose*. This did not stop him appointing the treasure-hunting hero as leader of an attack on Port Royal.

27 (*above right*): Renaming his stolen ship the *Fancy*, Henry Every decided to target the pilgrim ships that regularly took wealthy Muslims to and from Mecca. Before too long he captured the *Ganj-i-sawai*, owned by the Great Mogul Aurangzeb. Although this caused an international incident, he soon became a people's hero lauded in ballads and a popular play.

Captain Atherton in the Wigwam of Ninigret.

28 (*above*): Humphrey Atherton, a stalwart of the Boston community, had long-standing connections with Rhode Island's Narragansett lands. In 1644, when a captain in the Military Company of Massachusetts, he had led a campaign against the Niantic sachem, Ninigret. By 1660 he was major-general, a magistrate and superintendent of Indian affairs and determined to acquire prime Narragansett land illegally.

29 (*above left*): William Stoughton, twenty years Phipps' senior, 'was a steady administrator who had almost been forgiven for serving under Andros. But Stoughton was somebody whose certainty about the correctness of his own ideas was so steadfast that it left no room for empathy or imagination'.

30 (*above right*): Attorney General Sir Robert Sawyer, a distant relative of Phipps' by marriage, came up with some sharp legal footwork that meant English courts agreed to withdraw the Massachusetts Bay Colony's cherished charter.

31 (*above left*): Admiral Sir John Narborough was an investor in Phipps' *Concepcion* treasure-hunting venture and had himself appointed overall commander of the unsuccessful follow-up voyage. He was taken ill and died while anchored at the site of the wreck.

32 (*above right*): Sir Richard Haddock put money into Phipps' venture but inexplicitly sold out his stake shortly before Phipps' treasure-laden return.

Meanwhile, 'a couple of small vessels came in with Captain Phips lately from the wreck. Phips took from them a ton and a half of plate, and left them as much. They took as much more and brought it here. I took the King's tenths, and enclose an account thereof. They gave me five or six hundred pounds, and have carried fifteen or sixteen'.[16.18]

The 'small vessels' must have been those of Davis and Adderley. According to author Michael Jarvis,[16.19] Phipps had sworn the two captains to secrecy before departing for England, but Davis and Adderley did not stop their diving operation when Phipps left. 'News of the wreck reached Bermuda in midsummer, prompting a fleet of Bermudian salvagers to race to the site. Governor Robinson interrogated Adderley and Davis soon after they arrived in Bermuda. The two mariners officially declared raising three tons of money and plate worth £27,000, but it was widely rumoured that they and their crews had clandestinely landed another £15,000 to £16,000 in treasure.

Jarvis said that in all, thirteen Bermudian vessels officially reported raising more than 16,700 pounds of silver and a ton of gold, worth a minimum of £48,000 sterling in Bermuda. The treasure's value was roughly equal to that of the entire colony's tobacco crop over a decade. Jarvis again: 'Taking into account underreporting and smuggling, the treasure landed in Bermuda probably exceeded £70,000 – a dividend of roughly £12 sterling for every man, woman, and child on the island ... When he died in 1690, Adderley owned 1,856 ounces of bullion, £448 in cash, and a large collection of English-made silver spoons, tankards, plates, and candlesticks fashioned out of the Spanish coins he had raised. His three sloops, fine mansion, eighty-seven acres of recently purchased land, fifteen black and Indian slaves, and two herds of livestock reflect how he invested most of his earnings. Dozens of other mariners, 'all of them poor fellows until now', each gained hundreds of pounds from the wreck.'

King James would have recognised the name 'Phipps' when the bloated Albemarle bowed and scraped before him. This was the man who had been lent a ship and who had actually returned it on time. Here was a man that had annoyed the troublesome Bostonians, here was a man he had recently had bailed for charges arising for his support of one of his governors, and above all here was a man who had so recently paid a fortune into the royal coffers.

James was in much need of money, not least to pay his army of 'Irish brigands' kept camped on Hounslow Heath as a reminder to his subjects not to get too uppity. They showed signs of just that following publication of his *Declaration of Indulgence* which sought to suspend the *Test Act* requirements that then operated against non-conformists and Catholics. His actions could be seen as liberal, a championing of the freedom of religion. At the time they were seen as an illegal attempt by the Catholic king to overturn laws that had been enacted in Parliament, and an attempt to ensure the country returned to the church of Rome.

The storm clouds were gathering for James. Soon he would be in dispute with the bishops of the Church of England over his deeply unpopular declaration. Meanwhile, not too far away in his low-country stronghold, the ambitious (and seriously Protestant) William, Prince of Orange, was mustering his resources.

The other 'William' did not question such matters. The king was the king, and he accepted his knighthood without qualms. Other honours were to follow, including appointment as the provost marshal general of the Dominion of New England. This was a high-ranking post and no sinecure. Traditionally a provost marshal general is in charge of army discipline and policing. In New England the position had a wider community and policing context. The provost marshal general was in effect the chief of police, although there was no police force as such. Instead, there was a network of volunteer groups who took care of their own communities, dealing with such matters as payment (or avoidance) of duties, vagrancy, night-watch groups (as in Boston), and punishing petty theft. These groups were overseen by sheriffs appointed by the provost marshal general. Being effectively in change of law and order was a somewhat unexpected position for somebody who had been criticised (by John Knepp) for being unable to maintain order and discipline among the crew of his own ship (the *Golden Rose)*. But the eternal optimist Phipps had never before let lack of qualifications hold him back, and he didn't this time either.

Chapter 17

The Aftermath

PHIPPS WILL HAVE enjoyed his celebrity and being entertained about town. But there were aspects of his newfound fame that he would not have liked. Where there was money, there were bound to be people trying to claim a share. Various chancers now appeared, claiming they were owed money by the Gentleman Adventurers or by Phipps personally. One was Sir Richard White who had first persuaded Narborough and Haddock that he and Isaac Harmon knew where the wreck of the *Concepcion* lay (when later asked to direct Captain Stanley to the spot, they were unable to do so). He complained to the Spanish ambassador that Phipps had stolen information from him. That he didn't go to court suggests he knew he would have had difficulty substantiating the claim, but the Spanish ambassador did persuade James II to grant White a royal bounty.

Meanwhile merchant John Smith from whom the Gentlemen Adventurers had acquired the *Henry*, sued them all. He had been a full partner and deserved his share, he said. The Adventurers acknowledged a connection but said they had excluded Smith from the payout because he had never paid the balance due for his shares. On the contrary, they inferred, Smith had made money out of them by supplying the ships' needs.[17.1] The claim was eventually settled out of court, so Smith presumably received some sort of payout.

Phipps was pursued personally (but not sued) by Boston merchant Robert Bronson for £200 for his claimed loan of a servant to the *Golden Rose*. It seems Bronson never got paid. He was also the subject of a petition from Richard Covell, perhaps a relative of Phipps' long-time mate William Covell (or Covill). The 'mariner' wanted five hundredweight of silver he said had been allotted him 'for provisions supplied to Sir William and as a reward from the wreck' but which had been 'detained' by Phipps.[17.2]

He might also not have been too pleased about the clamour for a follow-up expedition; a return to the wreck of the *Concepcion* which, Phipps admitted, probably still clung to a good deal of its original treasure. Whether it was feasible to recover much more from the wreck was less certain, especially since Phipps would have realised its site was unlikely to have remained secret very long and it would almost certainly have already been picked over by others.

And besides, he had been away from home for about three years during which time he had achieved a long-held ambition and received an unexpected knighthood. He was anxious to return to his wife, to bask in the congratulations of his peers, and to take up his new appointment. He was now a man of some means and standing and he wanted his friends and acquaintances to know. And he wanted those who had dismissed him as nothing more than an ignorant backwoodsman to realise that he had made something of himself. He wanted to show off, to make his mother proud.

But the Gentlemen Adventurers had got the taste for treasure hunting. Narborough in particular wanted to lead his own squadron of search ships. He quickly applied for and received a new patent allowing the Adventurers to renew their hunt.

This acknowledged the previous patent had resulted in retrieval by Phipps of 'a considerable quantity of silver and other riches'. Phipps together with Albemarle, Falkland, Hayes, Narborough, Foxcroft and Nicholson intended 'another voyage for the recovery of more silver, gold and other riches which have been left, cast away, wrecked or lost', it said. The adventurers offered, in return for loan of a ship 'with her guns and tackle etc', to pay the king 'a full fifth of the proceeds up to £150,000 and one third of whatsoever proceed exceeding £150,000'. The king, who accepted the deal, was to bear the cost of the ship's wear and tear but the Adventurers were to pay 'the wages and victuals of the ship's complement, which is 200 in all'.[17.3]

The ship mentioned in the patent was the *Assistance*, then in the final stages of a rebuild. As it turned out the Adventurers ended up with the use of two ships, the *Assistance* and the *Foresight*, a thirty-seven-year-old fourth-rated ship of the line that was 120-feet long and had been upgraded to carry fifty-two guns.[17.4]

Narborough had himself appointed captain of the *Foresight*, and overall commander of the renewed treasure hunt. Meanwhile, the *Foresight*'s previous captain, Lawrence Wright, became captain of the rebuilt and recommissioned *Assistance*. Of similar size and complement to the *Foresight*, it had been adapted to provide additional cabins so that it might deliver Albemarle, his highly strung wife, their voluminous belongings and numerous servants to Jamaica.

The expedition now included a small flotilla of ships. Besides the *Assistance* and the *Foresight*, there was the *James and Mary*, now captained by Phipps' old first mate John Strong, and the *Good Luck*, a ship of 200 tons captained by Phipps himself. It might have left earlier had not the bloated and jaundiced Albemarle, after a round of farewell celebrations, been 'unwell'. So it was not until September 1687 that the *Assistance*, Albemarle's yacht and two merchant vessels left Portsmouth bound for Barbados. By then Narborough, Strong and

Phipps had already started their voyages to the rendezvous point in Barbados. At some point the *James and Mary* and the *Good Luck* got themselves separated from the group, so that only Narborough was there in time to greet the *Assistance* and its escorts when they arrived there a month later.[17.5]

Narborough escorted Albemarle to Jamaica and set sail for the wreck. A week later he was still looking. This was despite having brought along Edward Stanley, the former captain of the *Bonito* on whom Narborough had previously pinned such hopes. Perhaps at this stage he realised how skilled a seaman Phipps was, and how much success of the mission to find the *Concepcion*'s treasure had been down to Phipps' indefatigable leadership.

Narborough put into the north coast of Hispaniola where he waited for and eventually met up with Phipps. He also received the unwelcome news that there were approximately twenty-five vessels currently working the wreck.

There followed a frustrating few months. They had started off well enough with Narborough able to hire twenty-two divers. Following Phipps, he made it to the wreck site and shooed away the collection of small boats already there ('a small shallop with a tub and about twenty boats and canoes full of divers', said Stanley who had been dispatched to search them all).[17.6] Ominously Stanley found the wreck-fishers had retrieved almost nothing. Neither, over the next weeks and months, could Narborough's divers bring up treasure of any significance.

Soon the *Assistance* and Albemarle's yacht also turned up. They had been sent by Albemarle as reinforcements. He had received word from England that a Dutch expedition under Lord Mordaunt was on its way to the wreck. It looked as if there might be trouble. It didn't materialise. Although the Dutch did turn up, they must have realised what was on offer was not worth fighting for. After some forced cordiality they went away.

By April things were getting a little desperate. Narborough had sent home what had been retrieved so far. It amounted to £5,000, not enough to cover the costs of the expedition.

Phipps now attempted to move things along by using gunpowder to smash through the coral that he believed encased another treasure room in the wreck. It might have worked but it might also have sent a boat-sinking tsunami rushing around the pinball reefs, and caused major damage to the reef itself. It was probably fortunate that the attempt to ignite the explosives, and another that followed, was unsuccessful.

'Two days later a Dutch ship arrived, equipped with some special implements for diving, and Narbrough was so anxious to find more treasure that the Master had leave to try what he could do. But his effort, too, was a failure' reported Narborough's biographer Florence Dyer.[17.7]

Narborough and Phipps had all but given up hope of making a successful voyage. A last throw of the dice was to send Stanley off to search other nearby banks on the off chance of finding another wreck. When, in early May he returned empty handed, Phipps decided it was time to sail home.

Narborough stayed on two weeks more. On 26 May he wrote to Albemarle in Jamaica, 'we finding now but very little silver in the Wreck, and have used all our endeavours to get up the rock grown abaft but find them too strong for us'. They had, he said, 'taken up in all of silver, about thirty three hundred pounds Troy Weight, and four copper guns'. With 'bad weather coming on' he had put two sloops in charge of guarding the wreck site and was 'intending this day to sail with the *Prince* for England'.[17.8] The admiral admitted to Albemarle that he was currently 'very ill of a fever'. Early next morning he died. The treasure hunt was over.

It does seem a further patent was on offer with a John Hill standing in for Dame Elizabeth Narborough, the 'relict and executrix of Sir John Narborough'.[17.9] But nothing came of this. It was, after all, by now August 1688 when the reign of James II was in its final throes and William Prince of Orange was expected to land with an invasion force any day. He eventually did so on 5 November.

Phipps, meanwhile, had landed in Boston on 1 June. He came back to a new home. Diarist Samuel Sewall had noted that on hearing of her husband's financial success and knighthood the year before, the businesslike Mary Phipps had 'bought Sam Wakefield's House and Ground'. This was a brick-built house near the Charleston Ferry, purchased for £350.

On that June day, Mary happened to be in the company of Sewall listening to a sermon when 'word was brought in by the Coach-man of Sir William's being spoke with at Sea. By that time we got home, we heard that Sir William came in his Pinnace from Portsmouth [New Hampshire] this day. Many of the Town gone to complement Him'.[17.10]

Chapter 18

Andros Displaced

NOT ALL WERE pleased by Phipps' triumphant 1688 return to Boston. Even among those who craned their necks to see the lumbering giant come ashore, there would have been detractors, men he had crossed by ignoring or questioning their rules. After all, Phipps had caused havoc when last in Boston aboard the *Golden Rose.* And he had shown himself to be a 'king's man' at a time when the colony had been fighting to keep its charter and its claimed independence intact.

In his absence, things had deteriorated. Despite cancellation of its charter in 1684, the old administration had managed to keep itself in place for a further two years. Challenges to the process by which the charter had been cancelled, a change of king, the Monmouth Rebellion and other arguments and disturbances in England, had meant an increasingly distracted administration had concentrated on events nearer to home.

It was not until July 1686 that *The London Gazette* (issue 2159) was able to report that Edward Randolph (now secretary of the colony) had the previous month arrived in Boston aboard HMS *Rose*, bringing with him the king's commission 'to Joseph Dudley Esq, as President, and divers other Gentlemen of those Parts to be His Majesties Council for Government of that Territory, until the Arrival of Sirr Edmund Andross Governor in chief of New-England'. The commission, published as a proclamation, had been greeted with 'great Solemnity and Demonstrations of Joy'. If the 'joy' part was true, it was short-lived.

The charter had gone, and a royal governor, Sir Edmund Andros (also 'Andrews'), had been appointed to an extended 'Dominion of New England'. By the time Phipps turned up, opposing factions within the colony were at loggerheads. One group, old-school hard-liners, were for independence or nothing and for continued, if futile, resistance to change. The other, mainly the merchant classes with interests that often extended into England, were for greater cooperation with the motherland.

Andros was not in an enviable position. He had been commissioned to govern with the advice of an appointed council only. (New-England-born Joseph Dudley had been nominated president of the council with his some-time business associate, the much older William Stoughton, as his deputy. Both men were 'moderates' favouring cooperation with London.) There was no elected forum, something that meant every controversial innovation (and Andros had many) was open to criticism as being arbitrary and unjust.

His situation had been similar when, as governor of New York province from 1674 to 1680 Andros had been responsible for looking after the Duke of York's (by now James II's) North American interests. This had ended badly enough with Andros recalled to London to answer complaints from leading merchants about his financial probity.[18.1] Although a Protestant (and well off in his own right, with family interests in Guernsey), Andros was well in with James, and nothing further was made of these complaints. It was, after all, a time when governors were expected to be self-financing, raising locally all that was needed to cover their costs and pay.

What probably didn't help the situation in Massachusetts was that the unpopular, mendacious and prolific writer of complaining, anti-charter letters to London, Edward Randolph, had managed to get himself appointed secretary of the dominion government.

Wealthier Massachusetts landowners and merchants had initially given their support to Andros and his dominion government. But their backing was soon dissipated by a series of reforms 'threatening their vital interests, tightening up commercial regulations, and requiring landowners to take out new patents', according to the Colonial Society of Massachusetts.[18.2]

Had Andros been a more sympathetic character, less pompous, or a more alert administrator and less concerned with lining his own pockets, his governorship might have been more acceptable and more successful. But he was not, and it was not.

The outlying townships, where Andros had banned weekly community meetings, were among the most dogged members of the Andros depreciation society. Here local sheriffs were community leaders expected to keep the peace. Andros had appointed the incumbent sheriffs and presumably expected their loyalty. And now here was Phipps turning up with a royal warrant to usurp the governor's nominee for the position of provost marshal general and wanting to appoint his own sheriffs.

There was a stand-off of sorts. For more than a month Andros was 'too busy' to swear Phipps into office. And even after he had been sworn in, the governor declined to have the existing sheriffs step down. Phipps partly blamed Randolph for this. But in general, the governor's haughtiness was just the sort of behaviour that might have been calculated to inflame Phipps' rude sense of injustice.

Phipps had again placed himself near the centre of a political storm, but this time it was more personal. Andros had alienated his crown-appointed provost marshal general, somebody who might have been a much-needed ally, but a person whose natural predisposition was not to ignore any slight or to sit back and do nothing.

What Phipps did, was to sail for England. There he contacted Increase Mather, the prominent Puritan cleric who had campaigned for return of the Massachusetts Bay Colony's original charter and against the Andros regime. Mather had gone to England as a representative of the colony 'to see what might be done for his distressed Country'. The very day that Phipps had landed in Boston, Mather, along with other New England representatives Samuel Newel and Elisha Hutchinson, had 'the favour to wait on the King, and privately to acquaint him with the enslaved and perishing Estate of his'.[18.3]

The two, the bluff and boisterous mariner and the cerebral cleric, formed an unlikely friendship. What brought them together was their mutual dislike of Governor Andros, who in addition to his high-handed and unpopular measures, had insulted both personally. Phipps he had ignored and belittled, and Mather he had offended by requisitioning his meeting house for Anglican services.

Mather would have known Phipps by (dubious) reputation and perhaps shaken his hand after one of the few meeting house sermons Phipps had attended. He would have been better acquainted with Mary (Hull) Phipps who was a far more committed member of Mather's congregation.

The truth was that Phipps spent more time away from Boston than there. From the start of his marriage, he had turned to the sea for a living, first as a ship's carpenter and later as captain and probably owner or part-owner of commercial vessels that were increasingly used for treasure-hunting forays. He must have made at least a moderately good income even before he hit silver on the Ambrosia Bank, because Mary Phipps, who stayed home alone and looked after the paperwork, seems to have been able to afford an active social life. She was certainly known to Judge Sewall.

Now, with a common goal, Mather and Phipps slipped easily into an effective working partnership. Phipps may have lost the support of Narborough (through death) and Albemarle (through his governorship of Jamaica), but he had other London contacts to call on, including Hayes, Haddock, Falkland and Constantine Phipps. Above all, he was known to King James and was lauded about town as a hugely successful treasure hunter who had provided the Royal Mint with silver galore. Meanwhile Increase Mather had a network of supporters generated by his church, his writing and his presidency of Harvard College. Through the latter, and his work with the New England Company, he knew the Ashursts, father Henry and brothers Sir William and Sir Henry. All were City merchants and money men, the two 'Henrys' both serving terms as New England Company treasurers. They were also involved in politics, both the brothers holding Parliamentary seats at various times and Sir William serving as Lord Mayor of London in 1693.[18.4]

The unworldly Mather would have told Phipps that he had been received well by the king, whose *Declaration of Indulgence* may have been unpopular among English Anglicans but was potentially beneficial to Puritans. James may have been Catholic, but at least he was honest about it, and stood up for his religion. Perhaps that was better than being an Anglican or, worse still, a Quaker. Mather was sure something good would come of his meeting with the king and having the Massachusetts Bay Colony's charter reinstated was a definite maybe.

Whether Mather's assessment of James' intentions was accurate or not, it turned out to be irrelevant. He had lost sight of the bigger picture, which was that James' days as king were numbered. He had lost the confidence of his subjects.

Events in June, when he had listened to Mather's complaints, had sealed his fate. They had not been easy to miss. Six Anglican bishops had challenged the king's *Declaration of Indulgence* on the grounds that it had not been approved by Parliament. An outraged James had had the bishops arrested. Within the week it was being announced that the queen, Mary of Modena, had given birth to a son. This was widely disbelieved. It was conceded that the queen had been pregnant but it was said she was too old to produce a healthy child (she had already had an uncomfortable number of miscarriages). Obviously, an imposter baby had been smuggled into the birthing chamber so that James might have a Catholic heir. And then a jury acquitted the six bishops of any crime. 'Bonfires were made that night and bells rung, which was taken very ill at Court,' reported the diarist and courtier John Evelyn.[18.5]

William of Orange, stadholder of the Netherlands, nephew of James and married to his (Protestant) daughter Mary, had solicited an invitation to step in on behalf of the English people. This duly arrived and William, involved in a perpetual war to save his country from the French, quickly accepted. His fleet of over 400 ships brought his army to Brixham in Devon in November 1688. By December he was in London and James had thrown the Royal Seal in the Thames and scuttled off to France.[18.6]

Phipps may have been one of those many who lined the streets of London waving oranges on sticks and orange favours as William's army marched through the capital. The soldiers carried banners bearing the slogan 'The Protestant religion and the liberties of England'.

Certainly, Phipps and Mather were caught up in a swirl of activity and uncertainty. But they did not give up and although Parliament was in abeyance, government continued. Mather had published his complaints in the snappily named *A narrative of the miseries of New-England, by reason of an arbitrary government erected there under Sir Edmond Andross*. In this he argued that cancellation of the colony's original 1628 charter had been illegal as had the appointment of Andros who with 'four of his Council [perhaps all of them his absolute *Devotees*] are impowered to make Laws and raise moneys on the Kings Subjects, without any Parliament, Assembly, or Consent of the People'. Mather said unfair taxes had been introduced, property rights questioned, and town meetings limited to one meeting per year, 'whereas the Inhabitants have occasion to meet once a week for the Relief of the Poor; or other Town-affairs'. What is more, new laws were not printed 'so that the people are at a great loss to know what is Law and what not'.[18.7]

By February 1689 the Lords of Trade had before them a petition from Phipps and Mather forwarded them by the new king, King William. It outlined the complaints made by Mather, arguing that 'the charters and corporations of the four Colonies of New England were taken away in 1684 by illegal and arbitrary proceedings and Sir Edmund Andros was appointed Governor'. It asked for 'restoration of our ancient privileges and that Simon Bradstreet, Thomas Hinkley, Robert Trant, and Walter Clark may be re-admitted to their respective Governments'.

Both Phipps and Mather were called before the committee where they complained of a flaw in the process by which the original charter had been taken from them (by legal actions instigated by Sir Robert Sawyer, who was ordered to attend the next meeting of the committee two days later). At that meeting Phipps and Mather scored a significant win. No view was taken on the legality of cancelling the Massachusetts Bay charter but it was 'agreed to recommend the despatch of the governor to New England in lieu of Sir Edmund Andros with a provisional commission, to take charge of the administration till further order'. Andros was out, and he was to raise no more money.

Not only that, perhaps with a nod to the change of regime in England, the committee recommended preparation 'as speedily as possible, a new establishment for preserving the rights and properties of the people of New England'.[18.8]

To Phipps and Mather, it must have seemed they had won a major victory. They had, of course. But it was soon overtaken by events in Boston. In April, emboldened by the 'Glorious Revolution' in England, the people of Boston rose up in their own rebellion. In fact, they did not rise up as one, because there were certainly many against what went on, nor were they all people of Boston. Led by township sentiment, a coordinated assortment of out-of-town militias marched on Boston. It was an overwhelming show of ordered discontent that avoided (much) violence and it had Andros and his cronies, including Dudley and Randolph, thrown in gaol. Somewhere between twenty-five and fifty people were arrested, 'probably some were soon released, or were too obscure in rank to be recorded'. Dudley was put under house arrest for his own safety and Stoughton, 'whom the people could not yet forgive for his recent subserviency' soon stood down (reported historian and one-time American congressman John Gorham Palfrey).[18.9]

Job done. Phipps was soon on his way back to Boston. Mather, still focusing on obtaining revival of the Massachusetts Bay Colony's original charter, stayed on.

Phipps arrived home in May 1689, bringing with him official confirmation that James had vacated his throne and had been succeeded by the joint monarchs King William and Queen Mary. This, it was ordered, should be proclaimed without delay. If Phipps had been looking forward to telling Andros the news and the decision of the Lords of Trade and Plantations to replace him, he was disappointed. Andros was not at home – he had been locked up.

But, perhaps because of his appointment as provost marshal general under the old regime, Phipps does seem to have played a part in oversight of those carted off to gaol and to have monitored and censured correspondence that Andros attempted to send home. He would perhaps have enjoyed telling the haughty ex-governor about the celebrations that had accompanied his downfall.

'Never had such a pageant as, three days after, expressed the prevailing happiness, been seen in Massachusetts,' reported Palfrey. 'From far and near the people flocked into Boston; the Government, attended by the principal gentlemen of the capital and the towns around, passed in procession on horseback through the thoroughfares; the regiment of the town, and companies and troops of horse and foot from the country, lent their pomp and noise to the show; there was a great dinner at the Town-House for the better sort; wine was served out in the streets; and the evening was made noisy with acclamations till the bell rang at nine o'clock, and families met to thank God at the domestic altar for causing the great sorrow to pass away, and giving a Protestant King and Queen to England.'[18.10]

Chapter 19

Phipps Sees the Light

BY ARRIVING IN the aftermath of Boston's revolution, Phipps had put himself at the centre of political upheaval – again. Things had moved quickly over the previous month, quickly but not decisively. Although most colonists were pleased to see Andros deposed and locked up – he stayed just so until the following spring – there was no agreement about what should come next. The townships were for return to the old charter, but the moderates were still moderate.

In the rebellion's first flush a *Declaration of the Gentlemen, Merchants, and Inhabitants of Boston and the Country Adjacent* had struck a moderate tone. It deplored the snatching away of the colony's charter and declared the appointment of Andros and Dudley illegal. So far, so Matherish. But it went on to distance the dissenting council members from the actions of the Andros/Dudley administration. Council members who were 'true lovers of their country were seldom admitted to, and seldomer consulted at, the debates which produced these unrighteous things. Care was taken to keep them under disadvantages, and the Governor, with five or six more, did what they would'.

Those 'few ill men which have been (next to our sins) the grand authors of our miseries' had been arrested to await 'what justice, orders from his Highness, with the English Parliament, shall direct'.[19.1]

Shortly a provisional government, the 'Council for the Safety of the People and the Conservation of the Peace' was formed and the townships were consulted. The council's members elected the 87-year-old Simon Bradstreet as their president. In the end it was decided that the pre-Andros government should essentially be restored, with Bradstreet as governor, and that it should seek approval and authorisation from England. This authorisation arrived in December 1689. Bradstreet was to remain governor until a permanent solution could be found.

The Council for the Safety of the People had been aptly named. In 1689 Bostonians had thought themselves in real danger. The most immediate cause for concern was the possibility of Indian attack. King Philip's War, which had ended over a dozen years before, had dampened but not extinguished expressions of Native American resentment. Immediately after the conflict, colonists had withdrawn from more remote and unprotected areas, such as Phipps' own neck of the woods on the Kennebec River. But over the years the more adventurous (or more desperate) settlers had begun to reclaim 'Indian' land. Again, there had been friction as the two cultures clashed, with a growing number of raids and counter-raids by settler and Indian war parties.

Prior to his visit to gaol, Governor Andros had led an expedition to Maine which had helped to escalate hostilities. In April of 1688 he had attacked a trading station owned by Jean-Vincent d'Abbadie, Baron de Saint-Castin. He had picked the wrong man. Besides being French, de St. Castin was the son-in-law of Madockawando, chief sachem of the eastern Indians, the people of the dawn, the Wabanaki (or Abenaki). Subsequently there were Indian raids on the New Hampshire settlement of Dover, in part as payback for a cowardly 'massacre' of Indians in King Philip's War, and on Maine settlements in Newcastle and Yarmouth.[19.2]

The settler death count was rising, but worse was to follow. Indian groups belonging to the east coast 'Wabanaki Confederacy' formed something of an informal alliance with French settlers, including de St. Castin. New England settlers also formed allegiances with Iroquois groups and their deadly Mohawk clans around New York and nearer the Great Lakes. They probably all thought they were using each other for their own means.

In August 1689 Pemaquid (now Bristol), Maine, and its Fort Charles were attacked and destroyed. De St. Castin was around and there were certainly both French and Indian warriors involved in fighting in New Dartmouth (Newcastle), Maine and Pemaquid.

Schenectady in New York was attacked in the bitter winter of early 1690, Salmon Falls, Maine, a little later, followed by Falmouth (now Portland) in May 1690. And so it went on. This was the start of King William's War, an echo of conflict that had flared up in Europe and which was to continue for another nine years (the result in America was a score draw, except for those individual settlers and Native Americans unfortunate enough to be killed, maimed or enslaved).

England and the Netherlands had fought wars against each other in their struggle for commercial superiority. But by 1688 all that had ended with the two countries adopting shared leadership in the shape of William of Orange. He had long been engaged in a struggle against the ambitious 'Sun King', Louis XIV of France, to maintain the Netherlands' independence. Not too long after taking the English throne (jointly, to start with, with his wife Mary), he had persuaded England to ditch its support of France and change sides (Charles II had signed a secret treaty and was in the pay of Louis, James II was a professed Catholic and enthralled to France, to where he had fled).

By the end of 1689 England was part of a Grand Alliance that was at war with France. French and English North American colonies were now more than competitors, they were enemies.

The population of the New England colonies far outnumbered those in Acadia, the French colonies in north-east America that included most of Maine, Prince Edward Island, Nova Scotia and New Brunswick. There were probably about 2,000 Acadians against an estimated 50,000 Massachusetts colonists, 4,000 in New Hampshire and 7,000 in Plymouth.[19.3] But Acadia was closely in tune with Canada, the New France colony along the St. Lawrence River, including Quebec, which had around 15,000 colonists. Meanwhile New Englanders were in something of a state of chaos because of the Glorious Revolution and found difficulty reaching agreement even within their own Massachusetts Bay Colony. Numerical superiority was no guarantee of safety.

In Europe professional soldiers fought pitched battles. In New England the fighting was more up close and personal. As with King Philip's War, it was characterised by raids and counter-raids, ambushes and desperate defences, brutal murders and abductions. The numbers involved were not huge, but the effect was devastating and cumulative. In the outlying areas nobody was safe. Women and children were not spared, and at any moment farmers and their wives and children might be dragged from their fields, orchards or barns, carpenters killed as they worked, smiths cut down with their own tools, families murdered while sleeping in their own beds.

By September 1689 Benjamin Church was in the field. The captain who in 1676 had led the group that had stormed the Great Swamp and eventually tracked down and killed Metacom aka King Philip, was now Major Church. Holding a commission from the Plymouth Colony, he was made commander-in-chief of the combined forces of Massachusetts, Plymouth and Connecticut and ordered to take action 'against the common Indian enemy'. Church was to base himself and his forces in the vicinity of Falmouth and was to 'encourage your soldiers to be industrious, vigorous, and venturous in their service, to search out and destroy the enemy'. His commission assured him it had been agreed that his men were to receive a 'reward of eight pounds per head, for every fighting Indian man slain by them, over and above their stated wages'. But he was 'to take effectual care that the worship of God be kept up in the army; morning and evening prayer attended as far as may be, and as the emergencies of your affairs will admit; to see that the holy Sabbath be duly sanctified'. Also 'you are to take care as much as may be, to prevent or punish drunkenness, swearing, cursing or such other sins as do provoke the anger of God'.[19.4]

In October Church fought the 'Battle of Brackett's Woods' in defence of two dozen or so settler families living near Falmouth. He remained active in the area but could not prevent further massacres early the following year. In his diary Samuel Sewall recorded that it was on 21 March that he learned 'the dolefull news' that a surprise dawn attack on Salmon Falls had resulted in 'between 80 and 100 persons' being 'killed and carried away'.

In Boston, Bradstreet and his new government pondered what to do next. They were under pressure to be seen to do something. The something they decided upon, besides putting two companies under Church's command and mobilising their militia, was an attack on Port Royal, Nova Scotia, then capital of Acadia.

Immediately after the Salmon Falls attack 'Sir William Phips offers himself to go in person', said Sewall. 'The Governour sends for me, and tells me of it, I tell the Court; they send for Sir William who accepts to goe, and is appointed to Comand the Forces.'[19.5] Some in the council had apparently initially thought Phipps' participation unlikely because 'his Lady could not consent'.

The appointment coincided with Phipps' acceptance into the Mathers' North End church. In the Puritan world this was usually a drawn-out process in which incoming members had first to convince church elders of their faith as shown to them by revelation. A written statement was required. According to Cotton Mather, the minister who was to baptise Phipps, the bluff seaman had lately gone through a period of contemplation when 'like David, concerning the house of the God who had surrounded him with so many favours in his own', his thoughts had turned to religion. Today it might be termed a 'guilt complex'.

It could have been true that Phipps had been counting his blessings and had been encouraged by Mary to think of the religious implications of his (and their) great good fortune. He might also have thought that the religious certainty of his new friend Increase Mather was something to admire. But there was surely something more prosaic going on as well. Phipps might not have been a sophisticate when it came to politics, but he was astute enough to know where his interests lay. His period of contemplation must have allowed him to ponder why he had been treated better by kings Charles and James than by Boston's ruling elite. Perhaps the fact that he was not a member of a Puritan church had helped his relationship with the Catholic-leaning English kings? But now there had been a change and England was ruled by William and Mary, Protestants both, with William a Calvinist. Perhaps William and Mary would see him in a more favourable light if he were a member of a nonconformist church?

Phipps had achieved a more important position within Boston society than most would have thought possible. Even so, he was still an 'outsider'. To rise further he would have to become a freeman of Boston, and that also meant joining a church. Increase Mather and his church provided a route to membership of that elite ruling group. He would also have seen that leading an expedition against Acadia would do his prospects no harm. And perhaps he could sooth Mary's concerns about the dangers involved by providing her with the satisfaction of knowing his soul would be saved?

It is a matter of conjecture as to whether social pressure, marital concern or straight self-interest played a part in his candidacy for church membership. But it seems almost certain that the largely illiterate Phipps did not write the statement of faith he presented to the church elders. Mather said Phipps experienced something of a revelation when he heard a sermon asserting that 'to make a publick and an open profession of repentance, is a thing not misbecoming the greatest man alive'. That was it. He had resolved to be baptised into the church.[19.6] But then Mather also said Phipps had given him his statement of faith 'presented unto the pastor of the church, with his own hand-writing'.

It may have been his own handwriting, but even if so, the statement must have been copied from something written by Mary Phipps or Mather himself. It amounted to the best part of 1,000 eloquent words laced with biblical quotes and allusions. It had all started twenty-six years before, it claimed, when a young Phipps had heard Increase Mather preach. Alerted to his 'sins' he had 'a deep sence of my miserable condition' and began to think 'what I should do to be saved?'. He had been reminded of the scripture: 'come unto me, you that are weary and heavy laden, and I will give you rest'. And so it went on. It was heady stuff and it did the trick. Phipps was baptised and accepted into the church. The Mathers would have been pleased: Increase, still in London, because he had led his friend onto what he believed to be the path of salvation, and Increase and Cotton together because they had added an influential (and rich) Bostonian to their church.

Later in the month Phipps, now a freeman, was sworn in as major-general of Boston's Acadian expedition. He had no previous military experience although this was to be largely a seaborn attack. Simon Bradstreet, almost fifty years Phipps' senior, the revered merchant who had arrived in Boston aboard the Winthrop Fleet, and the man with whom Phipps had clashed when captain of the *Golden Rose*, had accepted him to lead the mission.[19.7]

It took a while for Phipps to assemble his fleet and muster his militiamen. But leaving on 28 April 1690, he turned up in Port Royal on 10 May with 'seven or eight hundred men in eight small vessels', according to Sewall.[19.8] Some of the flotilla may have comprised relatively small vessels but Phipps had two substantial ships in his fleet. His own vessel, the *Six Friends*, carried forty-two guns and 120 men. The *Porcupine*, captained by Cyprian Southack, had sixteen cannon besides six smaller guns, and a crew of one hundred and seventeen. Other ships in the flotilla were the *Mary*, a sloop with eight guns, the *Union* with four guns, the *Mary Ann*, a ketch with two guns, and two other small ketches, the *Lark* and the *Batchelour*. Altogether they carried 736 men, 286 sailors, 446 foot soldiers and four others.[19.9]

The size of the force and the element of surprise were such that it had little trouble taking Port Royal, its crumbling fort and its ill-supported governor, Louis-Alexandre des Friches de Menneval. A day after arriving, a Sunday, de Menneval, his priest and his officers came aboard the *Six Friends* and surrendered. 'The Soldiers laid down their Arms, and were gaurded to the Church, where they were kept as Prisoners,' the journal soon published by Josua Natsto recorded.

The following day the visitors 'went a-shoar to search for hidden goods, (for during the time of Parley they had broke open the King's Store, & Merchants Stores, and convey'd sundry Wares into the woods). We cut down the Cross, rifled the Church, Pu'lld down the High-Altar, breaking their Images: and brought our Plunder, Arms and Amunition into Mr. Nelson's Storehouse', according to Natsto.[19.10]

There was no battle, simply surrender, although Phipps insisted the governor had broken the terms of a treaty agreed between them by allowing what would have been legitimate spoils to be removed from the fort and hidden (as confirmed by Natsto). He used this as an excuse for allowing his men to lock up the inhabitants and loot and burn the place. Phipps also flattened the fort and insisted the inhabitants swear an oath of allegiance to the English crown. He was soon off back to Boston with his loot and prisoners of war, including de Menneval and the granddaughter of the Indian leader Madockawando.[19.11] Taking the girl is unlikely to have been an act of kindness. She was more likely seen by Phipps as a bargaining chip of likely use in future negotiations with his Wabanaki enemies. However, she was well treated, according to Baker and Reid, becoming a part of the Phipps household.

Being able to loot the place was important to Phipps. Church was busy seeking out and destroying Indian supplies, a tactic that had served him well in King Philip's War, and Phipps was determined to use similar tactics by disrupting the Wabanaki Confederacy/French supply lines. And it would also mean both he and his men would benefit financially as did Boston and many Bostonians. (Sewall's diary reported that on Monday 16 June, 'Notice is given by beat of Drum of the Sale of the Souldiers part of Plunder taken at Port-Royal, to be made next Wednesday'.)

Phipps' instructions, agreed by the governor and council of Massachusetts on 24 March, were that should the French not surrender under terms offered them, 'then (God succeeding our Arms) besides their Stated Pay, the just half of all Plunder taken from the Enemy, shall be *Shared* among the Officers and

Souldiers; Stores of War only Excepted'.[19.12] This was to encourage the soldiers to fight. As things turned out, there had been no fighting, but trying to hide away stores belonging to the king and merchants was sufficiently contrary to Phipps' terms that he believed he was thereby entitled to the king's stores as a prize, and the merchants stores too, as plunder. The loot was considerable and included several vessels as well as munitions, money and foodstuff.

According to Sewall, news of the taking of Port Royal arrived in Boston on 22 May. It could not have been more welcome, coming only a day after 'exceeding bad news from the Eastward. 'Tis believed Casco Garrison and Fort are burnt, and the Inhabitants destroyed; so that we do not understand that there is one escaped or shut up or left. We fear, if this be true, there may be so many French and Indians that we shall be obliged to raise 4 or 5 hundred Men to defend our Frontiers,' wrote Sewall.

The 'Casco' referred to was Fort Loyal, Falmouth. Church had defended the place the previous year but had moved on, leaving the settlers protected by their wooden stockade, Fort Loyal. On 16 May this had been attacked by a force of French and Indians that had previously attacked Salmon Falls. Their leaders included Baron de St. Castin. The fort soon surrendered. It and surrounding homesteads were torched, over 200 settlers were killed and the rest captured. Amidst the ensuing gloom, Phipps' return shone out as blinding light. The hero returned to news that in his absence he had been elected to the ruling council, a magistrate at last.

This did not stop the self-important and, in the case of John Nelson at least, the self-interested ruling Boston elite, expressing their disapproval of Phipps' sacking of Port Royal. Egged on by Nelson, de Menneval tried to take action against Phipps for return of his belongings. The attempt was quashed but Bradstreet wrote to Phipps on de Menneval's behalf advising him to return the Frenchman's clothes and personal effects. The courtesies extended de Menneval would have outraged Phipps. Despite his seeming jovial demeanour – tempered by occasional displays of anger – he was a hard frontiersman. He knew too well the realities of Indian wars and that the latest examples of Salmon Falls and Fort Loyal amply demonstrated the enemy's attitude towards those who surrendered. No quarter was given or expected. Phipps had been ordered to hit Port Royal hard, to stop the enemy in its tracks, to inflict a blow. For Bradstreet to give into the commercially biased attitudes of Nelson was an indication of just how out of touch the governor and his council had become.

Despite the criticism, within a month of arriving back from Port Royal there was news of further advancement for Phipps. At a session of the Massachusetts Colony's General Court held on 28 May, Phipps was appointed chief commander of an expedition to take Quebec. Major John Walley was to be second-in-command.[19.13]

Chapter 20

Disaster Breeds Success

PHIPPS' ATTEMPT TO take Quebec and put an end to the French/Indian alliance was a disaster.

If those who currently governed the Massachusetts Colony had taken a step back, they would have seen that it was all but inevitable New England would eventually prevail against its indigenous rivals. The numbers were simply stacked too much to their advantage.

While the Indian population, once masters of the land, continued to shrink through disease and deprivation, that of the more recent English arrivals continued to grow. Settlers were forever pushing further into traditional Indian lands, causing friction with insistence on their own values and their own ways of doing things. Before they knew it, many Native Americans had stepped out of their stone-age environment and become dependent on those ways, and the technology that went along with them. They could not produce but had become reliant on guns, ammunition, knives, scythes, spades, metal pots and pans and much more – things they could obtain only from the French or English newcomers.

Bradstreet's jittery council did not see it that way. Settlers were being butchered in unspeakable ways by a demonic enemy that appeared from nowhere and melted away at will. And they were in league with Catholic idolators. The colony needed men and money to combat the threat. And it needed another grand gesture to halt the French and the Indians in their tracks. In short, Bradstreet and his cronies were pinning their hopes on that brash, uncouth and often uncontrollable seaman, Sir William Phipps.

Appeals were sent to London requesting military supplies. The plan was for Phipps to lead an armada north along the coast and then into the St. Lawrence River as far as Quebec, there to batter its ramparts with a barrage of cannon fire. At the same time Major Walley's troops, who would already have landed, would mount a land attack on the city. Despite its position, partly atop a plateau 180 foot up, Quebec's defences were not thought to be particularly strong. And its defenders would be depleted by a second prong to the land assault coming out of New York and attacking Toronto.

Almost everything that could go wrong, did go wrong.

Overestimating (not for the first time) their importance to the English crown, the Bostonians waited in vain for their extra munitions to arrive. King William was obsessed with his European war against the French and was loath to deplete his resources in any way. He was happy for the New Englanders to provide a distraction for the French in Europe, but not to invest too much in their efforts. And while Phipps and his fleet waited, the winter got nearer and nearer.

By August it was go then or postpone for a year. Phipps went. There were storms and contrary winds to delay him further. There were no pilots to help him navigate the shoals and banks of the icy St. Lawrence. No extra supplies or ammunition. Walley's men were landed in the wrong place. There was an outbreak of smallpox among the sailors, and the joint colonist/Iroquois force sent from New York gave up and went home, allowing the French forces to regroup behind their Quebec ramparts.[20.1]

It was early October before Phipps reached Quebec. Aboard the *Six Friends* once again, his force comprised over thirty assorted ships and more than 2,000 cold and sickly militiamen and frozen-fingered sailors. All attempts to make headway against the near-3,000 French defenders failed. Phipps made do with using up his depleted powder to pepper the city with his remaining shot. It made little impression and at the end of the month he set sail for home with his much bruised and battered fleet in tow. Before leaving, Phipps negotiated return of settlers snatched in Salmon Falls and marched through the snow to be held for ransom in Quebec. Among them was Mercy Short, a prominent and much prayed over 'afflicted' accuser in the Salem witch trials (see later).[20.2]

'Thus, by an evident hand of Heaven, sending one unavoidable disaster after another, as well-formed an enterprize as perhaps was ever made by the New-Englanders, most happily miscarried; and General Phips underwent a very mortifying disappointment of a design which his mind was, as much as ever any, set upon,' reported Cotton Mather. 'He arrived November 19, at Boston, where, although he found himself, as well as the publick, thrown into very uneasie circumstances, yet he had this to comfort him, that neither his courage nor his conduct could reasonably have been taxed; nor could it be said that any man could have done more than he did, under so many embarassments of his business, as he was to fight withal.'[20.3]

Phipps reported thirty of his men killed in combat and seven ships lost. But the toll was much greater with 1,000 or more succumbing to hunger, disease, exposure or drowning. Cotton Mather noted that the last of the force to make it home unassisted did not arrive in Boston until 9 May the following year. In the retreat, a brigantine with sixty men aboard and commanded by one John Rainsford, had found itself stranded on a 'desolate and hideous island' at the mouth of the St. Lawrence. The men had taken the decision to eke out their slender provisions and overwinter on the island. They constructed 'nine small chimneyless things that they called houses' and hunkered down waiting for the ice to melt. Fewer than half their number survived the winter but in March five of the survivors set off for Boston in 'a little cuddy', a small open boat suitable for two or three people. Fighting their way through ice floes and around icebergs they lived on seal meat and fish, arriving in Boston fifty-five days later. A rescue mission for their comrades was mounted and the remaining survivors made it home sometime later.

Summing up, Cotton Mather of course put a brave face on it all. 'The serventest prayers were sent up to the God of armies, for the safety and success of the New-English army gone to Canada,' he wrote. 'The faithful … sometimes, in their devotions on these occasions, uttered their perswasion that Almighty God had heard them in this thing, 'that the English army should not fall by the hands of the French enemy.' Now they were marvellously delivered from doing so; though the enemy had such unexpected advantages over them; yea, and though the horrid winter was come on so far, that it is a wonder the English fleet, then riding in the river of Canada, fared any better than the army which a while since besieged Poland, wherein, of seventy thousand invaders, no less than forty thousand suddenly perished by the severity of the cold, albeit it were but the month of November with them.'[20.4]

Phipps had not escaped criticism for his part in the attack on Quebec, but he was not seen as the major culprit. Walley, the New Yorkers and Iroquois were seen in a less charitable light. Meanwhile the Massachusetts Colony found itself in some trouble. It had weak and uncertain government, no money and rampant enemies. The hardship, loss of life and of shipping was not all. The failed campaign 'plunged' the Massachusetts Bay Colony into 'extreme debt' – 'there being forty thousand pounds, more or less, now to be paid, and not a penny in the treasury to pay it withal'.[20.5]

An innovative solution to the colony's money problems was soon found. It had been used to minting its own money but by now its 'mint master' John Hull was long dead. However, somebody came up with the idea of issuing paper money. This was four years before the Bank of England did the same, largely to finance King William's European wars. It is tempting to think that Sir William Ashurst, who was to be one of the founding investors in the Bank of England and who knew and held discussions with William Paterson, one of the main promoters of the Bank, may have had some hand in the decision. It was certainly surprisingly bold for Bradstreet's council.

Cotton Mather explained the process: 'The general assembly first passed an act for the levying of such a sum of money as was wanted, within such a term of time as was judged convenient; and this act was a fund, on which the credit of such a sum should be rendered passable among the people. Hereupon there was appointed an able and faithful committee of gentlemen, who printed, from copper-plates, a just number of bills, and flourished, indented, and contrived them in such a manner, as to make it impossible to counterfeit any of them, without a speedy discovery of the counterfeit: besides which, they were all signed by the hands of three belonging to that committee.'

The bills, he said, were for values ranging from two shillings to ten pounds: 'The publick debts to the sailors and soldiers, now upon the point of mutiny, were in these bills paid immediately: but that further credit might be given thereunto, it was ordered that they should be accepted by the treasurer, and all officers that were subordinate unto him, in all publick payments, at five per cent, more than the value expressed in them.'

At first there was public uncertainty about the value of the bills, mainly because there was so little confidence in the longevity of the current administration, said Mather. At the start they were heavily discounted, the holders receiving only fourteen or so shillings in the pound. 'However, this method of paying the publick debts did no less than save the publick from a perfect ruin: and ere many months were expired, the governour and council had the pleasure of seeing the treasurer burn before their eyes many a thousand pounds worth of the bills which had passed about until they were again returned unto the treasury; but before their being returned, had happily and honestly, without a farthing of silver coin, discharged the debts for which they were intended.'

Phipps, he claimed was a supporter and 'at the very beginning, meerly to recommend the credit of the bills unto other persons, cheerfully laid down a considerable quantity of ready money for an equivalent parcel of them', claimed Mather. 'And thus in a little time the country waded through the terrible debts which it was fallen into.'[20.6]

Phipps must have realised that longer-term salvation for the colony lay in the gift of King William. The colony needed a new charter, and fast. It needed financial support, and it needed an end to the French/Indian aggression. And he hankered after being allowed another attempt on Quebec. All would be difficult to obtain but in the spirit of 'I will put right what I have allowed to go wrong', Phipps hurried off to London.

This was in no sense a running away from the consequences of failure in Quebec. Certainly, Phipps had been criticised for his part in the débâcle, but the criticism came mainly from the likes of Dudley and Nelson who had their own agendas. Despite what these two said, the commander of the New England forces had not initiated the assault on Quebec and had been asked to undertake a near impossible task. He had acquitted himself with stoic bravery and had not ordered outlandish or unwise actions. He could hardly be blamed for the disease that took so many of his men or the severity of the weather.

Although Phipps no doubt had the interests of Massachusetts at heart, he also had ulterior motives for his trip to England. He was, after all, now a businessman, a shipowner, merchant and landowner. Provided there was victory over the French/Indian alliance, or a satisfactory peace brokered, he saw potential in exploitation of New England's natural resources, especially its abundant wood and suspected mineral wealth. He had once been party to a patent to seek sunken treasure, now he would seek patents giving himself monopoly rights to prospect for other, more natural treasures.[20.7]

Phipps was hardly the only one to have spotted the potential of making a fortune from America's extensive forests. In the year he took up his governorship of Jamaica, Christopher Monck, Duke of Albemarle, had petitioned the king and seemingly been about to be granted letters patent giving him a fourteen-year monopoly on the construction of wind- or water-driven sawmills in any royal colony or plantation in America, 'except new England'. Nothing came of this as the duke died in early October 1688.[20.8]

Phipps made it to London in early 1691 where he quickly resumed his friendship with Increase Mather and no doubt contacted surviving shareholders of the joint-stock venture that had funded his *Concepcion* treasure hunt: the likes of Anthony Cary, Viscount Falkland, Sir James Hayes, Issac Foxcroft and Francis Nicholson. He would also have sought out the Massachusetts Bay Colony's London agents Elisha Cooke and Thomas Oates, and the New England Company's London-based treasurer Sir Thomas Ashurst and his brother, Sir William Ashurst, future governor of the New England Company, parliamentarian and soon-to-serve Lord Mayor of London. The New England Company connection may also have brought Phipps into contact with the charity's current governor, then in the last year of his life, Royal Society stalwart Robert Boyle.

The Massachusetts mariner's treasure-hunting success was well known, and he would have been a welcome guest wherever be chose to go. In England, at least, he was something of a celebrity, an exotic being whose immense good luck and God-given navigational skills had brought him (and others) untold wealth. He would no longer have been expected to wait in drafty anterooms to present his ideas and proposals.

Whether or not Phipps met Boyle during the year-plus that he spent in England, he is likely to have visited Jonathan's, the Change Alley coffee house that was the haunt of mariners and members of the Royal Society. It was also a magnet for 'projectors', such as William Paterson, wishing to finance their new schemes and for stockjobbers. These black-coated ravens stood about Jonathan's entrance door hawking their shares (having been shooed away from the nearby Royal Exchange because of their noisy behaviour).

The bulky Phipps would have brushed them aside with ease. But had he lingered to discuss their offerings, he would have been surprised and perhaps a little amused to learn that as well as the shares of long-established companies, such as the East India Company and the Hudson's Bay Company, the stockjobbers were pushing those of diving equipment makers and treasure-hunting adventurers. Once he had had trouble raising money for his planned treasure hunt. Now it seemed people were clamouring to be allowed a slice of such ventures.

In his many meetings and chance encounters, Phipps would have been pleased to discuss previous triumphs and outline future projects. With Falkland he would have talked about continuing treasure-hunting ventures. There had been talk of a third '*Concepcion*' attempt with Falkland and other original shareholders involved (Narborough's place being taken by his widow). Although it seems the group had a royal patent in place, the plans never matured.

But Falkland, now an Admiralty commissioner as well as a Member of Parliament, had caught the treasure-hunting bug and was currently financing a voyage to the South Seas. This was in the hands of Captain John Strong who had been Phipps' first mate on the *James and Mary*, a ship that Strong subsequently captained. He may well have been recommended for his latest venture by Phipps.

In 1689 Strong had received a royal commission to sail the *Welfare*, a ship of forty guns and a crew of ninety, through the Magellan Straights to Ecuador, repeating Narborough's 'secret' voyage of 1670. His mission was to find a Spanish treasure ship known to have sunk in the vicinity of his planned destination.[20.9]

By the time Falkland and Phipps are likely to have met (early to mid-1691), Strong was at or near 'Hawkins' Land', a group of islands in the south Atlantic named after the English adventurer Richard Hawkins who had visited them, but not landed upon them, a century before. On the charts carried by pirate-author William Dampier[20.10] they were put down as the Sibbel de Wards, otherwise known as the Islas Sebaldinas, visited by Dutchman Sebald de Weert a few years after Hawkins. Today these islands are known as the Falklands. Strong had found a convenient anchorage between the two main islands which he named 'Fawkland Channel' in honour of his sponsor Viscount Falkland. The name, but not its spelling, stuck and was eventually applied to the whole island group (over 700 of them).

Phipps does not appear to have made much headway with his own pet projects but was involved by Increase Mather in the push for a renewal of the Massachusetts Bay Colony charter.

Back in 1689, the new king, William III had referred Phipps' and Mathers' petition for renewal back to the Lords of Trade. There was little chance that the colonists would be granted the degree of independence to which they thought themselves entitled, but perhaps some compromise could be achieved? The committee had been asked to draft a suitable new charter 'with such Powers and Clauses, as may suite with, and be agreeable to the Laws and Government of this Kingdome, and may preserve the Rights and Properties of those Colonies, and reserve such a Dependance on this Crowne'.[20.11]

Nothing much happened until 1691. Then, in April, the Lords of Trade decided that before going any further, they needed the king to 'declare whether it be His Royall Pleasure to have a Governor or Single Representative of His own appointment from time to time to give His consent to all Laws and Acts of Government as in Barbados and the other Plantations, or whether His Majesty would leave the Power of making Laws to the People, or officers appointed by Them'.

William said he would nominate his own governor to take charge, thank you very much. The old charter had been 'legally Vacated' he said, and the colony's agents had themselves 'desired a new Charter from His Majesty with divers Variations from the former'. He ordered 'the Right Honorable the Lords of the Committee of Trade and Plantations do forthwith prepare the Draught of a new Charter upon that Foundation'.[20.12]

By July the committee was sending the king some last objections to its proposed charter from Massachusetts Bay agents. Among other things these concerned who should appoint judges and other legal offices and whether the governor should be able to blackball elected council members.

There was one further intriguing attempt to have the charter amended which involved Phipps, Mather, Sir Henry Ashurst and the projector William Paterson. Why Paterson should be involved is not clear although he, Ashurst and perhaps Phipps had some financial interest in the outcome. A further hint of what was going on was contained in a paper submitted by Phipps to the Lords of Trade a little time later. This listed the 'names of harbours and places suitable for townships in East New England and Nova Scotia'. They were 'Puttdumquoar, Penobscot, Muchyasse, Passamaquoddy, Meenus, Port Royal, Grand Passage, Cape Sable, Port La Have, Port Mattoon, Port La Flore, Chittabucto (which lies in the gut of Canseau and is the easternmost part fit for settlement)'. Could perhaps Paterson have been considering 'East New England and Nova Scotia' as possible sites for his scheme to establish a Scottish settlement in the Americas? About this time, he was much involved in creation of the Company of Scotland Trading to Africa and the Indies which was eventually responsible for a disastrous attempt to colonise the Darien.[20.13]

On 2 September 1691 the Lords of Trade took note of a petition from Mather ('by order from Sir Henry Ashurst') and Paterson asking that Nova Scotia be united to Massachusetts, 'also Maine, also New Hampshire'. They also wanted 'a clause providing that the passing of the charter may not deprive the people of any of the rights, privileges and properties belonging to them'. This last was an attempt to confirm property rights challenged by Andros.[20.14]

The upshot was that the committee agreed 'all former grants of land by the Governor and Council and all property legally vested in the inhabitants be confirmed'. (A few days later this was amended to apply to 'private persons only' since otherwise 'this will upset the whole Colony, for most of the towns have been erected by such conveyances'.)

The same 2 September meeting received a paper from Phipps pointing out that 'in Piscataqua and Nova Scotia there are vast quantities of timber fit for naval purposes, white oak, ash, and such abundance of pines that were they well improved they would supply the whole Navy with pitch and tar, better and cheaper than in Europe. I beg sufficient instructions and authority to prevent the waste of this timber'.

The committee agreed 'that all trees of the diameter of twenty-four inches and upwards at one foot from the ground be reserved to their Majesties for the Navy, on any land not already granted', and that the penalty for cutting such trees without a licence be £100 for every tree. Also, there should be 'no grant of land between the Sagadahock rivers, the St. Lawrence, the Gulf of St. Lawrence and the main sea' without royal approval.

By this time the Massachusetts agents had accepted there was no going back to the old charter. All was more or less decided except for the decision as to who would be the governor. 'The charter signed by King William III in October 1691 provided for royal appointment of a governor, lieutenant governor, and secretary, the continuation of a General Court lower house elected by freeholders, but without religious test, and a Council serving both as an executive power and legislative upper house, chosen by the General Court.' The governor could veto acts of the General Court, would serve as commander-in-chief, and appoint judges with Council consent, according to Massachusetts state archives.[20.15]

There had no doubt been a good deal of lobbying for the position of governor. There was no likelihood of the last governor of the 'Dominion of New England' Edmund Andros getting the job; that would have been asking for trouble. Joseph Dudley believed the governorship was his as of right, but his enthusiastic support for the Andros regime ruled him out. Edward Randolph had also made himself a hate figure in New England and could not be considered. Elisha Cooke was too committed to having the old charter revived. Simon Bradstreet, now approaching 90, also represented what had gone before. William Stoughton, twenty years Phipps' senior, was a steady administrator who had almost been forgiven for serving under Andros. But Stoughton was somebody whose certainty about the correctness of his own ideas was so steadfast that it left no room for empathy or imagination. There were also numerous colonial administrators and impoverished English gentry and petty nobles who believed they might be in the running.

But William Phipps was the obvious, hard-to-ignore choice. First and foremost, he was a made-in-Maine New Englander and on this score alone should be acceptable to the difficult colonists. He had proved his loyalty to the crown, not least by bringing it a fortune in recovered silver. He was an Indian fighter and admiral who had led a successful attack on Port Royal. True, he had been beaten back in Quebec, but King William was a general who knew not every battle could be won. As a member of Mather's church, Phipps had the right religious credentials, and he had the backing of Mather, Ashurst and, it seems, Paterson.

So, when, in late September the Lords of Trade had before them proposed appointees for governor, deputy-governor and assistants (until elections for the latter could take place in 1693), it was Sir William Phipps' name that headed the list. William Stoughton was proposed as his deputy, while Simon Bradstreet and Samuel Sewall were among those nominated as council members.[20.16]

By the end of the year, it was official. Sir William Phipps, the semi-literate-backwoodsman-made-good was to be the governor of the Province of the Massachusetts Bay which now included the territory of the former Massachusetts Bay colony, the Plymouth colony, Maine, Nova Scotia (until 1697) and the Cape islands, but not New Hampshire. He was also to be 'Commander-in-Chief of all forces, by sea and land of Massachusetts, Connecticut, Rhode Island, Providence Plantation, King's Province and New Hampshire'.[20.17]

By February 1692 Phipps and Mather were on their way back to Boston aboard the *Nonsuch*, a fifth-rated warship, ninety foot long with forty guns and a crew of 180.[20.18] Back in the 1660s and 1670s she had been captained successively by two future admirals, George Rooke and Cloudsley Shovell. But in February 1692 she had been recently refitted and her newly appointed captain, Richard Short, had handed his cabin over to Phipps.

Short, who was apparently disabled, his right hand having been injured in battle, described himself as 'an old servant in the Navy, having entered it in 1678 as lieutenant; and I hold good certificates from Sir Cloudesley Shovel and others'.[20.19] He was, it seems, also a drunk.

The ship was accompanied by a small flotilla of other vessels: the smaller *Edward and Mary* (fourteen guns and twenty-four seamen) carrying ammunition and stores, the *Jeremy* (with a crew of sixteen) and the *Thamer* (with twelve seamen).[20.20]

Phipps must have been feeling pleased with himself. In truth his appointment as governor was a poisoned chalice into which the seeds of his fall from grace had already been liberally sprinkled.

Chapter 21

Short Shrift

PHIPPS ARRIVED BACK in Boston in mid-May 1692. It was a Saturday and although late in the day he decided to give a speech to those who had come to greet him. God had sent him to serve his country, he said. He would protect the colony's ancient laws and customs, and, where practical (he was a politician now), all liberties and privileges would remain as before. He then began to read out his commission, but before halfway through he stopped. It was too late in the day, sunset was upon them and Saturday had transitioned into Sunday, he said. He would respect the Sabbath. There were to be no celebrations that evening and no firing of guns. All would have to be put on hold until Monday.

It sounds as if all this might well have been stage-managed to demonstrate what a pious man he had become. But on Monday it took his council six hours of debate whether he should begin his speech again from the beginning or simply continue where he had left off. It was eventually decided he should start again.

It was a sign of things to come. If Phipps had thought his council would give him an easy time, he was wrong. Andros-friendly council members who believed in cooperation with England had gone, only a mix of independent-minded councillors remained. Soon they were to be replaced by new nominees, but mostly they would comprise the same crew.

Phipps had come back to the usual Boston bickering plus a basketful of other problems. Joshua Brodbent, provost marshal of New Hampshire, pointed to one of them. 'No doubt you have heard of the wizards and witches,' he wrote to Francis Nicholson, lieutenant governor of Virginia and previously second-in-command in the Dominion of New England to Sir Edmund Andros. 'There are now over a hundred of them in gaol, but they betray each other so fast that they say there are seven hundred in all. One Burrowes, a minister at Easter, is imprisoned for a wizard. Most are church members, elders and deacons. Mrs. Moody, Parson Moody's wife, is said to be one, and many more very creditable persons.'[21.1]

Phipps also had the continuing King William's War to contend with and the colony's lack of money. On a personal front, he had no regular salary agreed by London or the colony, nor would he have. He was expected to be self-financing.

And his appointment as 'commander-in-chief of all forces, by sea and land of Massachusetts, Connecticut, Rhode Island, Providence Plantation, King's Province and New Hampshire' was an obvious source of future difficulties, blurring, as it did, the lines of command prevailing in the various colonies, each with its own governor and general council.

He would not have recognised it as such, but his own behaviour was also a problem. He was energetic, impatient and blunt. He was smart, clever but self-educated. Diplomatic, he was not. Well used to the sneers of those who continually harped back to his inability to read and write, he used his temper as a weapon to cover his perceived shortcomings, and his bulk to support his opinions.

Such behaviour no doubt played a part in his relationship with his nemesis Captain Richard Short. The two had obviously clashed from the start. Both were headstrong and neither was inclined to give the other leeway.

It had begun, perhaps, over an argument about prize money. While en route to Boston the *Nonsuch* had taken a French prize, the *Catharine*, loaded with sugar, cotton and cocoa. As captain, Short would normally have been entitled to the prize, but he was outranked by Phipps both on the *Nonsuch* and in the Admiralty Court of Massachusetts, where Phipps sat in judgement.

Both were later accused of 'breaking bulk', taking some of the cargo for themselves. Historians Emerson Baker and John Reid have suggested this may have been by some private arrangement between the two. But overall, and with some justification, Short would have felt hard done by, Phipps that the money would be helpful for the government coffers.

Not that Short was a paragon of virtue. He had some trouble keeping his crew intact and was soon busy using bully-boy tactics to force locals to sign on as crew members. In July the Lords of Trade heard that John Tomson, a member of the Council of Massachusetts, had complained to the governor about Short's behaviour: 'I was on the 30th of June in my quarters at the Green Dragon when Captain Short of H.M.S. Nonsuch came with several of his men and asked if any of his crew were there,' he wrote. 'I told them that there was no one in the house, but an ancient member of assembly. They searched the house and the men presently told me that they had the Captain's orders to pull me out of bed. On my going down the captain called me several ill names, and told his men to hale me away, without giving me time to put on my stockings. The Captain struck at me as I came out, and beat a man who fended off the blow. After taking me some way they let me go. I beg satisfaction for this affront.'[21.2]

Worse, much worse, was to follow.

When in London Phipps had pleaded that Massachusetts be given the protection of at least two warships. The result was that the Captain

Fairfax's *Conception Prize* was ordered to take up station in New England. And subsequently the *Nonsuch* received similar orders.

Short would have been aggrieved that, besides having to ferry Phipps and his party to Boston, he was now obliged to stay there supposedly at Phipps' beck and call.

The governor had grown up in what is now Woolwich, Maine, and, on paper at least, he and his family still owned property there. Pemaquid (now Bristol) was only twenty or so miles away (although the network of rivers and waterways in the area made any practical journey from one to the other a good deal longer (today the road journey is just under thirty miles). The news, in August 1689, that Pemaquid's wooden stockade, Fort Charles, had been attacked and destroyed by a joint Indian/French raiding party would have hit home.

When negotiating his appointment as governor, Phipps had managed to engineer an order to rebuild the fort at Pemaquid with something stronger. He wasn't, of course, given any money to do this but the order alone was sufficient for him to use colony funds for the rebuild. He must have seen this as a flagship project, a statement of his intent to defend the colony and a symbol of his power to do so. It was certainly a priority.

In July he had reappointed Benjamin Church as 'Major of the several companies of militia, detached for their Majesties' service against their French and Indian enemies'.[21.3] Soon he had taken him and his forces off to Pemaquid and asked him his opinion about erecting a fort there. They apparently spent some time surveying possible sites but the Indian-fighting hit-and-run specialist told Phipps that in his opinion a new fort would only provide a target for attack, forts 'being only nests for destructions'.

But Phipps had his orders, and his mind was made up. He needed a symbol that the Indians would understand. His stronghold, Fort William Henry, was to be stone-built and the best in the area. With up to eighteen mounted cannon, it would have a garrison of at least sixty men.

The preliminaries over, in August 1692 Church was sent off with the majority of his men 'to endeavour the destruction of the enemy'. Phipps was left to oversee the building work. For transport to and from Pemaquid, he apparently used the sloop *Mary* (the same as used in the attack on Port Royal). For protection during construction of the fort he relied on the *Nonsuch* and the *Conception Prize*. This was a duty that the *Nonsuch* captain, Richard Short, was reluctant to undertake.[21.4]

Further arguments between Phipps and Short followed. Phipps later put his side of the story in a letter to secretary of state (southern department), Daniel Finch, the Earl of Nottingham. This was after Short and Phipps had been involved in a scuffle on the Boston quayside, and Phipps had dismissed Short from his post.

'In September, 1692, I went to Pemaquid in a sloop kept in pay by this country, and left orders to Captain Short to follow me immediately; instead of which he delayed starting for four or five days and then stopped at Piscataqua on the way, whereby I lost the opportunity of surprising several French and Indians in some small islands near Pemaquid', wrote Phipps. 'After waiting several days longer than I had intended I was forced to return to Boston. Nor, though the wind was favourable, did Captain Short appear until some days after my departure … Soon after I reached Boston I received a report, which seemed likely to be true, that three French men-of-war were arrived on the coast. I sent written orders to Captains Short and Fairfax of H.M. ships Nonsuch and Conception, then lying at Pemaquid, to be in readiness, and directed them positively to fight the French ships if they met them, and otherwise not to leave the harbour but to stay and secure the fort. Notwithstanding this they both came to Boston, deserting the fort, which being unfinished to seaward would have been taken if attacked … They pretended that they were in want of provisions, but if so it was through their own fault, for I told them to send their pursers if they wanted any; but they did not send them because they needed the pretence.'

Phipps had more: 'In November last, I sent Captain Short my written order to go to Pemaquid, but he desired that the ship might be laid on shore at Boston, and voluntarily offered to supply a sloop with men, ammunition, and provisions to ply between Boston and Pemaquid during the winter as necessity might require. I consented; but, after I had ordered the ship to be laid up, on the second time when there was occasion to send to Pemaquid, Captain Short refused to send his men, though at the same time he suffered many of them to go to other quarters in merchant-ships, taking a reward of £20 a man out of their wages.

'I checked him, and threatened to deal with him according to his deserts, but he disdained to bear any reproof, gave me provoking language in public before several persons, and drawing near me shook his cane at me. This insolence provoked me to strike him a smart blow, which lit on the brim of his hat and on his shoulder, which I designed to warn him to keep his distance. Immediately he returned the blow and continued striking my head and body with his cane until I threw him on the ground. He rose, twice laid his hand on his sword, and then again assaulted me with his cane until I made him incapable of striking any more.

'He was free from drink, but he had the night before used threats against me. I suspended him the same day, and have sent him home. I have shewn all manner of respect to the King's captains and have tried to make their station easy and comfortable to them, but they have taken advantage of this to intrude upon my patience and take counsel with my enemies. I shall pass by in silence what only concerns myself, but so long as I am in my present station I cannot overlook neglect of duty.'[21.5]

Phipps was soon writing to the Admiralty asking for his complaints against the captain to be looked at: 'I will only add to them that he has neglected order of all kind on board his ship; has pressed men ashore without my warrant and afloat beyond his complement, making men pay for their release. I therefore forbade him to press at all without my warrant, for he has used his power to make a prey of the King's subjects. I have borne with much from respect to his commission, but my kindness has been misconstrued as weakness; and I now leave the matter to your justice.'[21.6]

Short had his own side of the story of course, painting Phipps as the aggressor. Accusations began to flow back to London from both sides. Among them was a submission from 'the warrant officers of HMS Nonsuch'. Captain Short, they said, 'is given to drunken habits, which makes him tyrannical both afloat and ashore. He has imprisoned most of his officers and driven many men to desertion by his cruelty, insomuch that we had determined to lay down our warrants rather than continue in such bondage. The Governor, however, has suspended him and appointed Thomas Dobbins in his stead, whom we hope you will confirm'. This was signed by 'the master, boatswain, purser, cook and gunner'.[21.7]

Meanwhile Captain Fairfax was also on the case. In March he wrote home in defence of Short, his 'brother officer'. The previous autumn he had been ordered to overwinter in Pemaquid, he said. 'I sounded the place with him, and found that it was impossible for him to winter there without certain ruin to the ship from touching the ground or the ice. This was the general opinion of the masters here and of his own officers, who were about to protest against it; but the Governor on further consideration laid her up at Boston, and requested Captain Short to send thirty men in country sloops with stores to Pemaquid, which the men voluntarily did, rather than hazard a King's ship.

'Since then some friends of the Governor having occasion to man a merchantman for a short voyage asked Captain Short to spare them some men while his ship was laid up, which he declined to do until they influenced the Governor to request him, saying that the voyage was short and would be a kindness to his men as well as to them, and promising never to thwart him with it. The ship sailed, and then the Governor ordered him to send four more men with the sloop Mary for Pemaquid, and thirty-six more for other service. Captain Short refused, for the men were unwilling and those that had already sailed were not yet returned. On this the Governor flew into a passion and gave him the lie, calling him lubber, rascal, etc. and laid him over the pate. Captain Short returned the blow with his left hand (his right hand being lame) but the Governor got him down and beat him most severely, breaking his head. He then went on board the ship and dispossessed him, putting the gunner in command and obliging the officers by threats to obey him. He then made out a mittimus and confined Captain Short to the common, nasty gaol, under such severe restraints, to my knowledge, as were more fit for the worst of villains than for a gentleman holding the King's Commission, barring him all help from friends or servants. Captain Short being much indisposed by ill lodging and the extreme cold, I waited, at his request, with two other gentlemen of considerable estates on the Governor, asking that he might be enlarged on their bail. The Governor refused, saying that Captain Short was lucky not to be laid in a dungeon in irons; and he also refused, though frequently requested by the most eminent gentlemen and merchants of the place, to give him some warmer lodging. I then went to the judge for a habeas corpus, which he was inclined to grant, when the Governor suddenly removed him to Castle Island, about a league from the town, where he is again deprived of any opportunity of settling his business or preparing his defence. The Governor said that he should be sent away in a day or two, which is now near two months since. I am well assured that Captain Short has behaved himself with great civility to Sir William Phips both during his passage and since then on shore, but has never met with other return than hard usage, though wanting not for large promises.'[21.8]

The argument soon spilled over to others that Phipps was having with his fellow New England governors.

Not only was Phipps 'commander-in-chief of all forces, by sea and land of Massachusetts, Connecticut, Rhode Island, Providence Plantation, King's Province and New Hampshire', he was also expected to act as the clearing house for money, munitions and other military supplies coming from England. Although required to support the other colonies, the Massachusetts governor was understandably frugal in distributing the men, money and munitions available to him beyond the frontiers of his own jurisdiction. Other colonies were equally reluctant to commit resources to help one another.[21.9]

The situation had provoked pointed exchanges between the various governors, none more vitriolic than those between Phipps and Benjamin Fletcher of New York, and between Phipps and John Usher of New Hampshire. Presence in the background of the deadly Joseph Dudley probably added spite to the exchanges.

One of the unexpected consequences of the failure of Massachusetts to push forward its prosecution of Andros and the others it had ejected in 1689 was that Dudley had been able to rehabilitate his career. When sent back to England he had met Colonel Henry Sloughter, who in 1689 had been appointed governor of New York. Sloughter and his entourage did not reach New York until December 1690, by when Dudley had joined his staff.

At the time New York, like Massachusetts, was being run by an 'illegal' government. Jacob Leisler had led a rebellion not dissimilar to that in Boston against its governing regime. Sloughter arrested Leisler and appointed Dudley to head a special court created to try Leisler for treason. Dudley found him guilty and Leisler was duly hanged, drawn and quartered. Meanwhile Dudley was named first chief justice of the newly established New York Supreme Court of Judicature. The appointment did not last long. Sloughter died unexpectedly and was replaced as governor by Benjamin Fletcher who in turn got rid of Dudley.[21.10] In 1693 he managed to get himself another job as lieutenant governor of the Isle of Wight off the south coast of England.

Even in Phipps' time as governor of Massachusetts, the property-ownership problems caused by competing charters for New Hampshire remained. In 1691 John Mason had finally sold on his inheritance rights to the colony to the merchant Samuel Allen, who the following year managed to get himself appointed royal governor. But much of the day-to-day running of the colony was put into the hands of lieutenant governor John Usher, Allen's son-in-law. Three years older than Phipps, Usher had been treasurer of the Dominion of New England under Andros. Perhaps more to the point, he must have worked closely with deadly Dudley.

Phipps and Usher involved themselves in a slanging match that soon came to involve allegations and counter-allegations concerning Captain Short. After Phipps arrested Short, he tried to have him packed off to London, putting him aboard 'a merchantship, Jeremiah Toy, master'. Phipps may have thought the ship would sail straight to England but he soon learned that it had stopped over at Piscataqua (now Portsmouth, New Hampshire) and that Short had been in contact with John Usher who was harbouring deserters from the *Nonsuch*.

In a rage Phipps took himself off to Piscataqua accompanied by 'fourteen armed men'. He confronted Toy, took his commission from him and tore it to shreds. He next went aboard Toy's ship, broke into Short's cabin (the captain being ashore) and, said Short, 'carried off my chest with all my clothes, money, papers, certificates, affidavits, journals and other matters which he knew that I had kept to vindicate myself before the Lords of Trade and Plantations'. He claimed 'a baser action was never done; it is termed piracy or robbery'.[21.11]

Phipps was soon writing to Nottingham complaining about both Toy and Usher. Several men had deserted the *Nonsuch* to go – presumably back to England with Short – in Toy's ship. John Usher had protected them in New Hampshire, he said. 'I sent letters to demand them and to the purser of the *Nonsuch* to seize them, but they were rescued out of his hands by Mr. Usher, and that they might be the better protected he obtained an order for their protection from the Council, on the ground that they had been discharged by Captain Short, though such discharge, being subsequent to his suspension, was invalid.'

Phipps admitted he had been to Piscataqua himself but said: 'When I came into the river, Toy, Short and the deserters at once went on shore before I could come up with them, whereupon I went ashore myself and desired to speak with the President but was refused. I also required Toy to produce Captain Short, but he would not, being encouraged by the Government and by the owner, who was then at Piscataqua.'

Phipps said he asked for a warrant for Short's arrest as an escaped prisoner but was refused. He had no option but to 'retire to Boston, leaving Short and the deserters under the protection of the Government'.[21.12]

Thomas Dobbins, the man Phipps had appointed as captain of the *Nonsuch* in place of Short also put his oar in. He wrote to the Admiralty saying that since his sacking Short 'has done all he can to obstruct the King's service by trying to draw away and corrupt the men of this ship'.

He had enticed four men to join him at Piscataqua. 'The purser was sent … to apprehend the deserters, but they were rescued by Lieutenant-Governor Usher, who threatened him for what he had done and finally committed him to prison for three days, during which time his ship was seized and condemned. Sir William Phips then went thither in person, who set the purser at liberty, but was refused delivery of Captain Short and the deserters'.[21.13]

Phipps and Short could both be bombastic and domineering. To what extent the expressions of support both received were spontaneous or obtained under pressure is difficult to say. Both were capable of being manipulative, Phipps had offered to return Short's confiscated possessions but only if he confessed his 'wrongdoing' and apologised. Here were shades of Phipps' treatment of de Menneval at Port Royal.

For his part, Short was accused by his boatswain and carpenter of refusing to sign their expense accounts unless they first certified that the ship was endangered by remaining at Pemaquid. If they had ever signed anything to that effect it was 'in ignorance', they said.[21.14]

The support given Short by Fairfax was no more than he, and the Admiralty, would have expected of a fellow long-term career officer. The *Conception Prize* was his first command, his last being in 1706 when, ironically, he was captain of the ninety-six-gun, second-rated ship of the line, *Albemarle*.[21.15]

In 1693 he seemed to be a little disillusioned by it all. 'I have before now hinted to you concerning my uneasiness in this station,' he wrote to the

Admiralty. 'It is known by every gentleman here that no one commanding one of the King's ships was ever used with common civility, but on the contrary basely abused. I have endeavoured to comply with the humours of those in authority here so far as becomes a gentleman, but find that nothing that bears the name shall be so treated. I wish that I could serve the King elsewhere, for I am sensible that I lie much out of the way of promotion, and beg your favour to obtain my removal from this station.'

And his ship was in poor shape. When it was laid up for the winter, he realised that without a new upper deck, fore and aft, it would be unfit for service. 'But I find that neither he [Phipps] nor any other persons have any instructions in the matter, and I receive little encouragement from him or from the country.'[21.16]

Whatever the rights and wrongs of the argument, retired admiral and one-time governor of Bermuda Sir Robert Robinson, summed things up when he wrote to William Blathwayt in January 1694: 'Surely it is very strange that the Captain of a man-of-war should be struck by any Governor whatsoever. I told Sir William how ill it looked on his part, and that if he had fault to find with Captain Short, he ought to have complained at home.'[21.17]

If Phipps was guilty of nothing more, he was certainly guilty of behaviour unbecoming of a governor. But then so was Robinson (see reference 23.2).

Chapter 22

Double, Double Toil and Trouble

WHILE ALL THIS arguing was going on, Salem Village, a parish in the north-west of the area administered by the town of Salem, was enthralled by delusions of witchcraft. Some young girls had been the victims of unseen attacks that had apparently left them gibbering wrecks, contorted by convulsions.

When medical help was sought, the diagnosis was that they had been bewitched. Some relatives made official complaints which led, in the last day of February 1692, to arrest warrants being issued against Sarah Good, Tituba Indian and Sarah Osborn. The pretext was 'suspicion of witchcraft' causing 'much mischief' to Elizabeth Parris, Abigail Williams, Ann Putnam and Elizabeth Hubbard.[22.1]

This was just over two months before William Phipps returned to Boston from England. In itself it was no big deal. People who believed implicitly in the existence of holy spirits were wired to accept there must also be unholy spirits emanating from the devil. Witches were the enemies within, otherwise ordinary people who served not holy but evil spirits and could conjure up spectral images of themselves and order these and devilish imps, 'familiars', to do damage to others.

Charges of witchcraft were not that uncommon in the New England courts. When Phipps was only 5 years old, Eunice Cole of Hampton, New Hampshire, had been convicted of witchcraft. She had been 'sentenced to receive corporal punishment and be imprisoned for life'. Six years later she was released having suffered 'so much punishment'. She said her property had been ruined and her 88-year-old husband needed looking after. The court agreed but 'she could not avail herself of the decision because she could not pay arrears or give bonds, and she remained in prison several years longer'.[22.2]

Only four years prior to the Salem arrest warrants, Ann 'Goody' Glover, an elderly cleaning lady of Irish descent (and Catholic) was tried, convicted and hanged for practising witchcraft. The presiding judge had been deadly Dudley. As in Salem, the initial accusers had been young girls. One, Martha Goodwin, had started an argument by insisting Glover's daughter had stolen some laundry. Soon after the argument the children became ill, the result of witchcraft, said a doctor.[22.3]

Cotton Mather, who had supported the prosecution, later wrote a 40,000-word text, *Memorable Providences*, describing the episode.[22.4] In it, he said the Goodwin family 'had no proof that could have done her [Goody Glover] any Hurt but the *Hag* had not power to deny her interest in the Enchantment of the Children; and when she was asked, *Whether she believed there was a God?* Her Answer was too blasphemous and horrible for any Pen of mine to mention. An Experiment was made, Whether she *could recite the Lords Prayer;* and it was found, that tho clause after clause was most carefully repeated unto her, yet when she said it after them that prompted her, she could not possibly avoid making *Nonsense* of it, with some ridiculous Depravations.'

Proof indeed.

In Europe there had also been outbreaks of what seemed to be witchcraft epidemics. The last in England had been during the Civil War when self-proclaimed 'Witchfinder General' Matthew Hopkins and his associate John Stearne had toured the Puritan heartland of East Anglia. They had developed something of a business, offering to expose local 'witches'. Their unique selling point had been an ability to obtain confessions from the accused, extracted mainly by sleep deprivation. 'Witches' were sat upon a stool and questioned for hour upon hour. Sometimes they were 'walked' to stop them nodding off.

The accused were mainly older women who were a drain on the poor box, at loggerheads with a neighbour, or just plain eccentric or odd. Their 'crimes' were known of by association rather than direct, observable deeds. They included causing illness in others (sometimes fatal), accidents (such as falling from a horse), or damage to farm animals (such as sudden death, milk drying up or chickens ceasing to lay eggs). The actual bad stuff was done by 'familiars': imps in the guise of animals or birds, even insects, to whom the 'witches' could talk.[22.5]

Having gained their confessions and collected their expenses, Hopkins and Stearne moved on, leaving the latest 'witch' to be locked up in the county gaol. Not a few died before they could make it to trial, victims of the dire conditions in which they were kept.

The surprising thing was that some of the 'witches' seemed to believe the 'confessions' that had been wrung from them and they basked briefly in their notoriety and supposed power. The less surprising thing was that once gaols were full and the cost of imprisoning, trying, and sometimes hanging the 'witches' became a burden, the whole thing stopped. It had lasted just two years.

'No one knows exactly how many suffered in the witch-craze of 1645 to 1647: as many as 300 women and men were interrogated, of whom more than 100 were put to death,' wrote Malcolm Gaskill in his book *Witchfinders: A Seventeenth-century English Tragedy*. 'It was a terrible tragedy; but it needs to be seen as part of something even more terrible, a civil war characterized by bigotry, brutality and bloodshed.'[22.6]

The Salem Village witch-hunt, which resulted in far fewer hangings, also took place during a brutal war, that between the New England colonies and the French/Indian alliance. It had exploded as something akin to a community nervous breakdown within a repressed group of uptight Puritans who considered themselves under siege from brutal enemies.

Indian/French raids had continued and if anything stepped up a gear while Phipps was in England. Colonists who lived at the outer limits of settlements, such as Salem Village, were in constant fear for their lives and liberty. They might at any moment be hacked down, shot or dragged off into slavery or to be held as hostages.

Some of the villagers knew this even better than others, having sought refuge in Salem after escaping previous Indian attacks. All of them lived on their nerves. Even when the enemy seemed occupied elsewhere, the settlers stayed close to their snow-covered homes, bereft of the sons and husbands who had been called to serve in the militia. Worried families tended their homesteads as best they could, but crop yields suffered and families went hungry and cold.

For those in Salem Village and its like, 1691 and 1692 were years of poverty, hunger and worry. Anxiety levels shot through the roof and community cohesion began to crack under the stress (in Salem village it had hardly ever been good). People struggled to pay their bills, even their expected contributions towards the cost of maintaining a village meeting house.

Samuel Parris, a merchant-turned-preacher, had only been ordained as Salem Village minister in November 1689 following a year of trial and negotiation. He had eventually agreed an annual salary of £60, paid partly in produce rather than cash, plus £6 worth of wood a year to burn in his four hearths.

In the bitter winter of 1691/92, the 38-year-old Parris (he was two years younger than Phipps) had complained continually about his lack of the promised wood. His salary was in arrears and some villages were questioning the ownership of the ministry house and the land around it, which Parris had thought had been given to him. All must have added to tensions within the Parris household.

The minister's pay might be slow in coming, but his job was considered unrelenting and important. It was to maintain constant vigil over the spiritual health of his congregation, to protect them from evil and from backsliding from their godly ways.

That the hysteria which led to the Salem witch trials of 1692/93 emanated from the minister's own home was extraordinary. The first of those 'afflicted' were Parris' own daughter, 9-year-old Elizabeth 'Betty' Parris, and his 10-year-old niece Abigail Williams. And the person they accused of causing their fits was the Parris' household slave Tituba.

Other less-than-commonplace features of the goings-on in Salem included the arrest of a 4-year-old (Dorothy 'Dorcas' Good) and the pressing to death of an 81-year-old man, Giles Cory (or Corey).

Under interrogation Dorcas confessed to being a witch and was gaoled. Her mother Sarah Good was hanged.

Giles Cory was an apparently well-off local farmer who was known to be something of a delinquent, fond of helping himself to other people's property. He was a petty thief who had once beaten a man to death (the man in question being an indentured servant, the crime for which he was convicted was unlawful killing rather than murder, and the punishment was a fine).

Both Giles Cory and his younger third wife Martha were brought to trial in September 1692. Martha, a self-proclaimed 'gospel woman' was found guilty but Giles refused to answer the charges in the prescribed form of words. Instead he 'stood mute'.

'Although pleading innocent to all the indictments as they were read, he refused to answer when asked the formality of how he would be tried. Giles was expected to answer, "By God and my country." Until he spoke those precise words, his case could not proceed,' explains Marilynne Roach in her day-by-day record of the Salem trials.[22.7]

In England this would have had legal significance since those found guilty of capital offences had their property confiscated and their heirs were thereby disenfranchised. In New England, which now had a new charter, the position was not so clear. But Giles certainly had concerns about his legacy to the fore when, at the last, he had taken the bother to draft a new will.

The new charter did make one thing clear: the court could now use the 'English' solution to such impasses – those 'standing mute' could be 'pressed' into making a plea. This was not the application of strong arguments but a much more literal, physical, not to say barbaric option. The 'pressed' accused would be stretched out on the ground and heavy weights placed on his or her body, added to regularly, until bones cracked, organs exploded and all air was forced out. This happened to Giles Cory. He had a choice, enter a formal plea to the charges against him, or die. He chose to die.

When William Phipps arrived home from England in May 1692, two dozen or so suspected 'witches' had been formally arrested. Only a week before George Burroughs had been added to the list. He was a former Salem minister who had held the position now occupied by Parris from 1680 to 1683. He had barely been back to the village in the nine years since leaving, but his spectre had, according to various of the afflicted villagers. This was enough for an order to be issued for his arrest.

Although the number of 'witch' arrests was still not huge, the goings-on in Salem had attracted much attention (as is witnessed by Joshua Brodbent's letter, see above). This was partly because those arrested had been questioned in well-attended public hearings.

Magistrates John Hathorne and Jonathan Corwin, both wealthy Boston merchants utterly convinced of their godly status and impeccable good judgement, had harangued the accused with a torrent of leading questions.

The events had been spectacular. Damp and steaming villagers, even more jumpy than usual given the supposed presence of witches, had packed into the Salem Village meeting house. So many were pressed against the windows that the resulting gloom had added to the foreboding. No doubt there had been some jostling for places with many of the women sitting together. They would have gossiped while they waited for proceedings to begin, perhaps nibbling at the bread and cheese they carried in their pockets or fingering the pocket bibles they had brought for protection.

At the back would have stood the constable, ready to refuse entry to or eject the unwelcome, and some of the men. Outside there were perhaps militiamen guarding against unrest and attack. At the front were seats reserved for the 'afflicted' and the accused, and a table for the magistrates and Samuel Parris, who had been asked to take notes.

Proceedings began with prayers. Audience participation in the hearings that followed was boisterous, with hissing, jeering and calling out. The 'afflicted' girls stared relentlessly at the accused, screaming, flinching, convulsing or fainting in response to their every move. If questioned they fitted, claimed dumbness or pointed to invisible spectres sitting in the rafters or patrolling the fields outside.

At the beginning of March, Sarah Good was interrogated. She was asked: 'Why do you not tell us the truth? Why do you thus torment these poor children?'

'I do not torment them,' she replied.

'Who do you employ then?' asked Magistrate Hathorne.

Good said she did not know who was tormenting the girls, but it was not her.

'Who was it then that tormented the children?' asked Hathorne.

'It was Osborn,' said Good.

Tituba Indian, another of the accused had been harassed by the magistrates into saying that she had been pursued by spectres, two of which resembled Sarah Good and Sarah Osborn.

Hearing Good name Osborn, 'the girls recovered, only to say that Osborn and Good were hurting them', reported Marilynne Roach in her account of the

Salem witch trials.[22.8] Good was hanged two months later but not the sickly Osborn who died in gaol. And so it went on. 'Went to Salem, where, in the Meeting-house, the persons accused of Witchcraft were examined; was a very great Assembly; 'twas awfull to see how the afflicted persons were agitated,' wrote Samual Sewall in his diary for 11 April 1692.

Soon Cotton Mather had also weighed in, warning his North Church congregation again the dangers of complacency in the face of the challenge of witchcraft. In April 1692 he published his sermon as *A Midnight Cry*, 'an essay for our awakening out of that sinful sleep, to which we are at this time too much disposed'. In this he called upon his congregation to be alert to the dangers of witchcraft. 'Tis well known, that the *Devils* make a Compact with some *Witches*, to be the Masters of their *Souls* … ; and such *Witches* have been among our selves,' he wrote.[22.9]

Phipps' arrival with his new commission and a new charter threw something of a spanner into the Salem witch trials works. The number of accused was increasing daily but there were for the moment no courts with the authority to try them. As of May, the new charter applied and the mandates of the courts and of their judges and magistrates were in temporary abeyance. But the need to do something about the supposed Salem coven was urgent.

The new governor's own priorities seem to have centred around his plans for a new fort at Pemaquid and allocation of resources to the New England colonies. He chose to pass the 'Salem problem' over to his deputy, William Stoughton.

Two weeks after Phipps' arrival, he established a special court to deal with the Salem accused, a so-called court of 'Oyer and Terminer'. Six judges were appointed, including John Hathorne and Samuel Sewall, to serve under chief justice William Stoughton. Samuel's brother Stephen, who lived in Salem Town, was clerk to the court. There seems to have been some family connect between him and Samuel Parris, the minister wisely packing his 'afflicted' daughter Betty off to live with Stephen and his wife soon after the start of court hearings.

The attitude of the new court was little changed from that displayed during the magistrates' interrogations. Only days after its appointment the court returned a 'guilty' verdict against the first of the accused to be tried, Bridget Bishop. Eight days later she was hanged in a field between Boston and Salem.

The evidence against Bishop had been the reaction of the 'afflicted' to her (their fits and convulsions) and their insistence that a spectral image of Bishop had appeared to them and admitted criminal acts. Staunton, who presided at the trial and signed Bishop's death warrant, had warned the jury not to be fooled by the healthy appearance of the 'afflicted'. All those present had seen the effects of the accused on their demeanour, he said.[22.10]

In June five more women, including Sarah Good, were found guilty. They were all hanged on 19 June. In early August five more (four witches and the wizard, George Burroughs) were found guilty and four of them – Elizabeth Proctor was spared for the time being because she was pregnant – were hanged just over two weeks later.

In September, fifteen more people were found guilty and sentenced to hang, eight of whom, including Martha Cory, were hanged on 22 September. This was two days after Giles Cory's flattened body had given up the ghost.

Enough was enough. Perhaps the turning point was the hanging of George Burroughs, dragged over sixty miles from his home in Wells, Maine to face outlandish charges. He had left Salem on bad terms. His treatment by the fractious villagers was much the same as that afforded Parris. His pay failed to arrive as promised, meaning that when his wife died, Burroughs had been forced to borrow money to pay for her funeral. The loan came from John and Rebecca Putman, with whom his family had at one time lodged, and remained outstanding when Burroughs left Salem – apparently a cause of friction between him and the Putmans.

Having moved to Falmouth (now Portland) he escaped the 1690 Indian attack on the settlement, helping others to survive. Apart from his supposed superhuman strength, the evidence against Burroughs was spectral: supposed visions of the 'afflicted' that resembled him and confessed to being in league with the devil and to having murdered his first two wives (although by different methods, depending on which of the 'afflicted' was asked).

At his hanging Burroughs had recited the Lord's Prayer, something that most committed Puritans believed impossible for a witch or wizard to do. In fact, although the judges claimed otherwise, 'spectral evidence' had been the deciding factor in most of the 'guilty' verdicts (that, and the antics of the 'afflicted'). Its use was now at the heart of the controversy that followed.

Some of the accused went near to questioning the motives of the 'afflicted' and the veracity of their visions. Although there was the possibility of an element of payback in the claims made, such suggestions were generally taken only to confirm a lack of sympathy for the 'afflicted'. The judges certainly refused to consider the possibility that 'spectral evidence' had been made up. Their continual response to anything along these lines was to ask the accused: 'Can't you see how these children suffer?'

The 'afflicted' seem to have been affected by some form of group hysteria, but so too did the judges. They found it impossible to act impartially, to look beyond the accusations made, to listen to any of the arguments of the legally unrepresented accused, or to question any of the obvious inconsistences in the 'evidence' given.

The idea behind 'spectral evidence' was that it was impossible for the devil to misrepresent an innocent person in an incriminating dream. Only the guilty could appear in such spectral form.

The counter view, now expressed by Increase Mather, among others, was that this understated the power of the devil to deceive. If he, she, or they could transform his, her or their own forms into any chosen likeness, and everybody 'knew' this was the case, then it would certainly be possible for the devil or devils to appear in any guise in the dreams or spectral visions of anybody. So, it follows that spectral visions could not be relied upon as foolproof evidence.

This change from accepted wisdom was outlined by Increase Mather at an October 1692 meeting of the Cambridge Association,[22.11] an ecclesiastic group of Puritan thinkers who met regularly at Mather's Harvard College. This was soon published as *Cases of Conscience concerning Evil Spirits Personating Men.*[22.12]

In this Mather said, 'the Devil has frequently appeared in the shape of famous Persons to the end that he might seduce men into Idolatry [a sin equal to that of witchcraft).' Of this, no man who 'has made it his concern to enquire into things of this nature can be ignorant'. Mather went further: 'This then I Declare and Testify, that to take away the life of any one; meerly because a *Spectre* or Devil, in a Bewitched or Possessed person does accuse them, will bring the Guilt of Innocent Blood on the Land, where such a thing shall be done. Mercy forbid that it should, (and I trust that as it has not, it never will be so) in *New-England.* What does such an Evidence amount unto more than this. Either such an one did afflict such an one, or the Devil in his likeness, or his Eyes were bewitched.'

It was brave stuff. After all, all church members would have believed themselves at some point to have experienced a revelation, often in the form of a vision or visitation. For a leading cleric to chip away at even a corner of the validity of the invisible world was at the least challenging. But Mather was careful not to go too far. He did not criticise the Salem witch trial judges for their decisions (including that to hang Burroughs). 'The Judges affirm that they have not Convicted any one meerly on the account of what Spectres have said, or of what has been Represented to the Eyes or Imaginations of sick bewitched persons,' he said.

Phipps and Mather had probably had conversations about the goings-on in Salem and had come to the same conclusion: something had to be done to put an end to the excesses. Phipps' wife Mary, at one time rumoured to be a witch herself, would also have counselled restraint.

Phipps didn't do restraint, he did action. To his eternal credit, a few days after Mather had published his *Cases of Conscience*, Phipps banned the use of 'spectral evidence'. And three weeks later, at the end of October 1692, he dissolved the Court of Oyer and Terminer and ordered release of accused witches.

In his report back to the Lords of Trade he was forthright in condemning what had gone on but also careful to blame his deputy Stoughton for most of it. The Court of Oyer and Terminer had been established after 'loud cries and clamours of the friends of the afflicted, together with the advice of the Deputy-Governor and Council,' he said. 'The chief judge was the Deputy Governor, and the rest people of the best prudence and figure that could be pitched upon. At Salem in Essex County they convicted more than twenty persons of witchcraft, and some of the accused confessed their guilt.'[22.13]

Phipps 'was in the East of the Colony throughout almost the whole of the proceedings, trusting to the Court as the right method of dealing with cases of witchcraft'. But when he returned, he 'found many persons in a strange ferment of dissatisfaction', the devil having 'taken upon him the name and shape of several persons who were doubtless innocent'. Phipps said he had now forbidden the committal of any more accused persons, 'and them that have been committed I would shelter from any proceedings wherein the innocent could possibly suffer wrong'.

Phipps' actions in reining in the excesses of the Salem judges was given official approval and in January 1693 the king in council ordered a letter written him to this effect. It also directed 'that in all future proceedings against persons accused of witchcraft or of possession by the devil, all circumspection be used so far as may be without impediment to the ordinary course of justice'.[22.14]

After this Phipps went further in his criticism. In a letter to Nottingham, he said the Court 'had condemned and executed some twenty persons, some of whom were believed by many to be innocent'. Yet, he said, the Court still proceeded in the same method of trial.

'The judges, on enquiry, told me that they had begun thus, but had human testimony against such as were condemned, and undoubted proof of their being witches; but at length I found that the devil took upon him the shape of innocent persons, some of the accused being of unblameable life to my own knowledge.'[22.15] In another letter to Nottingham he wrote that stopping the witchcraft trials had 'averted the ruin of this province'.[22.16] Phipps may have averted ruin, but he had made even more enemies, Stoughton among them.

Chapter 23

London Calling

'THE ONE THING that seems certain is that he [Phipps] was absolutely unfit to occupy the place in which he was seated, or to wield the power with which he was entrusted.' So concluded British military historian and editor of state papers, the Honourable Sir John William Fortescue. 'All evidence points to the fact that he was ignorant, brutal, covetous and violent, and that his appointment to the Government of Massachusetts was a very grave misfortune,' he said.[23.1]

Well, that was one view. Written in 1903, it is both untrue and unfair. Phipps may have been uneducated, but he was not ignorant. He was a skilled boatbuilder and an experienced mariner who had ventured an Atlantic crossing probably more times than he could remember. It was true he argued a lot. Fortescue lists his quarrels with the governor of New York, Benjamin Fletcher, with New Hampshire lieutenant-governor, John Usher, and with Captain Richard Short. He could have added others. Phipps upset people. This is because he was a force for change, some might say a force of nature. And he certainly stood up for both his own and especially his colony's corner.

He had to. He was under scrutiny from London, he had 'enemies' in council who criticised his every move, he had governors of neighbouring colonies fighting for a larger share of the resources shipped from England and a larger share of any praise coming the way of New England. And he had Richard Short and the Admiralty nibbling at his heels, and Joseph Dudley sniping from the sidelines, telling anybody who cared to listen that he could do the job better. It was no wonder Phipps' seemingly impregnable shell sometimes cracked and he had his 'dog days'[23.2] when he slunk into depressive mode. Always infuriating to some, he must have been impossible to deal with on such days.

For sure, Phipps was no angel. But by the appalling standards of the seventeenth century, when exploitation went unnoticed and corruption hardly raised an eyebrow (provided you had the right parentage), neither was he a crook. Like others in his position, he did blur the lines between personal and public profit and loss (particularly in the use of ships and their crews). But then it was not unexpected he should do this to subsidise the personal cost of funding his office. He probably viewed his own and his colony's finances as inextricably linked. His will, which detailed accumulated wealth amounting to less than the amount he had gained from his pre-appointment spectacular treasure hunting, suggests his claimed 'covetous' behaviour was somewhat restrained – exceedingly so in comparison with other governors.[23.3]

Phipps had become governor at a time when the colony had been under considerable threat. Its own intransigence had brought it to within a hair's breadth of being lumbered with a much more restrictive charter than eventually emerged from Phipps', Increase Mather's and Sir Henry Ashurst's negotiations with the English government. It was under attack from the Indian/French alliance and it was broke. In addition, it was apparently infested with witches, or so many seemed to believe.

As a member of the colony's pre-new-charter council, Phipps must take some of the blame for this dire state of affairs. But although he had gone about his duties with his usual gusto, he was not a prime mover in the decisions made, or not made. Once he became governor, he took no time to shake the governing council (most of whom had been re-appointed) out of its stupor. He had moved to introduce English laws, as required to do, and to establish a new supreme court. Against resistance from other New England colonies, he had reinvigorated the militia with the appointment of Major Church to a more all-encompassing command. He had obtained limited financial support from the king, and the protection of the two warships now stationed in New England. He had put an end to the pyscho-delusional antics in Salem, and he had built his new fort at Pemaquid.

Although the fort was criticised for its cost, exact positioning and design (and was indeed later overrun), it served the purpose which Phipps had discerned necessary. It had been a symbol of determination and power which had bought at least a temporary lull in the fighting.

In September 1693 he wrote to the Earl of Nottingham boasting: 'I have caused a large stone fort, called Fort William Henry, to be built at Pemaquid, and have kept a force ready to attack the Indians whenever they appear on our frontiers, which it has done with success. The fort is strong enough to resist all the Indians in America and has so much discouraged them that they have laid down their arms and sent their Sagamores to beg for an everlasting peace. I went to Pemaquid accordingly and concluded articles of peace, of which copy is enclosed. This province will now be better able to help the others, though much impoverished by the war.'[23.4]

The peace treaty had brought immediate criticism from Usher who complained that he should have been consulted (although the Lords of Trade had made the point that Usher's commission 'must not be understood to derogate from Sir William Phip's authority in reference to military matters'[23.5]).

Phipps' argument with Usher came in the context of a governance tussle between New Hampshire and Massachusetts. In 1693 'many inhabitants' of

New Hampshire had petitioned its council to have their colony annexed to the Massachusetts Bay Colony. Its 'owner', the absentee proprietor/governor Samuel Allen, Usher's boss and father-in-law, objected to the idea saying that if that were to happen 'the whole of his proprietary rights and profits will be lost'. It was in his and Usher's personal interests to denigrate everything Phipps did.[23.6]

The argument with Fletcher came in the context of misunderstandings about who was in charge of the local militia. According to Phipps' commission, he was in charge. But in May 1693 King William or the Lords of Trade had realised this arrangement would be fraught with difficulty and decided to make Governor Fletcher 'Commander-in-Chief of the militia of Connecticut … revoking the former commission to Sir William Phips for the same'.[23.7] Unfortunately this was not recorded in the minutes until September and nobody seems to have told Phipps about it. There was also misunderstanding about who governed Martha's Vineyard, the avaricious Fletcher thinking it came under his control while Phipps knew it had been included in his commission.

Meanwhile Phipps had upset Jahleel Brenton, the 'Collector, Surveyor and Searcher of the Customs in New England', an 'Edward Randolph' mark II. Initially Phipps and Brenton had clashed over events that took place before Phipps had become governor, but the argument spilled over into a dispute over the severity with which the English *Navigation Acts* should be applied to Massachusetts shipping. Phipps, for once given the full backing of his council, wanted dispensations for local traders. As often happened, he went too far and, claimed Brenton, fists had flown. The upshot was that a much-put-out Brenton wrote to London 'begging' that he be allowed to bring a prosecution against Phipps.

Taking his 'searcher' duties seriously, Brenton, had, in 1691, seized three vessels and their cargoes, on the grounds that they had contravened the *Navigation Acts*. The three ships were the two pinks, the *Two Brothers* and the *Three Brothers*, and the brigantine, *Mary.* Brenton had trouble making his case stick. He had won in the local county court but then had been hauled before the Court of Assistants in Boston, where he lost. Outraged by the Court of Assistants' decision, Brenton appealed to the Privy Council naming Phipps as a defendant.[23.8] It was some years before the case was eventually decided in Brenton's favour.[23.9]

While Brenton waited for his 1691 case to be heard in London, he continued to demand that local vessels comply with the letter of the *Navigation Acts*. Phipps and his council convinced themselves that this would be so invasive that it would be 'contrary to the royal instructions that there should be [no] hindrance to trade'. They were, they decided, entitled to offer local ships some leeway.

'The Governor and Council have lately issued an order forbidding me to enter and clear vessels, saying that this duty lies only in the Naval Officer, which is a great encouragement to illicit trading,' Brenton claimed. Worse, 'Sir William Phips himself is carrying on private and illicit trade, but finding this order insufficient to conceal it he has prevailed with the Assembly to pass an Act exempting all ships trading from Colony to Colony from entering or clearing, in the teeth of the *Acts of Navigation.*'

When Brenton seized the sloop *Good Luck* – presumably Phipps' own ship of that name – for illicit trading, 'Sir William Phips came with about fifty persons and laid violent hands on me, dragging me about the wharf, striking me with his cane and his fists, and threatening to break all my bones and commit me to prison if I did not give up the ship and goods, which I was forced to do'.[23.10]

By January 1694, when Brenton's complaints against Phipps reached the ears of the Lords of Trade, the committee established a board of enquiry to investigate them further.[23.11] It would hardly have pleased him to see that Joseph Dudley and John Usher had somehow got themselves appointed members. The Lords of Trade had also decided that some of Captain Short's complaints were worth looking at. These included the claim that following a scuffle with Captain Short, Phipps had imprisoned him illegally. Also 'he did break open Captain Short's chest and carry off his goods' and 'condemned a French prize, sitting himself as judge, and that it does not appear that he ever accounted for the King's share nor the ship's company's'. He also condemned another ship, the *St. Jacob* captured by privateer ships which he had ordered to be manned and armed 'on pretence of His Majesty's service'.

By February 1694 Phipps had been summoned to London 'to answer the original charges of Jahleel Brenton and Captain Short, and the additional charge of having condemned the prize St. Jacob without reserving the King's share'.

The Lords of Trade ordered Phipps to take the first available ship home and that, probably in recognition of his known explosive temper, also made a point that 'free liberty be given to all concerned to collect authenticated copies of records and depositions, wherein Sir William shall not intermeddle except in respect of such proofs as he may himself require'.[23.12]

The recall was serious enough for Phipps to appoint Benjamin Jackson as his London agent and, through him, to promise 'a full account of affairs in Massachusetts'. Before that, the agent needed to see copies of the complaints made against his client, said Jackson.[23.13]

Phipps now resorted to a tried and tested Massachusetts tactic: delay. In July Phipps wrote to Nottingham telling him he had received the summons home. 'As soon as the preparations therein directed are complete I shall embark, and I hope no delay will arise through a journey which I am making to the Eastern parts, which is judged absolutely necessary to secure the peace with the Indians. But if it should retard my coming for a few weeks I hope that I shall be excused, the matter being of the greatest importance to the Colony'.[23.14]

But in September Stoughton wrote to London: 'I have received the King's letter, summoning Sir William Phips home to answer the charges against him. I caused it to be read in Council; the necessary notices have been given, and myself and Council have given up several days to the receiving of evidence. No delay shall be in the proceeding with this matter.'

A day later Phipps felt obliged to tell Secretary of State (northern and southern departments) Sir John Trenchard: 'I am so near shipping myself for the voyage that I shall defer all further matters until I can wait on you in person.' However he also used the opportunity to lay blame for his delay in departure on Thomas Taylor, the most recent captain of the *Nonsuch* (his own choice after the sacking of Short, Thomas Dobbins, having lasted only nine months in the job). 'Lately,' Phipps said, he had ordered Taylor to St. Johns, New Brunswick, 'to await the arrival of a considerable French ship that was expected there. On frivolous pretences Taylor delayed so long that the French ship arrived before him, and though she was once so near him as to prepare to fight him, he pretended that he never saw her; and so the Frenchman despatched her errand and weighed anchor.'

The result of this failure had been that the French, 'now supplied with vast stores for war', had 'fitted out a party of French Indians for blood and spoil upon our frontiers' and had 'made cruel depredations upon a place called Oyster River [New Hampshire], and after that upon another secure plantation, slaughtering the inhabitants'.

His recall home had hardly helped the colony's relationships with its Indian adversaries, Phipps complained. On hearing news of this 'the Eastern Sagamores' seem to have abandoned 'that good regard for the English to which I had brought them'. Phipps added for good measure that 'Captain Dobbins has since burned a considerable French ship in the place where Taylor failed'. Finally, he asked Trenchard to 'pray give no heed to the malicious accusations of my enemies until I have been heard'.[23.15]

Meanwhile Deputy-Governor Stoughton, who had been belittled by Phipps' intervention in the Salem witch trials, must have taken personal satisfaction in forwarding to London, in November 1694, his collected evidence. It was substantial, and Stoughton let it be known that Phipps had done 'all that he could' to hinder the collection of 'proof' against him. This included 'threatening the witnesses that they ought to have their ears cut off'.[23.16]

The same month the Lords of Trade noted that a pamphlet had been published 'giving first a brief summary of the history of New England, and then developing into a bitter attack upon Sir William Phips'. The anonymous authors repeated the supposed slur that Phipps had 'learned to write since he was married and cannot yet read a letter'. But it went much further, claiming misconduct by Phipps when acting as a judge 'both in Admiralty and in Chancery', his 'maltreatment' of Short and Brenton, 'his quarrel with the Assembly and his manner of overriding it'. Finally *A letter from New England* had described his treaty with the Eastern Indians as a 'fraud' and as simply a 'means of monopolising the beaver-trade to himself'.[23.17]

Phipps' enemies certainly had it in for him and it is not too hard to draw up a shortlist of likely authors of *A letter from New England.* Presumably they were going for the kill, as if the evidence submitted by Stoughton were not enough. Perhaps they worried that it was not? Certainly, it was substantial in volume. Brenton alone listed fourteen claimed offences in his sworn affidavits. Among assaults and the like, Phipps was claimed to have colluded with the local naval officer, to have released a ship seized by Brenton, buying part of cargo himself, and to have 'encouraged masters of ships to rescue forfeited goods, and refused redress to the Collector'. Brenton also claimed the governor had 'permitted the loading of enumerated articles, collected the customs, converting them to his own use, and gave a certificate in order to protect them from the Collector'.[23.18]

It looked bad, but Phipps did have his supporters. In October 1694, the month before Stoughton sent his collected complaints against the governor off to London, the Council and Assembly of Massachusetts took the trouble to send their own petition to the king and queen begging that 'no complaints of a personal concern may be improved to deprive us of the services of Sir William Phips as Governor'.[23.19] Signed by Isaac Addington, secretary to, and Nehemiah Jewett, speaker of, the Massachusetts House of Representatives, this contained partial answers or at least suggested mitigating circumstances to some of the charges against Phipps.

'We beg to lay before you our deplorable state owing to fresh incursions of the Eastern Indians, who despite the late treaty have perfidiously risen, and have murdered or taken more than 150 people since July,' they said, continuing: 'This has obliged us to a reinforcement of all our frontiers, which compels the greater part of the inhabitants to leave their homes and betake themselves to garrisons. The French by unwearied solicitations and presents have also prevailed with the Five Nations to agree to a neutrality, portending no little disquiet to us, who are already exhausted by the expense and losses of the war … For these reasons, as well as owing to the drain on us for the protection of New Hampshire, we cannot spare a quota of men for New York. Our Agents will lay matters more particularly before you.'

By the end of January 1695, Phipps was back in England and asking for more time to prepare his defence against the 'false accusations' made against him.[23.20]

Phipps never did have the chance to present his defence. On 18 February 1695 he died, the victim of an unknown flu-like illness. Perhaps his non-stop and combative lifestyle had worn down his defences to the point that he had no resistance left. Whether he would have won through against his accusers is an open question. In the seventeenth century the outcome of such challenges often depended more on position, standing, sponsorship and largesse than on a strict examination of the evidence.

There might be a long list of powerful men ranged against him, men such as Dudley, Stoughton, Fletcher, Usher, Allen and probably the ever-cautious Blathwayt. Against this, Phipps had a royal connection. He had met, negotiated and corresponded with, and probably tried the patience of, King William (Mary had died the previous December). He had achieved great success in his face-to-face dealings with the English establishment and probably believed he could win through force of character alone. That may well have been the case.

The Navy, which looked after its own, did not act on Phipps' claims about Short. A drunkard or not, Short went on to captain three other ships, although none was more powerful than the *Nonsuch*, all being fifth-rated ships of the line. His career ended in 1702. His supporter, Captain Robert Fairfax, had a more illustrious career, captaining a further fifteen ships, the last a second-rated ship of the line. Ironically perhaps, having commanded the *Conception Prize*, he ended his career in 1707, as captain of the *Albemarle*.

Phipps believed he would be exonerated. He was proposing more schemes and ventures until the end, such as renewed attempts on Quebec and patents giving him a monopoly on parts of the beaver-pelt trade.

Massachusetts had done well out of Phipps. He had made mistakes and he was an awkward character, but he had always stood up for the colony and made himself a rallying point at difficult times, always approaching his task with great energy and bravery where called for. His governorship was tumultuous but cannot be said to have been a failure, especially from the point of view of his fellow Massachusetts citizens. He was a charismatic figure and always popular enough in some quarters to mustering a crowd of supporters when he chose to do so (as Jahleel Brenton had found out to his dismay).

Certainly, the deadly Dudley, who eventually achieved the governorship in 1702, was less popular and no more successful. He had faced much the same problems as Phipps: lack of a fixed salary, Indian wars and a stubborn council.

Phipps' friend and supporter Increase Mather was convinced the colony had lost somebody with its interests at heart, although his eulogy did go somewhat over the top. 'This province is beheaded, and lyes a bleeding,' he said. Phipps was 'a merciful man; some think too merciful', and 'a zealous lover of his country'. New England 'knows not yet what they have lost', he concluded.[23.21]

Phipps does seem to have been more of a patriot than he was given credit for; perhaps even too much the little-New-Englander. But he had never fitted in with his colony's ruling elite who found it impossible to overlook his humble beginnings. However polite they might have been about him after his death, to them he had always been an outsider. He was more (the Disney version of) Davy Crockett than Davy Crockett himself: just too slap-your-back, too can-do, too roughhouse, too wear-your-heart-on-your-sleeve, and just too American.

PART III

THE DIVING BELL BUBBLE

'No individual raindrop ever considers itself responsible for the flood.'

John Ruskin

'The law of unintended consequences, often cited but rarely defined, is that actions of people, and especially of governments, always have effects that are unanticipated or "unintended".'

Rob Norton

Chapter 24

Curse of the *Concepcion*

FOR THOSE WHO care to believe in such things, the *Nuestra Senora La Pura y Limpia Concepcion* must seem to have been cursed. So few of those closely involved in breaking open its silver-filled secrets survived for too long afterwards.

Narborough had died while still anchored at the wreck. The royal beneficiary King James had soon lost his throne. Abraham Adderley who, along with fellow Bermudian mariner William Davis had turned up at the *Concepcion* wreck site and helped Phipps recover its contents, died a rich man in 1690.[24.1] Anthony Cary, Viscount Falkland, one of the investors in Phipps' treasure-hunting venture, died of smallpox in 1694 aged thirty-eight. By this time, he had lost most of his *Concepcion* fortune, having invested it in other similar but abortive ventures. A few months earlier he had been briefly imprisoned in the Tower of London accused of using Admiralty funds to bribe members of Parliament. His fellow investor in the *Concepcion* expedition, Lord Albemarle, was already dead. He had died in Jamaica in October 1688, aged thirty-five. His death was largely the result of his own excesses.

Albemarle, badgered by his wife into making a new will in 1687, had not been too careful about completing the legal niceties. The result was an old will that might still be valid and a new will that might not, and two sets of potential beneficiaries willing to test the matter in the courts. The mentally unstable duchess, who had been well provided for in any case, soon complicated matters further by marrying the avaricious and widowed Lord Montagu. She had previously said she would only marry a royal suitor. It was claimed that to win the skittish hand of the wealthy widow, Montagu had kitted himself out in the guise of the emperor of China.[24.2] He and the Earl of Bath, who had been Albemarle's confidant and principal beneficiary in the old will, now engaged in a long running face-off. During this, new claimants alleging Albemarle's parents had not been legally married had to be dealt with and the mad duchess was declared insane by the Lunacy Commissioners. In the end she outlived all the original claimants to her husband's fortune. John Granville, Earl of Bath, died in 1701, followed within two weeks by his son and heir Charles Granville, aged nineteen. Very briefly the second Earl of Bath, he had committed suicide 'apparently horrified by the legacy of debt and deceit engendered by the dispute'.[24.3] Montagu died in 1709. Albemarle's estate was finally wound up in 1734, the year that his 80-year-old wife, the 'mad duchess', died.

Captain John Strong, Phipps' chief mate on the *James and Mary*, died in 1693. He was thirty-nine. After a brief spell as captain of Phipps' old ship, he had moved on to command the forty-gun *Welfare*, sent by Falkland in search of south seas treasure. By July 1693 he was in command of the *Charles II*, the forty-six-gun lead ship in another treasure-hunting venture mounted principally by the Houblon brothers, of whom more later. The plan was to rendezvous at 'the Groyne' (La Caruna in north-west Spain), there to await a commission from the Spanish crown (the then incumbent was the ailing Carlos II, in whose honour the *Charles the Second* had been named). The commission did not arrive and Strong took sick and died. The captaincy of the *Charles the Second* passed to Captain Charles Gibson with calamitous consequences (see later).

It was barely eighteen months later, in February 1695, that Phipps himself died, aged forty-four. His 'fruitful' mother still lived, as did his enterprising wife Mary, his 10-year-old adopted son Spencer (by now Spencer Phips) and the father of his adopted son Dr David Bennet, who was by now approaching 80 (still another twenty-four years to go).

Phipps' worth at the time of his death was in the region of £5,000, say historians Emerson Baker and John Reid.[24.4] Of this, almost £3,400 was held as belongings, including a yacht and a share in the merchant vessel *Friendship*, plus his brick-built home and several other properties along the Boston waterfront, together with land in Maine and elsewhere. Phipps had died a wealthy man. 'His clothing and furnishings alone were appraised at £400, which was more than twice the value of the entire estate of the average contemporary Bostonian,' say Baker and Reid.

News of Phipps' death did not reach Boston for some weeks. It was on 5 May that Samuel Sewall logged it in his diary, saying that 'people are generally sad'.[24.5] The following morning 'Guns are fired at the Castle and Town for the Death of our Governour'. It was the day of the council elections.

People 'generally sad' was hardly an indication on widespread colonial grief for the death of its champion. And two days later Sewall visited widow Phipps whom, he said, 'takes on heavily for the death of Sir William. Thinks the Lieutenant [Stoughton] and Council were not so kind to him as they should have been'.

Phipps' remains were interred in the St. Mary Woolnoth churchyard where it was recorded that his tombstone stated: 'near this place is interred the Body of Sir William Phipps, Knight; who, in the year 1687, by his great industry, discovered among the rocks near the Banks of Bahama on the north side of

Hispaniola, a Spanish Plate-ship, which had been under water 41 years, out of which he took in gold and silver to the value of £300,000 sterling; and, with a fidelity equal to his conduct, brought it all to London, where it was divided between himself and the rest of the adventurers: For which great service he was knighted.'

It went on to say that Phipps had 'discharged his trust [as governor] with that zeal for the interest of his country, and with so little regard to his own private advantage'.[24.6]

St. Mary Woolnoth was later rebuilt. In 1857 its crypt was reinforced to allow the City and South London Railway Company to construct the Bank underground station immediately below its foundations. The remains of those buried in the old churchyard had already been reburied in the City of London Cemetery.

It seems Phipps was better appreciated in London than he was in his hometown. It is particularly apt that he should be buried in the City of London not only because his reputation was higher there than it was among those bickering Bostonians with whom he had lately worked, but because this was the place that benefitted most from his legacy.

Chapter 25

Unintended Consequences

IT WAS AS if seventeenth century England had suddenly woken itself up to a new reality. There were discoveries, inventions and new ways of working. Application of logic and reason meant the world was no longer so incomprehensible.

By 1660 like-minded 'natural philosophers' had gathered to probe and question all before them. Within three years they had received royal approval and were able to call themselves members of 'The Royal Society of London for Improving Natural Knowledge' (the 'Royal Society'). Christopher Wren, an astronomer, architect and founder member, gave the first lecture.

Creation of this influential grouping was only one of several developments that combined to encourage a surge in the design and production of new-fangled devices, machines, gadgets and processes. Another was a 1624 change in the law that made it easier for inventors to profit from their work. Prior to this, letters patent giving monopoly of use of virtually anything had been in the grant of the monarch. James I had been much criticised for using charters and patents as a means of raising money, through fees and levies on applicants, that bypassed parliamentary scrutiny. Charters and patents had been granted creating monopolies in all manner of trades, processes and lands.

The outcry was such that James was obliged to agree to the *Statute of Monopolies 1623* (in fact passed in February of the following year, according to the current convention that the official year starts on 1 January and not as formerly 25 March, 'Lady Day'). Its polite introduction suggested 'Misinformacions and untrue pretences of publique good' had led to many patents being 'unlawfullie putt in execucion, to the greate Greevance and Inconvenience of your Majesties Subjects, contrary to the Lawes of this your Realme, and contrary to your Majesties royall and blessed Intencion'.[25.1]

All existing monopolies, grants and dispensations from penalties were declared void. But the act allowed new monopolies for up to fourteen years to be granted to 'the true and first Inventor and Inventors' of 'any manner of new Manufactures within this Realme'. Obtaining such patents was made easier and the cost less.

As he had done on the battlefield, Prince Rupert, by the 1670s in his fifties, led the charge to make the most of his discoveries. From his workshops within Windsor Castle, he had produced a stream of inventions including painting methods, guns, improved gunpowder, new metal alloys, glass droplets, lifting, mining, diving and gun-boring devices and methods.

This was not simply the result of an esoteric hobby: the prince was also trying to make money. In 1670 he was granted a fourteen-year exclusive licence to exploit his process for 'converting into steele all manner of edged tooles, files, and other instruments forged and formed in soft iron'.[25.2] The following year he took out a patent for a super-sized cannon made of improved iron. He was able to sell this idea to the government of the day although the cannon was never produced.[25.3]

According to Anderson's *History of Commerce*,[25.4] the prince was also responsible 'for a floating machine, worked by horses, for the towing of great ships against wind and tide', a diving machine and 'a machine for the raising of ballast; though found insufficient even before Prince Rupert's death'.

Another factor in the drive towards innovation was the growing use of 'joint-stock companies as vehicles for business endeavours. Individual merchants and adventurers often joined together to finance manufacturing and trading ventures, for example a trading or even privateering voyage. Such arrangements were in the nature of partnerships. And they were understood to be temporary and only to last as long as the venture for which they were created – such as a particular voyage. The next voyage or venture would need a new set of investors, or the original investors to recommit their involvement.

By the 1680s, a new form of more permanent financial arrangement was taking centre stage. The joint-stock company was all the rage.

There had been companies in existence for a long time. They worked on the general principle that they had their own entities in law, and this was separate and different from that of their individual shareholders. Until the joint-stock companies became fashionable, companies were usually formed in one of two ways: by act of Parliament or by grant of a royal charter. Both routes to incorporation were tortuous, tedious and expensive.

Acts of Parliament were used most often for incorporation of towns, charters for creation of major, national-scale ventures, such as the opening up of trade with the West Indies, with the East Indies, the Levant, Muscovy or North America (the Hudson's Bay Company was a chartered company, as was the Royal African Company). To the extent that these companies usually had shareholders, they were also joint-stock companies (the Virginia Company of London, the Hudson's Bay Company and the Royal African Company were examples of such arrangements). But unlike the newer version of joint-stock companies, they were regulated by their charters, and were cumbersome outfits, granted monopolies and usually offering the crown a stake in profits in return. Some, such as the East India Company, were highly successful, but this did not stop the company later launching an unchartered joint-stock version of itself.

Most joint-stock companies formed in the latter half of the seventeenth century were at the other end of the scale. They were smaller, freewheeling enterprises, and sometimes highly speculative. Their structure was much like a modern-day public or private limited company, except that investors were not protected by limited liability, nor by regulation of any sort (there was no *Companies Act*).[25.5] Such joint-stock companies (the Albemarle/Phipps treasure-hunting company was an example) were created by private legal agreement, usually made between a 'projector' (the person raising money and usually the person who drew up the agreement) and the investors. There were shareholders but no shareholders' rights, except those that the initial agreement might or might not say about this in the constitution and by-laws of the company. There were directors, or 'governors', but no limitation on their powers except those written into that same constitution or by-laws.

But joint-stock companies had important advantages over simple partnerships. First, once formed they continued in being indefinitely (or at least until they went broke and folded). Secondly, they could call on large numbers of individual investors who need have no previous contact with the others involved and who were not expected to take an active part in the running of the company. Nor did investors necessarily have to stump up too much (they might buy just one share in the company or as many more as were available).

The notion of 'limited liability' – that shareholders could not be asked to pay any more than their original investment– had yet to be hit upon: investors in all types of company were ultimately liable for their company's debts. But given a substantial number of subscribers/shareholders, those putting money into joint-stock companies had the comfort of knowing their liability was shared with many others. Third, shareholders could cash in at any point by selling their shares in the company (provided they could find a buyer).

Author, bankrupt and part-time fraudster Daniel Defoe (of *Robinson Crusoe* fame) had a good deal to say about the joint-stock phenomenon in his *An Essay Upon Projects.* He conceded that well-founded, honest projects were 'doubtless in general of public advantage, as they tend to improvement of trade, and employment of the poor, and the circulation and increase of the public stock of the kingdom'. But there were too many, he claimed, that had been formed by dishonest, 'contemptible' projectors. These men – for they were invariably men – were driven by their own desperate fortunes 'to paint up some bauble or other … and then cry it up for a new invention'. The project 'gets a patent for it, divides it into shares, and they must be sold. Ways and means are not wanting to swell the new whim to a vast magnitude; thousands and hundreds of thousands are the least of his discourse, and sometimes millions, till the ambition of some honest coxcomb is wheedled to part with his money for it, and then (*nascitur ridiculus mus* [an absurd mouse will be born]) the adventurer is left to carry on the project, and the projector laughs at him.'[25.6]

As usual with Defoe, he was telling his readers to 'do what I say, not what I do', since he had already lost money investing in a speculative joint-stock company. But in any case, whatever he might say, the joint-stock format was popular with investors because of the relative ease with which they could become involved in what most would have understood to be something of a gamble. They were even more popular with projectors and their associates because of the substantial control they were able to retain over their creations.

To start with, the number of new companies was not huge, no more than twenty-five or so. But even this number probably doubled the trading company count of former years. And then something else happened to boost the number: the 'Glorious Revolution', or more accurately, William of Orange's invasion and his accession, along with his wife, to the thrones of England, Scotland and Ireland.

Suddenly England had a more certain outlook. William and Mary accepted constitutional limits to their powers. Religious uncertainties, reopened by James II, seemed to have been settled in favour of a more tolerant Protestant regime, and the country had the benefit of a lasting coalition with Holland and its ingenious population.

Holland was no longer the enemy as in recent wars, but France was.

Everything Dutch was now in vogue, including Dutch ideas on finance, investment and share trading. Among the examples now acted upon in England was that of the world's first functioning stock exchange. Beginning in 1602, this was based on dealing in shares of Holland's own version of an East India Company, the Vereenigde Oost-Indische Compagnie, or VOC, founded that very year. Unlike the shares in its English equivalent, launched in 1600, VOC shares were traded from almost day one. They were treated as financial securities that could be bought and sold, both for immediate delivery or at some specified future date. The share price had a life of its own, rising and falling on rumour and speculation (since little information was released by the company itself). Certainly, dividends paid had little bearing on share price since none were declared for the first eight years of the VOC's existence. Even then the dividend was paid in kind, each shareholder receiving an entitlement to a quantity of the spice mace.[25.7]

Chapter 26

Not Without Honour

WHEN, IN 1687, William Phipps anchored at Gravesend, his holds brimming with silver, he had once again placed himself at the centre of political and economic upheaval. Scientific and financial advances were shifting society away from unquestioning loyalty to a medieval system of government. James II continued to alienate most of his subjects while trying desperately to cling to his throne. The following year he would be gone. William of Orange was waiting at the sidelines, quietly assembling the massive flotilla that would carry his invasion force to England.

The nation was in an excited state. It was ready for change, and it was captivated by the romance of Phipps' story. Here, it was thought, was an uneducated backwoodsman who had somehow happened upon a massive fortune, hidden for years in the depths of the ocean. If he could do it, people thought, anybody could.

For Phipps himself, the most immediate result of his treasure-hunting success was personal wealth, a knighthood, and soon, governorship of Massachusetts. For England it was something else. It was a boost to the economy, renewed fascination with diving bell technology and in treasure-hunting opportunities, and demand for joint-stock investment opportunities in both. Inventors and projectors got to work to make the most of the opportunity.

There had been a long fascination with diving bells, which had been known about for hundreds of years. But until Phipps arrived in Gravesend, relatively little attention had been paid to possible improvement in the basic design. In the seventeen years between 1672 and 1689 there had been only five new diving bell-related patents issued, reported Christine Macleod in a 1986 article in *The Economic History Review*.[26.1] By contrast, seventeen applications were made for such patents in the two years 1691 to 1693, of which eleven were granted. 'Alone they accounted for almost one-fifth of all patents issued in 1691 to 1693,' said Macleod. These patents included a 1692 grant to Isaac Thompson, Captain Benjamin Graves, Thomas Joell and Joux Cuthbert 'of a invention whereby a man may be let down under water, either in the sea or elsewhere, engine, by the assistance of a certain diving; habit, which does well secure them from the pressure of the water, and leaves their armes and legs naked and at liberty ; and thereby, and with the help of another engine for pumping of air, the said person so lett downe may safely continue for an hour at least under water with great freedome and clearnesse of sight, and be capable of doeing any manner of worke during all that time.'[26.2]

Another 1692 patent was that granted to John Overing for his engine 'to convey air into pipes by new contrived bellows, with plates covered with leather for securing the head and reteyning the air about the upper pte of the body, and gives liberty for a man to see, walke, and worke a considerable time in many fathom under water'.[26.3]

Some diving machine inventors had made a business out of their ingenuity. John Tyzack, for example, besides holding a patent for a diving machine also held patents for 'an engine … for the well and more easy oyling and dressing of leather and cloth' and for a 'night engine', an early attempt at a burglar alarm.[26.4]

Cornish inventor Joseph Williams also held a patent for an 'engine, consisting of screws, wheeles, and wrenches, whereby he is able to draw and raise great weights with much more ease and advantage then by any other waies and meanes now practised'. This, he said, would be of 'great use in raising mineralls, buildings, and merchants goods, loading and unloading shipps, &c'.[26.5]

The chancer, opportunist and friend of Daniel Defoe, Thomas Neale, held patents for a means of making verdigrease, 'and of boyling the same in wooden or other panns, and alsoe of making panns or vessells of wood for boyling of verdigrease' as well as a process for 'makeing of Steele equivalent to Corinthian Steele'. His portfolio included patents for making 'brasse and thereof plates for kettles and the like', and for a 'sort of table to be played upon with balls to fit into small hollows'. The latter was to be 'inlaid with chances of dice as may prevent all cheating'.[26.6]

Others, such as John Williams, had fewer inventor credentials. Nevertheless, he was successful in obtaining a patent for a diving engine 'for the carrying of foure men fifteene fathom or more under water in the sea, whereby they may worke 12 houres together without any danger; which said engine will be of 'great use for the taking upp of wrecks and shipps that have been and shall be lost in the sea'.[26.7]

Known for his discoveries rather than his inventions, Royal Society member Edmund Halley (of Halley's Comet fame) cooperated with Stephen Evance, Francis Tyssen and John Holland to come up, in 1691, with a diving engine 'whereby by conveying aire into a diveing vessell they can maintaine severall persons at the same time to live and worke safely undr water at any depth for many houres, for the retreiveing & regaining of gold, silver, bullion, money, and all manner of goods and merchandize wreckt and lost at sea'.[26.8]

There were others. In 1691 John Hooke, Samuel Atkinson, Samuel Weale and Nicholas Nicholls obtained a patent for an engine 'by which a man may worke a considerable depth under water for many houres, being made of tymber with glass windows, a doore, and severall air pipes, united leather sieves, and iron braees affixed thereunto'.

In 1693 John Stapleton (gentleman) became the owner of a patent for an engine 'contrived as to pmitt a pson, inclosed in it, to walk under water; and of a new invented way to force air into any depth of water, to supply the pson in the said engine therewith, and for continuing a lamp burning'.

The following year Samuel Winball, (also gentleman) patented his 'diveing engine, framed and consisting of brasse, lead, iron, and other mettalls and materials, by which said engine one or more pson or psons may descend into the sea, altho' at the depth of 20 fathom or more, and there remaine by the space of 24 houres ; and by means of the strength and contrivance of the said engine, the pson or psons within the said machine are safely secured from any pressure or inconveniencye of the water, and have pfect freedome of air and breathing, and likewise free liberty of seeing whatever is in the water, and of useing his or their handes and bodyes, whereby any thing may be fastned to whatever is in the bottom.'[26.9]

Many of these patents were used as the bases for joint-stock company offerings. In his 1912 major work on early joint-stock companies,[26.10] political economist Professor William Scott listed four companies owning 'diving-engines': those invented by John Williams, Joseph Williams, John Tyzack and John Overing. Other companies promised their investors returns from the recovery of wrecks from places where they had been granted treasure-hunting rights: in England, off Bermuda, off Broadhaven, and 'in other places' (the last two being companies projected by Thomas Neale), and in Spanish waters (seeking to profit from the Houblon brothers' hoped-for patent).

'Some of the engines seem to have served their purpose, but there is no record of any repetition of Phips' success,' said Christine Macleod, who reported that when sued by an unhappy investor, John Williams had apparently absconded. She might have added that those companies offering an opportunity to become involved with actual recovery of treasure – nine are listed by Scott – seemed also generally to have failed to make any significant finds.[26.11]

But two of the companies listed by Scott seem to have had more substance than their competitors. All except one had been established by private agreement ('deed of settlement', said Scott) and were therefore not regulated. The exception was 'The Governor and Company for Recovering Wrecks from England', which had obtained a royal charter. This was the company that planned to make use of a diving bell designed by Edmund Halley and patented by him and his collaborators: Member of Parliament Stephen Evance, who besides being receiver of poll tax and commissioner of various duties, was governor of the Hollow Blade Company and a Royal African Company investor; Francis Tyssen, slave plantation owner and East India Company and Royal African Company investor; and John Holland. Among other shareholders was businessman Thomas Jett, named in 1692 papers concerning his management of a saltpetre works in Marylebone, as a 'citizen and merchant taylor'. The work's articles of agreement were also signed by Stephen Evance.[26.12]

Halley kept the Royal Society informed of his diving bell achievements, including its design, its construction, a personal test dive in the Thames, and his involvement in the attempted recovery of 'elephants teeth' from the wreck of the *Guynie*, sunk off Chichester. This was a Royal African Company slave ship that had sunk while in the process of returning a consignment of treasures to England.[26.13] The commission likely came via Tysen's and Evance's RAC connections.

The second company to have more backing than the others, and the most spectacular failure, was that of the Houblon brothers, City merchants all. Sir James was a Member of Parliament and a friend of Samuel Pepys. Soon-to-be-knighted John was a City alderman and Master of the Grocer's Company, who later became the first governor of the Bank of England, lord mayor of London and an Admiralty commissioner. Abraham was later also a governor of the Bank.

The Houblons intended to make use of their Spanish business connections to obtain treasure-hunting licences from the Spanish king, Carlos II. Raising money from their merchant and parliamentary friends, the brothers bought four vessels, the *Charles the Second*, the *Dove*, the *James* and the *Seventh Son*. They thought that their masterstroke was to man them with mariners who had sailed in the Caribbean and preferably had had treasure-hunting experience, inevitably a rough-and-ready lot.

In the autumn of 1693 the ships and their complement of 300 freebooters were sent off to La Coruna, in Spain, to await the expected licences. They didn't get any further.

Things had begun to go wrong from the start. John Strong, Phipps' former chief mate who had been appointed captain of the *Charles the Second*, took sick and died and was replaced by Charles Gibson. Meanwhile the men fretted through the winter months in their damp and rainswept ships. By May the weather had changed but there was still no sign of their licences, nor their pay.

At this point, *Charles the Second* mate Henry Every led a mutiny. While Gibson was asleep, the disgruntled seamen seized the ship, cut its cables and made for the open seas. Next day Gibson was set ashore with other refuseniks, leaving Every to sail off for the Indian Ocean in command of a crew of eighty-four.

Renaming his stolen ship the *Fancy*, Every – who was one or two years younger than Phipps and also went by various aliases, including John Avery and Benjamin Bridgeman – decided to target the pilgrim ships that regularly took wealthy Muslims to and from Mecca. Before too long he captured the *Ganj-i-sawai*, known to English courts as the '*Gunsway*', an armed dhow owned by the Great Mogul Aurangzeb.

In Surat the attack was seen as the outrage that it was, sacrilege on the high seas. There were riots with mobs intent on taking revenge on anybody daring to call him- or herself English. Aurangzeb, who was 77 at the time and ruler of most of India, was not a man to be crossed. His rage was directed mainly towards the East India Company, some fifty of whose Surat factory employees were arrested and placed in irons.

Back in England there was a degree of panic in the company's Leadenhall headquarters. Using its considerable lobbying power, it managed to secure a Royal Proclamation against Every – a cross between a 'wanted dead or alive' poster and an international arrest warrant. This called for the 'outmost diligence' to be used 'for seizing, and apprehending' Every, alias Bridgeman, and twenty-five named 'accomplices'. A price of £500 was placed on Every's head and £50 on each of his accomplices.

The ensuing manhunt yielded only meagre results. The cabin boy Philip Middleton, arrested in Ireland, told how after taking the *Gunsway*, Every had sailed to the Bahamas where the governor, Nicholas Trott, had agreed to allow the pirates ashore on payment of twenty pieces of eight and two pieces gold per man (there were 100 on board) plus the *Fancy* and all that was in her.

There the trail ran cold. Every had disappeared, never to be seen again. He may have been murdered, lived out his life in some distant land in a degree of luxury, or perhaps, as Daniel Defoe suggested, was cheated out of his ill-gotten gains and died a pauper.

The authorities, however, knew that somebody had to pay for what had happened. Of the eight suspected pirates arrested, Middleton and another had turned king's evidence. In mid-October 1696, the remaining six were put on trial at the Old Bailey (sitting as an Admiralty court). Seven names were on the indictment. Every had not been captured, nor would he ever be, but his name was added to the list of those charged.

It was a show trial, held to show the world in general, and Aurangzeb in particular, that England would no longer tolerate piracy on the high seas. Unfortunately for the authorities it took three attempts to obtain guilty verdicts against those charged. But in the end, they were convicted and the six on whom the authorities could lay hands were duly hanged in Wapping's Execution Dock.[26.14]

It was not until early 1695 that the Houblon's expedition was put to rest and the remaining ships were allowed to sail back to England. By 1696 'mariners, carpenters etc in the squadron of the "Spanish Expedition Shipping"' were suing investors in the Houblons' company for return of property. The case dragged on for another six years and was not settled until after the death of several of the litigants.[26.15]

Lack of success did not seem to blunt the enthusiasm for investment in diving-related concerns nor the growing number of joint-stock companies with interests in other fields. Like Dutch investors, English investors had discovered that movements in the price of shares traded in a more or less open market was not dependent wholly on the results of the company concerned. These markets moved not according to past results but to future expectations.

The wherewithal of a stock market was being created and publications were beginning to appear that advised would-be investors and speculators on prices; the two most prominent were Houghton's *Collection for the Improvement of Husbandry and Trade*, and Castaing's *Course of the Exchange,* both begun in the early 1690s. By 1694, when its coverage was extended further, Houghton's was already listing prices for sixty-four of an estimated 150 joint-stock companies. These listings were posted in Jonathan's coffee house which has claims to being the birthplace of the London Stock Exchange.[26.16]

According to William Scott, shares prices of three diving companies appearing on Houghton's list held steady between 1692 and 1693. 'It shows how long the expectation of success continued, that as late as May 18, 1694, a writer as staid as John Houghton mentioned that "there was great hope of gain from a Spanish wreck",' he said.[26.17]

It was understandable that there should be such interest in investing in companies, including those intent on more fanciful 'opportunities'. The country was at war with France and much silver was being shipped to Europe to pay the wages of King William's army. Meanwhile England's existing coinage was much battered, defaced and clipped. There was a shortage of money; not wealth (although there was undoubtedly a shortage of that too) but the means of spending wealth. Merchants were being obliged to use various forms of security (such as bills of exchange, promissory notes, goldsmiths' receipts, and share certificates) as currency. Soon, in 1696 there would be a reminting of the coinage under the auspices of Issac Newton, and sooner still, in 1694, creation of the Bank of England with its own bills and of the Million Lottery whose tickets were also used as quasi-money.[26.18]

In the meantime, foreign trade was somewhat curtailed, not least by the number of ships seized by French privateers, and shortages were causing rising demand for British-made alternatives. The prospects for companies serving the home market looked good.

And there was another factor: a new appetite for speculation. Perhaps it was a wartime attitude. Why not take a risk, after all, tomorrow we might find foreign troops knocking at our doors?

'Witness Sir William Phips' voyage to the wreck; it was a mere project; a lottery of a hundred thousand to one odds; a hazard which, if it had failed, everybody would have been ashamed to have owned themselves concerned in,' wrote Daniel Defoe. And yet success had 'sanctified' such unlikely projects and 'it would be a kind of blasphemy against fortune to disallow them,' he said.[26.19]

Defoe was talking about speculation verging on gambling, but also about hope, something that Phipps had had in abundance. Coupled with a fierce determination and unwavering tenacity, he had won through against what might have seemed insurmountable odds. Those in New England had declined to honour his achievements to the extent that they deserved. But in England they were celebrated. Here they provided the spark that lit commercial adventures – a diving bell bubble that bred a generation of investors. Their heirs would create a worldwide business empire that, for better or worse, painted the map of the globe red.

Appendices

Phips or Phipps?

William Phipps answered to both 'Phips' and 'Phipps'. In England, official and other papers (court cases, citations, agreements and appointments) often referred to him as 'Phipps'. In New England papers it is perhaps more the other way; 'Phips' trumps 'Phipps'. But there are examples of both spellings in both English and New England references.

Phipps was around when most things were far from standardised. Spelling was one discipline that was not. There are numerous examples of people known by names spelled in more than one way. Some feature in this book (Phips or Phipps, Cony or Coney, White or de Vite, Covell or Covill, Cory or Corey, Narborough or Narbrough).

Phipps himself was famously challenged when it came to literacy. He may not have cared about whether he had one or two 'p's in his name, or even noticed. His own signature, see below, is somewhat ambiguous. His mother and father were Phipps, his stepson Phips.

For the sake of consistency in the text I have used Phipps throughout, although direct quotes have retained whatever spelling was in the original.

Indians or Native Americans?

In his book about King Philip's War, author Daniel Mandell* acknowledged 'a long and often acrimonious debate over whether to use the term "Indians" or "Native Americans"'. Surveys of tribes in the United States suggest a preference for use of the description 'Indian', he said. 'To avoid being overly

* Mandell, Daniel R., *King Philip's War: Colonial Expansion, Native Resistance, and the End of Indian Sovereignty* (Witness to History) (pp. 178–179). John Hopkins University Press.

repetitive in this book, I use both "Indians" and "Natives" when not referring to a particular tribe or community. Similarly, I refer to the newcomers as English (which is what they usually called themselves), colonists, or settlers.'

In this book, I have aimed to follow the approach adopted by Mandell.

Dates, Days, Spelling and Sources

As noted above, little if anything was standardised in the seventeenth century. Spelling and grammar were matters of personal choice, dates varied according to the preferred calendar, the value of coins was a matter of assessment of their gold or silver content. People often had more than one name, or more than one spelling of the same name. Place names, also, had a habit of changing. Mapmakers drew precise charts of a world whose topography was uncertain and prone to revision. As far as possible place names have been given both in the form used at the time and their modern rendition.

To reflect this, quotations in this book have been repeated as written at the time, idiosyncratic spelling intact. Dates have been given as recorded at the time. The exception to this is that each year has been taken to start on 1 January and not 25 March, Lady Day, which was the first day of the official administrative year in England and New England.

Much that is a common feature of life today had not even been thought of in William Phipps' time. Income tax was one of them. Life was lived at a different pace, and many 'necessities' of today were unknown. This makes assessing the present-day equivalent of seventeenth-century money so difficult. In this text the currency converter available via The National Archives has been used where some idea of comparative value is needed. This gives values in terms of purchasing power and wages at the time.

In researching this book, I have made full use of the internet and particularly those websites offering access to archives and other database. These have included The National Archives, the official archive and publisher for the UK Government, and British History Online. These have given access to minutes and reports of various committees and councils, civil court cases involving Phipps and others, warrant books with details of payments and much more of an official nature.

References and Notes

Chapter 1: Predestined

1.1 www.parliament.uk/about/living-heritage/evolutionofparliament/parliamentaryauthority/the-gunpowder-plot-of-1605/collections/thanksgiving-act/ - Parliamentary Archives, HL/PO/PU/1/1605/3J1n1.

1.2 The 1628 Parliament was the first to which one Oliver Cromwell was elected. He was an East Anglian gentleman farmer whose family had a history of sending its menfolk to sit in Parliament and was a man with a reputation for sticking up for those who had been unjustly treated. Cromwell, a Puritan, was of plain dress and manners. His oratory was laced with biblical references and delivered with the force of an Ian Paisley. Had he lived in the twenty-first century he might well have been a television evangelist.

1.3 Cromwell 'worried seriously whether to go to New England in 1638 and start a new life', according to Fraser, Antonia. *Cromwell, Our Chief of Men*. Orion.

Chapter 2: Coming to America

2.1 Craven, Wesley Frank, *The Virginia Company of London, 1606–1624*, Virginia 350th Anniversary Celebration Corporation, Williamsburg.

2.2 Named to honour William Phipps, the subject of this book, Phippsburg, is about ten miles south of Woolwich, the community in which William was born and spent his childhood.

2.3 Macinnes, C. M., *Ferdinando Gorges and New England*, Bristol Branch, Historical Association, 1965.

2.4 *Bible*, King James Version, Matthew 5:14, 'A city that is set on a hill cannot be hid. Neither do men light a candle, and put it under a bushel, but on a candlestick; and it giveth light unto all that are in the house. Let your light so shine before men, that they may see your good works, and glorify your father which is in heaven.'

2.5 Winthrop, John, *A Modell of Christian Charity*, 1630, Collections of the Massachusetts Historical Society, Boston, 1838, 3rd series 7:31–48. Accessed via University of Virginia, https://xroads.virginia.edu/~DRBR/winthmod.html.

2.6 Banks, Charles Edward, *Topographical Dictionary of English Emigrants to New England 1620 – 1650*, Genealogical Publishing Co., 1937.

2.7 Baker, Emerson W. & Reid, John G., *The New England Knight; Sir William Phips, 1651–1695*, University of Toronto Press, 1998.

2.8 This almost tallies with the 1937 findings of Colonel Charles Edward Banks in his *Topographical Dictionary of English Emigrants to New England 1620–1650.* This lists John Brown as leaving Bristol for 'Pemaquid, Maine' and James Phipps as leaving the same city for 'Sheepscot, Maine' ('Sheepscot could be a reference to a region or river'). The places named are all in the same general vicinity and could easily refer to the same destination. No date is given for their departure, but it seems likely this was just before Brown bought land in Pemaquid in 1625. See also: Banks, Charles Edwards, *Genealogical Dictionary of Maine and New Hampshire,* New England Historic Genealogical Society, Boston, 2012.

2.9 Apprenticeships were generally only available to boys who were the children of 'freeholders', people of some standing. Completion of an apprenticeship ensured the sobriquet of 'master' craftsman and a reasonably comfortable, if hard-worked, living. But the apprenticeship itself was akin to a form of slavery with the young apprentice bound to obey his master's every command.

2.10 Otis, James, *The Story of Pemaquid*, Thomas Y. Crowell & Co., 1902.

2.11 Pope, Charles Henry, *The Pioneers of Maine and New Hampshire 1623 to 1660*, published by Charles H. Pope, 1908.

2.12 Spencer, Wilbur D., *Pioneers on Maine Rivers*, republished by Genealogical Publishing Co. Inc., 1973 (original 1930).

2.13 Pope, Charles Henry, *The Pioneers of Maine and New Hampshire 1623 to 1660*, published by Charles H. Pope, Boston, 1908.

2.14 Mather, Cotton, *Magnalia Christi Americana* (Great American Christ), Vol 1 (of 2), first printed 1702, reprint 1853–1855, The Library of Early American literature.

2.15 Fraser, Antonia, *Cromwell, Our Chief of Men*, p. 455, Orion.

2.16 Baker, Emerson W. and Reid, John G., *The New England Knight; Sir William Phips, 1651–1695*, University of Toronto Press, 1998.

2.17 Lounsberry, Alice, *Sir William Phips*, Charles Scribner's Sons, 1941.

Chapter 3: Living the Dream

3.1 Mather, Cotton, *Magnalia Christi Americana* (Great American Christ), Vol 1 (of 2), 1702, reprint 1853–1855, The Library of Early American Literature.

3.2 Mather, Cotton. *Cotton Mather: Magnalia Christi Americana*, Vol 1 (of 2), 1702, p. 118.

3.3 Repeated in Sprague, John Francis and Packard, Bertram E., *Three Men From Maine: Sir William Pepperrell, Sir William Phips, James Sullivan and A Bit of Old England in New England,* Maine Collection, *1924*. 96. https://digitalcommons.usm.maine.edu/me_collection/96.

3.4 Connor, L. G., *A brief history of the sheep industry in the United States*, Agricultural History Society Papers 1 89–197, 1921. www.jstor.org/stable/44216164. 'Sheep were introduced into Massachusetts between 1624 and 1629. In 1642 there were 1,000 sheep in Massachusetts, and 3,000 by 1652,' according to this paper.

3.5 Spencer, Wilbur Daniel, *Pioneers on Maine rivers, with lists to 1651*, Lakeside Print. Co., 1930. Accessed via Internet Archive. A bushel is a measure of volume and in the case of wheat, ten bushels equate to between 560 and 600 pounds in weight, in the case of other grains and pulses, the figure varies.

3.6 *The Charter of New England: 1620*, Yale Law School, Lillian Goldman Law Library, The Avalon Project, https://avalon.law.yale.edu/17th_century/mass01.asp.

3.7 Letter from John Winthrop, Governor Massachusetts Bay Colony, The Golder Lehrman Institute of American History, 1634.

3.8 Although the two owners of Clarke & Lake, Major Thomas Clarke and Captain Thomas Lake, habitually used their army ranks as part of their names, neither was a career soldier. Both held commissions in the Military Company of Massachusetts. This volunteer force, based in Boston, subsequently morphed itself into the Ancient and Honorable Artillery Company of Massachusetts. It had been created by the colony's General Court in 1638. Clarke is first mentioned as a lieutenant in 1639, only a year after the company's formation. Lake is first listed as a captain in 1662.

3.9 Baker, Emerson, *The Clarke & Lake Company: The Historical Archaeology of a Seventeenth-Century Maine Settlement,* Maine Historic Preservation Commission, 1985.

Chapter 4: Unforgotten and Unforgiven

4.1 Charles II, *An Act of Free and General Pardon Indemnity and Oblivion, 1660,* in *Statutes of the Realm: Vol 5, 1628-80*, ed. John Raithby, pp. 226–234.

4.2 *1660: The Regicides, The Society of Colonial Wars in the State of Connecticut*, www.colonialwarsct.org/1660.htm#:~:text=Regicides%2C%20in%20English%20history%2C%20were,by%20the%20Act%20of%20Indemnity.

4.3 The man that Hannah Hull married was Samuel Sewall. The same age as Phipps, he benefitted from a better education, graduating from Harvard in 1671. He married Hannah in 1676. His career was illustrious. He is credited with being a minister, printer, merchant, magistrate, member of the colony's governing body, member of the Military Company of Massachusetts, diarist and, in 1700, author of an early anti-slavery pamphlet, *The Selling of Joseph*. On the downside, he was a judge in the Salem witch trials, although he was the only judge to apologise for his part in sentencing nineteen people to death. Sewall did not doubt the existence of witches but said the evidence on which he had based his decisions had been too weak.

4.4 'America and West Indies: April 1664' in *Calendar of State Papers Colonial, America and West Indies: Vol 5, 1661–1668*, ed. W. Noel Sainsbury, London, 1880, pp. 196–205.

4.5 'America and West Indies: April 1664' in *Calendar of State Papers Colonial, America and West Indies: Vol 5, 1661–1668*, ed. W. Noel Sainsbury, London, 1880, pp. 196–205.

4.6 Quoted by John Gorham Palfrey. *History of New England During the Stuart Dynasty* Vol 2, Little, Brown.

Chapter 5: Boston Bound

5.1 Mather, Cotton, *Magnalia Christi Americana* (Great American Christ), The Library of Early American literature Vol 1 (of 2), 1702, reprint 1853–1855.

5.2 Allison, Robert J., *A Short History of Boston*, Commonwealth Editions, 2004. New England had been named as such by Captain John Smith, by his own account a leader of the 1606 expedition to establish a colony in Jamestown, Virginia. He had subsequently explored the coastline north of Virginia and produced a chart on which he named both New England and 'Plimouth', some six years before the Pilgrim Fathers set sail from Plymouth, England. He may have chosen the name to humour his business acquaintance Ferdinando Gorges, who had Plymouth connections and was an advocate of American colonisation. Smith pre-empted settlers' weakness for naming their new villages after their old hometowns. Immigrants were soon giving settlements names such as Boston (Lincolnshire), Arundel (West Sussex), Barnstable (Devon), Braintree (Essex), Ipswich (Suffolk), Norwich (Norfolk), Salisbury (Wiltshire), Southampton (Hampshire) and Weymouth (Dorset).

5.3 Record Commissioners, *List of tax-payers in the town of Boston, 1674–1695,* Rockwell & Churchill, 1881. https://hdl.handle.net/2027/uc1.31158004191382.

5.4 Woods, Robert Archery, *Americans in process; A settlement study*, Houghton, Mifflin & Co., 1903. Accessed via https://archive.org/details/americansinproce00wood.

5.5 Mather, Cotton, *Magnalia Christi Americana*, Vol 1, 1702. A portrait of Phipps painted by Thomas Child at about the time Phipps received his knighthood (illustration 3), shows a healthy-looking 30-something fixing the artist with a somewhat challenging stare. Phipps' clothing is not elaborate but neither does it have the plainness favoured by Puritans nor the clerical look adopted by some of his contemporaries such as Samuel Sewall or William Stoughton. Phipps has a firm chin and a defiant look in his eyes. This image contrasts with another thought to have been etched in the early 1690s. This shows a portlier man, much fuller of face and dressed in much more elaborate clothing, including a many-buttoned waistcoat and lace protruding from his substantial cuffs of his jacket sleeves. He is perched on the edge of his chair as if ready to leap up at any moment (illustration 4).

5.6 Folsom, George, *History of Saco and Biddeford, with notices of other early settlements, and of the proprietary government, in Maine, including the provinces of New Somersetshire and Lygonia*, A. C. Putnam, 1830.

5.7 Mather, Cotton, *Magnalia Christi Americana,* Vol 1 (of 2), 1702.

5.8 Baker, Emerson W. & Reid, John G., *The New England Knight*, University of Toronto Press, 1998, reporting on inventory of the estate of John Hull, 2 May 1673, Suffolk County Probate File, 661; Noyes, Libby, and Davis *Genealogical Dictionary of Maine and New Hampshire*, 357,651. Mary's sister Rebecca and brother-in-law David Bennet had a son, Spencer Bennet, who was later adopted by his childless uncle and aunt. He took the surname Phips and went on to serve as the Lieutenant Governor of Massachusetts from 1732 until his death in 1757.

Chapter 6: King Philip's Revenge

6.1 'An Act for the promoting and propagating the Gospel of Jesus Christ in New England, July 1649' in *Acts and Ordinances of the Interregnum, 1642–1660*, ed. C. H. Firth & R. S. Rait, London, 1911, pp. 197–200.

6.2 Natick Historical Society, www.natickhistoricalsociety.org/naticks-beginnings.

6.3 *New England Company*, The City of London, www.cityoflondon.gov.uk/things-to-do/history-and-heritage/london-metropolitan-archives/

collections/new-england-company. During this time John Eliot also translated the bible and other religious texts into the Algonquin language. In 1663 over 1,000 copies of *Mamusse Wunneetupanatamwe Up-Biblum God, aka* 'The Eliot Indian Bible', were printed, using the Harvard College press in Cambridge, Massachusetts. The cost was covered by The President and Society for the propagation of the Gospel in New England, which by then had transformed itself into the New England Company. In 1664 a copy of the bible was presented to King Charles II by the NEC's then president, Royal Society stalwart Robert Boyle. The relationship between Harvard and the New England Company was enduring. It became significant for Phipps when later characterised by personal contacts between Harvard's sixth president and NEC commissioner, Increase Mather, and the company's London bankers, the influential Ashurst family.

6.4 *Journal of Richard Mather, 1635, His Life and Death*, Dorchester Antiquarian and Historical Society, 1670. The three faster ships in the flotilla that took Humphrey Atherton and Richard Mather to New England were the *Elizabeth*, *Mary* and *Diligence.* All made it safely to Newfoundland. But arrival in New England of the *James* and its remaining escort, the *Angel Gabriel*, coincided with that of a hurricane, later known as 'The Great Colonial Hurricane'. The *Angel Gabriel*, which was anchored at Pemaquid with most of its passengers and crew ashore for the night, was 'burst in pieces' by the winds, never to be seen again. The *James* made it to Boston. It was 'a ship 100 passengers, besides 23 seamen, & 23 cowes and heyfers, 3 sucking calves & eight mares, yet not one of all these dyed by ye way, neither person nor cattell, but came all alive to land', reported Richard Mather. But 'most of ye cattell and other goodes' carried aboard the *Angel Gabriel* was lost, along with 'one seaman and 3 or 4 passengers'. The flotilla had been seen off from Bristol by the ever-enthusiastic would-be colonialist Sir Ferdinando Gorges.

6.5 Brooks, Lisa, *Our Beloved Kin: Remapping a New History of King Philip's War*, https://ourbelovedkin.com/awikhigan/namumpum.

6.6 Bailyn, Bernard, *The New England Merchants in the Seventeenth Century*, p. 172, Read Books Ltd.

6.7 Mandell, Daniel R., 'King Philip's War', *Witness to History*, p. 121, Johns Hopkins University Press,

6.8 *The Historical Marker Database*, www.hmdb.org/m.asp?m=191736

6.9 Mandell, Daniel R., 'King Philip's War', *Witness to History*, pp. 161–162, Johns Hopkins University Press.

6.10 Mather, Cotton, *Magnalia Christi Americana*, Vol 1 (of 2), 1702, p. 118.
6.11 Mandell, Daniel R., 'King Philip's War', *Witness to History*, pp. 173–174, Johns Hopkins University Press.
6.12 Mandell, Daniel R., 'King Philip's War', *Witness to History*, pp. 155–156, Johns Hopkins University Press.
6.13 Natick Historical Society, www.natickhistoricalsociety.org/naticks-beginnings.

Chapter 7: Randolph Arrives

7.1 'America and West Indies: November 1671' in *Calendar of State Papers Colonial, America and West Indies: Vol 7, 1669–1674*, ed. W. Noel Sainsbury, London, 1889, pp. 271–282.
7.2 Hall, Michael G., *Edward Randolph and the American Colonies 1676–1703*, University of North Carolina Press, 1960 which in turn relies heavily on *Edward Randolph, Letters and Official Papers*, The Prince Society, Boston 1909.
7.3 'America and West Indies: July 1677, 16–31' in *Calendar of State Papers Colonial, America and West Indies: Vol 10, 1677–1680*, ed. W Noel Sainsbury and J. W. Fortescue, London, 1896, pp. 116-138.
7.4 Estelle Frances Ward, *Christopher Monk, Duke of Albemarle*, chapter 'The king visits Newhall', John Murray, London, 1915. In 1676 secretary of state (southern department) Henry Coventry pursued the king and his court to Newmarket, where it had gone to watch the horse racing and to enjoy the hospitality of the former secretary of state (southern department) and current lord chamberlain, the Earl of Arlington, at his mansion in Euston, Suffolk. Coventry had hoped that since most of the Privy Council would be with the king, there might be time for some state business. But it was not to be. He wrote Joseph Williamson, secretary of state (northern department) that after delays caused by lack of rain, by rain, hunting, socialising and a surprise visit to the Duke of Albemarle's Newhall Manor, 'I perceive there will be no direction… We have had no committee of the Council. … Nor, I believe, shall before our departure'.

Chapter 8: Captain Phipps Goes to Sea

8.1 Baker, Emerson W. & Reid, John G., *The New England Knight*, University of Toronto Press, 1998.
8.2 Mather, Cotton, *Magnalia Christi Americana* Vol 1 (of 2), 1702. Deer Island is a peninsula that is now a designated part of the Boston Harbor

Islands National Recreation Area. Cotton Mather demonstrated his 'Christian' compassion when he wrote that 'an association of profane Indians near our Weymouth set themselves to deter and seduce the neighbour Indians from the 'right ways of the Lord'. But God quickly sent the small-pox among them, which like a great plague soon swept them away'.

8.3 Hubbard, Reverend William, *General History of New England, from the Discovery to 1688*, Second Edition, Charles C. Little & James Brown, Boston, 1848, digitised version University of Connecticut Libraries.

8.4 Pond, Enoch, *The Lives of Increase Mather and Sir William Phipps* Vol 5, Massachusetts Sabbath School Society.

8.5 Pond, Enoch, *The Lives of Increase Mather and Sir William Phipps* Vol 5, Massachusetts Sabbath School Society.

8.6 Pond, Enoch, *The Lives of Increase Mather and Sir William Phipps* Vol 5, Massachusetts Sabbath School Society.

8.7 Harvard University, The Graduate School of Arts and Sciences, *The Fight Over Inoculation During the 1721 Boston Smallpox Epidemic, https://sitn.hms.harvard.edu/flash/special-edition-on-infectious-disease/2014/the-fight-over-inoculation-during-the-1721-boston-smallpox-epidemic/.* To give him his due, Cotton Mather was later a champion of inoculation against smallpox. He said that his West African slave Onesimus had told him of the custom in his homeland to expose people to a less dangerous strain of smallpox, thereby giving them protection from more deadly versions of the disease. When, in 1721 and 1722, 6,000 of Boston's then 11,000 inhabitants contracted smallpox, Mather faced much public anger and criticism because of his advocacy of inoculation. Some 850 Bostonians died in the epidemic.

8.8 *A Treaty For the Composing of Differences, Restraining of Depredations, and Establishing of Peace in America, Between the Crowns of Great Britain and Spain, Concluded at Madrid the 8th/18 Day of July, in the Year of our Lord 1670, Translated out of Latin,* Published by His Majesties Command In the SAVOY, Printed by the Assigns of John Bill and Christopher Barker, 1670. Accessed via the Text Creation Partnership, http://name.umdl.umich.edu/A32671.0001.001.

8.9 'America and West Indies: September 1670, 16–30' in *Calendar of State Papers Colonial, America and West Indies: Vol 7, 1669–1674*, ed. W. Noel Sainsbury, London, 1889, pp. 94–110.

8.10 *Charles II, 1672: An Act for the incouragement of the Greeneland and Eastland Trades, and for the better secureing the Plantation Trade,* in *Statutes of the Realm: Vol 5, 1628–80*, ed. John Raithby, 1819, pp. 792–793.

8.11 The New Englanders were not the only American colonists to be outraged by the so-called Plantation Trade Act of 1673. In Carolina, where Albemarle County had been a proprietorial colony since 1664 and had become an exporter of tobacco via Massachusetts and Rhode Island, settlers were at odds with their Lords Proprietors over the fairness of the law. In 1677 this led to a minor revolt (Culpepper's Rebellion) which overthrew the then governor.

Chapter 9: An Idea is Formed

9.1 Cotton, *Diary of Cotton Mather: 1681–1708,* Massachusetts Historical Society. Cotton Mather later wrote in his diary: 'About fifteen years ago, I bought a Spanish Indian, and bestowed him for a Servant, on my Father [Puritan minister Increase Mather]. About three Years ago, Sir William Phips, our Governour, bestowed a Spanish Indian for a Scant on myself. My Scant affecting the Sea, I permitted him, to go to Sea; and being an ingenuous Fellow, I gave him an Instrument for his Freedom, if served till the End of the year 1697.' A year later the man's ship was captured by the French but was later recaptured by an English man-o-war and the man was eventually restored to Mather. But still he was not freed. 'My Servant being so strangely returned, I sett myself to make him a Servant of the Lord,' said Mather.

9.2 Dampier, William, *A New Voyage Round the World,* Penguin Books Ltd., pp. 55–59. In this groundbreaking book William Dampier, one of those who took part in the 1680 raid on Portobello, wrote about visiting the Island of Aves the following year. Now a Federal Dependency of Venezuela, the island has a reef to the south. 'The Count d'Estree lost his Fleet here in this manner,' he wrote. 'Coming from the Eastward, he fell in on the back of the Riff, and fired guns to give warning to the rest of his Fleet: But they supposing their Admiral was engaged with Enemies, hoisted up their Topsails, and crouded all the Sails they could make, and ran full sail ashore after him; all within half a mile of each other. For his light being in the Main-Top was an unhappy Beacon for them to follow; and there escaped but one Kings-Ship, and one Privateer.' The men from the privateer had got themselves ashore and lived happily on the contents of barrels that had floated across the reef. 'They lived here about 3 weeks, waiting an opportunity to transport themselves back again to Hispaniola; in all which time they were never without 2 or

3 Hogsheads of Wine and Brandy in their Tents, and Barrels of Beef and Pork.' When another privateer turned up, intending to careen his ship, the captain was delighted to find more than wine, brandy, pork and beef had been washed up. 'For here lay driven on the Island, Masts, Yards, Timbers, and many things that he wanted.'

9.3 *The Lead Mines at Tantiusque, Vol 61: The Pynchon Papers, Vol II,* Colonial Society of Massachusetts, www.colonialsociety.org/node/832.

9.4 Bailyn, Bernard, *The New England Merchants In The Seventeenth Century,* Read Books Ltd, p. 28.

9.5 Jarvis, Michael J., *In the Eye of All Trade,* Omohundro Institute of Early American History and Culture and the University of North Carolina Press, p. 19.

9.6 Mather, Cotton, *Cotton Mather: Magnalia Christi Americana*, Vol 1 (of 2), 1702, pp. 118–119.

9.7 *Records of the Court of assistants of the colony of the Massachusetts bay, 1630–1692*, Vol 1, Printed under the supervision of John Noble, Clerk to the Supreme Judicial Court, Boston, 1901, Court of Admiralty, June 1682, *Theophilus Poole and others v William Phipps, Erasmus Steevens and Nicholas Hayword.* Accessed via Internet Archive.

Chapter 10: It Had Been Done Before

10.1 Bryce, George, *The Remarkable History of the Hudson's Bay Company,* bz editors, p. 9.

10.2 Andra-Warner, Elle, *Hudson's Bay Company Adventures,* Heritage House, pp. 14–15.

10.3 Charles River Editors, *The Hudson's Bay Company: The History and Legacy of the Famous English Trading Company in Colonial America,* Charles River Editors.

10.4 'America and West Indies: April 1664' in *Calendar of State Papers Colonial, America and West Indies: Vol 5, 1661–1668*, ed. W. Noel Sainsbury, London, 1880, pp. 196–205.

10.5 'America and West Indies: April 1664' in *Calendar of State Papers Colonial, America and West Indies: Vol 5, 1661–1668*, ed. W. Noel Sainsbury, London, 1880, pp. 222–231.

10.6 Carteret was a royalist and something of a rogue. His family, of French origin, had substantial interests in Jersey where he served as lieutenant governor. During the Civil War he made the most of the appointment, racking up a fortune supplying arms and ammunition to West Country royalist forces. Jersey was the last royalist stronghold to surrender. Carteret went off to France, returning to England after the restoration in 1660, when he was appointed treasurer to the Navy. There he made another fortune, charging threepence for every pound that passed through his hands. But his creative accounting methods brought criticism and censure. Things would have turned out worse for him but for a personal endorsement from the king. His American lands were named New Jersey in recognition of his connections with the Channel Island of that name.

10.7 'America and West Indies: April 1664' in *Calendar of State Papers Colonial, America and West Indies: Vol 5, 1661–1668*, ed. W. Noel Sainsbury, London, 1880, pp. 119–122. Prince Rupert and Carteret were also both founder-shareholders in the original 1663 version of the Duke of York's slave-trading outfit, the Company of Royal Adventurers Trading into Africa.

10.8 *The Royal Charter for incorporating The Hudson's Bay Company, A.D. May 2, 1670*, The Solon Law Archive, Canadian Constitutional Documents, www.solon.org/Constitutions/Canada/English/PreConfederation/hbc_charter_1670.html.

10.9 Gough, Barry M., *The 'Adventurers of England Trading into Hudson's Bay': A Study of the Founding Members of the Hudson's Bay Company, 1665–1670*, *Albion: A Quarterly Journal Concerned with British Studies*, vol. 2, no. 1, 1970, pp. 35–47. Accessed via *JSTOR*, https://doi.org/10.2307/4048440.

Chapter 11: A Right Royal Welcome

11.1 www.historyofparliamentonline.org/volume/1660-1690/member/sawyer-robert-1633-92. Six years younger than William, Constantine Phipps was in 1683 at the start of an illustrious legal career (which involved him in several high-profile trials and culminated in his appointment as lord chancellor of Ireland). That the older Phipps should have been able to maintain far distant family contacts, at a time when the only option would have been to do so by way of hand-written correspondence, suggests the barely literate William had help with his paperwork. The most obvious source was his wife Mary who seems to have been a full partner in every aspect of their life together.

11.2. *The Deadliest Atlantic Tropical Cyclones, 1492–1996*, National Hurricane and Central Pacific Hurricane Center, www.nhc.noaa.gov/pastdeadlyapp2.shtml.

11.3 1641 was a bad year for the Spanish economy. The treasure carried by the *Concepcion* was lost and so was another massive treasure: the pay for Spain's 30,000 Flanders-based army. This fortune in gold and silver slipped beneath the waves when the ship tasked with carrying it to Antwerp sank in deep water somewhere off Land's End, Cornwall. Returning from the West Indies, Captain John Limbrey had taken his leaky ship, the *Merchant Royal,* into Cadiz in south-west Spain. While his ship was being patched up, a Spanish vessel contracted to ferry the wage money to Antwerp had gone up in flames. Limbrey stepped in. He had a substantial, well-armed ship and a consort vessel, the *Dover Merchant*, for support. But none of this was any help when, in September, his still-leaking ship was caught in a storm. Some eighteen sailors drowned although Limbrey and most of his crew made it to the *Dover Merchant*. The money was lost.

11.4 Earle, Peter, *The Treasure of the Concepcion* (where the story of the *Concepcion* and its sinking is told in some detail), Viking Press, New York, 1979.

11.5 The National Authority for Maritime Affairs of the Dominican Republic, https://dominicantoday.com/dr/north-coast/2022/06/22/state-of-concern-dominican-north-coast-reefs/. The area which now includes the Dominican Republic's Banco de la Plata and Navidad Marine Mammal Sanctuary, is described by the country's National Authority for Maritime Affairs as 'an open water reef complex'. The sanctuary is located sixty-five nautical miles north of the Dominican Republic from the nearest point of land and averages thirty-five nautical miles in width and thirty in length, an area of over 1,000 square miles.

11.6 *Admiralty papers*, National Archives, ADM 106/367/184.

11.7 Hacke, William, *A Collection of Original Voyages (1699)*, reprint published by John Carter Brown Library, New York, 1993, pp.13–14.

11.8 Narborough certainly had no love for the Spanish. In 1670 he had led his own 'secret' expedition to the south seas. Charged with establishing trading links with towns along the Chilean coast, he reached as far as Valdivia before having to admit that there was no hope of success given the intransigence of local officials. But Narborough scored a navigational success. Rather than round Cape Horn to reach the south seas, he had found his way through the treacherous Magellan Straights, publishing his charts of the area in 1673.

11.9 *Admiralty records*, National Archives, ADM 106/367/184.

11.10 Three Decks, British sloop 'Bonetta' (1673), https://threedecks.org/index.php?display_type=show_ship&id=3361.

Chapter 12: A Rose by Any Other Name

12.1 Mather, Cotton. *Magnalia Christi Americana*, Vol 1 (of 2), 1702, pp. 118–119.

12.2 *Calendar of State Papers, Colonial, America and West Indies: Vol 12 1685–1688* and *Addenda 1653–1687*, ed. J. W. Fortescue, London, 1899, pp. 71–86.

12.3 Royal Collection Trust, www.rct.uk/collection/405178/the-action-of-the-kingfisher-with-seven-algerine-ships-1-june-1681.

12.4 https://english.elpais.com/elpais/2019/03/01/inenglish/1551436896_082581.html.

12.5 Hall, M. G., *Edward Randolph and the American Colonies 1676–1703*, W. W. Norton, 1969, pp.79–99. Cranfield was something of a disaster as a governor. His opportunities to enrich himself from his appointment were disappointingly small and he soon fell out with almost everybody: with Randolph, with Mason, with the settlers and with his own council, which he dissolved. His attempts to raise taxes resulted in a short-lived rebellion led, at the start of 1683, by former council member Edward Gove, whom the vindictive Cranfield had had carted off to England for execution. Cranfield was replaced in 1685 and Gove was subsequently pardoned.

12.6 Randolph, E, *Edward Randolph: Including his letters and official papers from New England, middle, and southern colonies in America, with other documents relating chiefly to the vacating of the royal charter of the colony of Massachusetts Bay, 1676–1703*, Prince Society, Boston, 1858.

12.7 *Records of the governor and company of the Massachusetts bay in New England, 7 November 1683*, W. White, printer Boston, 1853. Accessed via www.sec.state.ma.us/arc/arcdigitalrecords/mbcolony.htm.

12.8 *Records of the governor and company of the Massachusetts bay in New England*, 5 December 1683, W. White, printer Boston, 1853. Accessed via www.sec.state.ma.us/arc/arcdigitalrecords/mbcolony.htm.

12.9 Karraker Cyrus H., *The Hispaniola Treasure*, University of Pennsylvania Press, 1934, pp. 26–43.

12.10 'America and West Indies: February 1684' in *Calendar of State Papers Colonial, America and West Indies: Vol 11, 1681-1685*, ed. J. W. Fortescue, London, 1898, pp. 581-601.

12.11 'America and West Indies: February 1684' in *Calendar of State Papers Colonial, America and West Indies: Vol 11, 1681–1685*, ed. J. W. Fortescue, London, 1898, pp. 645–664.

Chapter 13: Laying the Groundwork

13.1 'America and West Indies: September 1683, 1–15' in *Calendar of State Papers Colonial, America and West Indies: Vol 11, 1681–1685*, ed. J. W. Fortescue, London, 1898, pp. 486–495.

13.2 Sir Henry Morgan was a famed buccaneer, the leader of the Brethren of the Coast who twelve years previously had sacked Panama, bringing home riches for the crown and wealth to the island. Rewarded with a knighthood and deputy-governorship of Jamaica he had by 1683, when in his late forties, become something of a besotted embarrassment to Lynch.

13.3 'America and West Indies: November 1680' in *Calendar of State Papers Colonial, America and West Indies: Vol 10, 1677–1680*, eds. W. Noel Sainsbury & J. W. Fortescue, London, 1896, pp. 623–635.

13.4 'America and West Indies: November 1683, 2–15' in *Calendar of State Papers Colonial, America and West Indies: Vol 11, 1681–1685*, ed. J. W. Fortescue, London, 1898, pp. 532–545.

13.5 'America and West Indies: November 1683, 2–15' in *Calendar of State Papers Colonial, America and West Indies: Vol 11, 1681–1685*, ed. J. W. Fortescue, London, 1898, pp. 532–545.

13.6 'America and West Indies: November 1684, 17–30' in *Calendar of State Papers Colonial, America and West Indies: Vol 11, 1681–1685*, ed. J. W. Fortescue, London, 1898, pp. 726–740.

13.7 'America and West Indies: February 1685' in *Calendar of State Papers Colonial, America and West Indies: Vol 12 1685–1688 and Addenda 1653–1687*, ed. J. W. Fortescue London, 1899, pp. 1–8.

13.8 'America and West Indies: September 1684' in *Calendar of State Papers Colonial, America and West Indies: Vol 11, 1681–1685*, ed. J. W. Fortescue, London, 1898, pp. 682–694.

13.9 'America and West Indies: September 1684' in *Calendar of State Papers Colonial, America and West Indies: Vol 11, 1681–1685*, ed. J. W. Fortescue, London, 1898, pp. 682–694.

13.10 'America and West Indies: July 1685' in *Calendar of State Papers Colonial, America and West Indies: Vol 12 1685–1688 and Addenda 1653–1687*, ed. J. W. Fortescue, London, 1899, pp. 61–71.

13.11 'America and West Indies: February 1685' in *Calendar of State Papers Colonial, America and West Indies: Vol 11, 1681–1685*, ed. J. W. Fortescue, London, 1898, pp. 765–769.

13.12 'America and West Indies: May 1685' in *Calendar of State Papers Colonial, America and West Indies: Vol 12 1685–1688 and Addenda 1653–1687*, ed. J. W. Fortescue, London, 1899, pp. 38–47.

13.13 'America and West Indies: June 1685' in *Calendar of State Papers Colonial, America and West Indies: Vol 12 1685–1688 and Addenda 1653–1687*, ed. J. W. Fortescue, London, 1899, pp. 47–61.

13.14 'America and West Indies: December 1685' in *Calendar of State Papers Colonial, America and West Indies: Vol 12 1685–1688 and Addenda 1653–1687*, ed. J. W. Fortescue London, 1899, pp. 123–135.

13.15 'America and West Indies: January 1686, in *Calendar of State Papers Colonial, America and West Indies: Vol 12 1685–1688 and Addenda 1653–1687*, ed. J. W. Fortescue, London, 1899, pp. 135–147.

13.16 Earle Peter, *The Treasure of the Concepcion*, Viking Press, New York, 1980.

13.17 'America and West Indies: June 1685' in *Calendar of State Papers Colonial, America and West Indies: Vol 12 1685–1688 and Addenda 1653–1687*, ed. J. W. Fortescue London, 1899, pp. 47–61.

13.18 'America and West Indies: October 1685' in *Calendar of State Papers Colonial, America and West Indies: Vol 12 1685–1688 and Addenda 1653–1687*, ed. J. W. Fortescue, London, 1899, pp. 99–114. Bysshe, a lawyer, had arrived in Bermuda with Cony but was soon advocating Bermudians establish a 'free government'. *In the Eye of All Trade: Bermuda, Bermudians, and the Maritime Atlantic World, 1680–1783* reports that having been sent back to England with Phipps, Bysshe and the like-minded Sarah Oxford spent time in the Tower of London before being released without trial. (Jarvis, Michael J., *In the Eye of All Trade: Bermuda, Bermudians, and the Maritime Atlantic World, 1680–1783,* Omohundro Institute of Early American History … and the University of North Carolina Press, p. 497). Colonel Richard Cony (or Coney) was the last governor under Bermuda's private charter, which expired in 1683, and the first crown-appointed governor under its new charter. He remained governor until 1687.

Chapter 14: Albemarle Steps In

14.1 'America and West Indies: August 1685' in *Calendar of State Papers Colonial, America and West Indies: Vol 12 1685–1688 and Addenda 1653–1687*, ed. J. W. Fortescue, London, 1899, pp. 71–86.

14.2 'America and West Indies: June 1685' in *Calendar of State Papers Colonial, America and West Indies: Vol 12 1685–1688 and Addenda 1653–1687*, ed. J. W. Fortescue, London, 1899, pp. 47–61.

14.3 Mather, Cotton, *Cotton Mather: Magnalia Christi Americana*, Vol 1 (of 2), 1702, p. 119–120.

14.4 Hopkins, Leon, *The Pirate who Stole Scotland*, Pen & Sword 2023.
14.5 George, Robert H., *The Treasure Trove of William Phips*, *The New England Quarterly* 6, No. 2, 1933 pp. 294–318, https://doi.org/10.2307/359127.
14.6 'Entry Book: January 1686,15–31' in *Calendar of Treasury Books, Vol 8, 1685–1689*, ed. William A. Shaw, London, 1923, pp. 525–546.
14.7 'Entry Book: March 1686, 21–31' in *Calendar of Treasury Books, Vol 8, 1685–1689*, ed. William A. Shaw, London, 1923, pp. 664–684.
14.8 'Entry Book: November 1686, 21–25' in *Calendar of Treasury Books, Vol 8, 1685–1689*, ed. William A. Shaw, London, 1923, pp. 1014–1031.
14.9 Karraker, Cyrus H., *The Hispaniola Treasure*, University of Pennsylvania Press, 1934.
14.10 George, Robert H., *The Treasure Trove of William Phips*, *The New England Quarterly* 6, No. 2, 1933 pp. 294–318. The start of the disastrous reign of James II was its highpoint. Despite being Roman Catholic and therefore in theory disbarred from many offices, James' promises of tolerance and understanding to followers of all Christian religions (soon broken) meant he was accepted with little dissent other than that of his nephew, James Scott, Duke of Monmouth. Scott was the eldest of Charles II's army of illegitimate offsprings. His justification for opposing his uncle's right to the throne was his claim that Charles had secretly married his mother, Lucy Walter (or Barlow). Therefore he, Monmouth, should be declared the rightful king. Lucy Walter, or Barlow, or Stuart, was long dead, so couldn't comment. Monmouth had only recently been implicated in an alleged 1683 plot to kill his father (the 'Rye House Plot') and had found it convenient to decamp to Holland, his birthplace. But now he was on his way back, confident malcontents would flock to his side. As it turned out he had badly misjudged the situation. At this stage relatively few people were that unhappy with James and in under a month Monmouth's rag-tag band had been routed at the Battle of Sedgemoor and the would-be king had met his gory and botched end. The battle was a mismatch between professional soldiers and a larger force of 'pitchfork volunteers'. Of the latter, a third were killed or wounded on the battlefield and most of the rest were captured. Judge Jeffrey's 'Bloody Assizes', which followed, found over 400 of the prisoners deserving of a death sentence and just short of 900 of transporting to America or the West Indies. Among the beneficiaries was Sir Richard White to whom the king gifted seventy convicts as indentured servants.
14.11 Mather, Cotton, *Magnalia Christi Americana*, Vol 1 (of 2) pp, 1702, 119–120.

14.12 Ward, Estelle Frances, *Christopher Monck Duke of Albemarle*, Book 1, chapters 2 and 3, John Murray, London, 1915.
14.13 *History of Parliament,* www.historyofparliamentonline.org/volume/1660-1690/member/howard-philip-1631-86.
14.14 Ward, Estelle Frances, *Christopher Monck Duke of Albemarle*, Book 6, chapter 11, John Murray, London, 1915.

Chapter 15: A Company is Formed

15.1 Ward, Estelle Frances, *Christopher Monck, Duke of Albemarle*, p. 275, John Murray, London, 1915.
15.2 Anderson Adam, *An Historical and Chronological Deduction of the Origin of Commerce from the Earliest Accounts to the Present Time*, originally two volumes, London, 1764. Accessed via the Internet Archive, https://archive.org/details/historicalchrono01ande.
15.3 Carr, Cecil T., *Select charters of trading companies, A.D. 1530–1707*, Bernard Quaritch, London, 1913.

Chapter 16: What Phipps Did Best

16.1 Dyer, Florence E., *The Life of Admiral Sir John Narbrough*, Philip Allan, London, 1931.
16.2 Karraker, Cyrus H, *The Hispaniola Treasure*, University of Pennsylvania Press, 1934.
16.3 Earle, Peter, *The Treasure of the Concepcion*, Viking Press, New York, 1980.
16.4 London Metropolitan Archives, Harben Bequest, HB/C/077.
16.5 *Lester v Foxcroft*, National Archives, C 10/250/51 1998.
16.6 *A Calendar of Inner Temple Records*, F. A. Inderwick ed., Published by order of the Masters of the Bench, London, 1896.
16.7 *Lester v Foxcroft*, Parliamentary Archives, Reference: HL/PO/JO/10/6/12/1603.
16.8 Ward, Estelle Frances, *Christopher Monck Duke of Albemarle*, John Murray, London, 1915.
16.9 Ward, Estelle Frances, *Christopher Monck Duke of Albemarle*, John Murray, London, 1915.
16.10 Mather, Cotton. *Magnalia Christi Americana*, Vol 1 (of 2), 1702, p. 120.
16.11 Karraker, Cyrus H., *The Hispaniola Treasure*, University of Pennsylvania Press, 1934.
16.12 Dampier, William, *A New Voyage Round the World,* p. 50, Penguin Books Ltd. In his book, Dampier wrote about a pirate visit to Riohacha

(he called it 'Rio La Hacha'): 'The Pearl-banks lye about 4 or 5 leagues off from the shore, as I have been told; thither the Fishing-Barks go and anchor; then the Divers go down to the bottom, and fill a Basket (which is let down before) with Oysters; and when they come up, others go down, two at a time; this they do till the Bark is full.' The pirates later 'took some of the Indians', presumably as slaves.

16.13 Jarvis, Michael J., *In the Eye of All Trade: Bermuda, Bermudians, and the Maritime Atlantic World, 1680–1783,* p. 81, Omohundro Institute of Early American History and the University of North Carolina Press.

16.14 *Winthrop's Journal, History of New England 1630–1649*, ed. James Kendall Hosmer, Vol 2, p. 67, Charles Scribner's Sons, New York, 1908,

16.15 Pritchard, R. E., *Captain John Smith and his Brave Adventures*, Haus Books, London, 2008.

16.16 *An Exact and perfect relation of the arrival of the ship the James and Mary, Captain Phipps commander with 200000 lb in gold and silver taken up in nine fathom water from the bottom of the sea*, reproduction of original in the Huntington Library. Accessed via the University of Michigan Library, https://quod.lib.umich.edu/e/eebo2/A38885.0001.001/1:1?rgn=div1;view=fulltext.

16.17 Bank of England inflation calculator, www.bankofengland.co.uk/monetary-policy/inflation/inflation-calculator.

16.18 *Calendar of State Papers, America and West Indies: Vol 12 1685–1688* and *Addenda 1653–1687*, ed. J. W. Fortescue, London, 1899, pp. 71–86.

16.19 Jarvis, Michael J.. *In the Eye of All Trade: Bermuda, Bermudians, and the Maritime Atlantic World, 1680–1783*, pp. 81–82, Omohundro Institute of Early American History and the University of North Carolina Press.

Chapter 17: The Aftermath

17.1 *Smith v Duke of Albemarle*, National Archives, C 10/227/63, 1687.

17.2 *Acts of the Privy Council (Colonial), Charles II, vol 16, 1 June 1680–31 May 1683.* Accessed from Ames Foundation, https://amesfoundation.law.harvard.edu/ColonialAppeals/images/APC2_all/APC2_1_918.pdf.

17.3 *Calendar of Treasury Books, Vol 8, 1685–1689*, ed. William A. Shaw, London, 1923, pp. 1414–1436.

17.4 Three Decks, https://threedecks.org/index.php?display_type=show_nation&id=1.

17.5 Karraker, Cyrus H., *The Hispaniola Treasure*, University of Pennsylvania Press, 1934, p58.

17.6 Quoted by Dyer, Florence E., *The Life of Admiral Sir John Narbrough*, Philip Allan, 1931, p. 223.

17.7 Dyer, Florence E., *The Life of Admiral Sir John Narbrough*, Philip Allan, 1931, p. 225.

17.8 Dyer, Florence E., *The Life of Admiral Sir John Narbrough*, Philip Allan, 1931, p. 227.

17.9 'Entry Book: August 1688, 16-31' in *Calendar of Treasury Books, Vol 8, 1685–1689*, pp. 2041–2059, ed. William A. Shaw, London, 1923.

17.10 *Diary of Samuel Sewall. 1674–1729, Vol 1.* Accessed via Massachusetts Historical Society, https://archive.org/details/diaryofsamuelsew01sewaiala.

Chapter 18: Andros Displaced

18.1 Whitmore, William Henry, *A Memoir of Sir Edmund Andros, Knt, Governor of New England, New York and Virginia, &c., &c*, reprinted from the Andros Tracts, published by the Prince Society of Boston, Boston, 1868. DigiCat version.

18.2 *Massachusetts: The Revolution of 1689 and the Charter*, Colonial Society of Massachusetts, hrrps://www.colonialsociety.org/node/1784.

18.3 *Calendar of State Papers Colonial, America and West Indies: Vol 17, 1699 and Addenda 1621–1698,* addenda July 1688, p. 605, ed. Cecil Headlam, London, 1908.

18.4 *Index to Original Subscribers*, Bank of England, chrome-extension://efaidnbmnnnibpcajpcglclefindmkaj/www.bankofengland.co.uk/-/media/boe/files/archive/original-bank-subscribers/1694.pdf. The Ashursts had a nice line in looking after the New England Company's financial interests and acting as London bankers of convenience for a number of Boston merchants. While Sir Henry was something of a 'projector', proposing ideas for exploiting New England's natural resources, Sir William was more interested in City investment opportunities. As a member of the Merchant Taylors' livery company he was acquainted with fellow member William Paterson, who came up with a plan for creating a Bank of England. Ashurst was one of the founder investors in the Bank, investing £3,000. He was also a director.

18.5 Evelyn, J., *Diary and Correspondence of John Evelyn*, ed. William Bray, Vol 3, p. 49, Bickers & Son, London, 1906.

18.6 *Glorious Revolution 1688*, National Archives, www.nationalarchives.gov.uk/education/resources/significant-events/glorious-revolution-1688/.

The invitation to William of Orange to come to England and save the day was signed on their own authority by seven lords, one a bishop (the 'Immortal Seven'). They told William that 'the people are so generally dissatisfied with the present conduct of the Government in relation to their religion, liberties, and properties (all which have been greatly invaded), and they are in such expectation of their prospects being daily worse that your Highness may be assured there are nineteen parts of twenty of the people throughout the Kingdom who are desirous of a change'. It was the sort of thing that might have been written by Mather concerning New England.

18.7 Mather, I., *A narrative of the miseries of New-England, by reason of an arbitrary government erected there. Under Sir Edmond Andross*, Text Creation Partnership, Evans Early America, https://quod.lib.umich.edu/cgi/t/text/text-idx?cc=evans;c=evans;idno=N00368.0001.001;view=text;rgn=div1;node=N00368.0001.001:2.

18.8 'America and West Indies: February 1689' in *Calendar of State Papers Colonial, America and West Indies: Vol 13, 1689–1692*, ed. J. W. Fortescue, London, 1901, pp. 4–11.

18.9 Palfrey, J. G., *The Atlantic*, May 1864 edition, www.theatlantic.com/magazine/archive/1864/05/the-new-england-revolution-of-the-seventeenth-century/628204/. Palfrey had no sympathy for Dudley. He wrote that the chief justice had been away when the rebellion happened and had attempted to hide in the home of a Major Smith. 'But a party got upon his track, and took him to his home at Roxbury. "To secure him against violence", as the order expresses it, a guard was placed about his house.' Dudley's previous host, Smith, was lodged in gaol at Bristol. 'Among the oppressors, he [Dudley] it was whom the people found hardest to forgive. If Andros, Randolph, West, and others, were tyrants and extortioners, at all events they were strangers; they had not been preying on their own kinsmen. But this man was son of a brave old emigrant Governor; he had been bred by the bounty of Harvard College; he had been welcomed at the earliest hour to the offices of the Commonwealth, and promoted in them with a promptness out of proportion to the claims of his years. Confided in, enriched, caressed, from youth to middle life by his native Colony beyond any other man of his time, he had been pampered into a power which, as soon as the opportunity was presented, he used for the grievous humiliation and distress of his generous friends. That he had not brought them to utter ruin seemed to have been owing to no want of resolute purpose on his part to advance himself as the congenial instrument of a despot.'

18.10 Whitmore, William Henry, *A Memoir of Sir Edmund Andros, Knt, Governor of New England, New York and Virginia, &c., &c.* Andros was eventually sent back to England. Charges were brought but nobody cared to testify against him. In 1692 he was appointed governor of Virginia. 'That his government was distasteful to the citizens of Massachusetts is undeniable, but no man sent here to perform the same duty would have been acceptable,' claimed his biographer, William Whitmore. 'We may class Andros rather among those statesmen, unwelcome but necessary, whose very virtues and abilities are detested in their lifetime, because they do so thoroughly their appointed work and initiate new periods in national history.'

Chapter 19: Phipps Sees the Light

19.1 Palfrey, J. G., *The Atlantic*, May 1864. www.theatlantic.com/magazine/archive/1864/05/the-new-england-revolution-of-the-seventeenth-century/628204/, and *The Glorious Revolution in Massachusetts*, Colonial Society of Massachusetts, *Massachusetts: The Revolution of 1689 and the Charter*, pp. 1–4, www.colonialsociety.org/node/1784.

19.2 Church, Thomas, *Benjamin Church, History of Philip's War, Commonly Called the Great Indian War of 1675 and 1676: Also, of the French and Indian Wars at the Eastward, in 1689, 1690, 1692, 1696, and 1704*, Thomas B. Waite & Son, Boston, 1827. In 1676 Major Richard Waldron persuaded Indians congregated at his trading post to take part in a sham training exercise. This gave the opportunity to Massachusetts units, commanded by captains Syll and Hawthorne, to kill or capture in the order of 400 Indians. 'Those that were not found to have been in the former war were dismissed, and the rest were sent to Boston. About 8 or 10 were hanged as murderers, and the rest sold into slavery,' according to a report of the event. Thirteen years later (in late June 1689), the Indians repaid the compliment. A Native American woman who had asked to lodge in Waldron's garrison, feigned illness during the night before opening the outer doors. 'The enemy rushed in with great fury. They found the major's room as he leaped out of bed, but with his sword he drove them through two or three rooms, and as he turned to get some other arms, he fell stunned by a blow with the hatchet. They dragged him into his hall and seated him on a table in a great chair, and then began to cut his flesh in a shocking manner. Some in turns slashed his naked breast.' The 80-year-old's nose and ears were then cut off and forced into his mouth. At the last Waldron was run through with his own sword.

19.3 Davies, S. J., *Estimated population of American Colonies: 610 to 1780*, Vancouver Island University, https://web.viu.ca/davies/H320/population.colonies.htm.

19.4 Church, Thomas, *Benjamin Church, History of Philip's War, Commonly Called the Great Indian War of 1675 and 1676: Also, of the French and Indian Wars at the Eastward, in 1689, 1690, 1692, 1696, and 1704*, Thomas B. Waite & Son, Boston, 1827.

19.5 Sewall S., *Diary of Samuel Sewall 1674–1729, Vol 1 1674–1700*, Boston, Massachusetts Historical Society, https://archive.org/details/diaryofsamuelsew01sewaiala.

19.6 Mather, Cotton, *Cotton Mather: Magnalia Christi Americana,* 1702, Vol 1 (of 2) p. 127.

19.7 'America and West Indies: May 1690, 19–31' in *Calendar of State Papers Colonial, America and West Indies: Volume 13, 1689–1692*, ed. J. W. Fortescue, London, 1901, pp. 263–276. In May 1690 the journal of Benjamin Bullivant concerning affairs New England was presented to the Lords of Trade. Bullivant, a doctor, had moved to Boston in about 1685, becoming the first church warden of King's Chapel. He was soon appointed attorney general under the Andros regime and was one of those arrested and imprisoned following the 1689 Boston revolt. 'The Council and deputies are debating a descent on Port Royal,' Bullivant wrote. 'Mr. Nelson laid his plans before them, and it was thought that he would be Generalissimo, but the deputies said he was a merchant and not to be trusted, so Sir William Phips is appointed. Nelson refused with scorn to serve under him. Drums beat for recruits; some few enlist and then change their minds and desert; and no one dares to question them' … 'April 3. General Phip's men mustered at the town-house, mostly without arms. About eighty in a body deserted with huzzas on being told that they must find their own arms. One of the officers appointed by Phips was hooted by his company, which had chosen another captain' … 'April 28. Sir W. Phips sailed for Port Royal.'

19.8 Sewall, Samuel, *Diary of Samuel Sewall. 1674–1729,* Vol 1 (of 3), Massachusetts Historical Society, https://archive.org/details/diaryofsamuelsew01sewaiala.

19.9 Natsto, Joshua, *A Journal of the Proceedings in the late Expedition to Port-Royal, On board Their Majesties Ship, the Six-Friends, The Honourable Sr William Phipps Knight, Commander in Chief,* Boston 1690. Accessed via the Text Creation Partnership, https://quod.lib.umich.edu/cgi/t/text/text-idx?c=evans;idno=N00414.0001.001.

19.10 John Nelson was the Boston merchant who had hoped to lead the raid on Port Royal himself. His resentment at being passed over, and the loss of an opportunity to see that his trading interests in Port Royal, including his 'storehouse', were protected, were at the root of his later troublemaking for Phipps.

19.11 Baker, Emerson W. & Reid, John G., *The New England Knight*, p. 149, University of Toronto Press, 1998.

19.12 Massachusetts, Governor (1689–1692: Bradstreet), Bradstreet, Simon, 1603–1697, Massachusetts. Council, 1689, Text Creation Partnership, https://quod.lib.umich.edu/e/eebo2/B09481.0001.001?rgn=main;view=toc.

19.13 *Governor Bradstreet and Council* (at a session of the General Court of the Massachusetts Colony, in Boston, 28 of May, 1690, Anno Regni Regis & Reginæ Gulielmi & Mariæ secondo, (whereas the Honourable Sir William Phipps knight is appointed to take the command of such forces as shall be raised for Their Majesties service in the present expedition against the French at Nova Scotia, and L'Accadie), printed by Samuel Green, 1689. Access via University of Michigan Library, www.lib.umich.edu/.

Chapter 20: Disaster Breeds Success

20.1 Several Phipps' escapades were affected by smallpox but the farm lad who no doubt sometimes milked the family cow, seems to have been immune to the disease.

20.2 Roach, Marilynne, *The Salem Witch Trials: A Day-by-Day Chronicle of a Community Under Siege*, Taylor Trade Publishing, p. 892.

20.3 Mather, Cotton, *Cotton Mather: Magnalia Christi Americana*, Vol 1 (of 2) 1702, p. 131. For a more detailed description of the assault, see Baker, Emerson W. & Reid, John G., *The New England Knight*, pp. 86–109, *The Expeditions of 1690*, University of Toronto Press, 1998.

20.4 Mather, Cotton, *Cotton Mather: Magnalia Christi Americana*, Vol 1 (of 2), 1702, p. 133.

20.5 Mather, Cotton, *Cotton Mather: Magnalia Christi Americana*, Vol 1 (of 2), 1702, p. 132.

20.6 Mather, Cotton, *Cotton Mather: Magnalia Christi Americana*, Vol 1 (of 2), 1702, pp. 132–133. The scheme described is very similar to that concerning the Bank of England, devised by William Paterson and others in England as a means of financing the country's war efforts. Just as in Massachusetts, there was an early crisis of confidence in

Bank of England bills, which were initially heavily discounted. There were two main differences between the Massachusetts scheme and that adopted in England. These were that the Bank of England was a private company owned and financed by shareholders and that it was never intended that the loan to the government should be redeemed. The Bank of England lent the money it raised from shareholders to the government at a guaranteed rate of interest. The Bank then issued bills, effectively paper money, that were secured on its government-guaranteed loan interest. As termed by Paterson, it had created a 'perpetual fund of credit'; a national debt that has continued to rise ever since.

20.7 Baker, Emerson W. & Reid, John G., *The New England Knight*, University of Toronto Press, 1998. Authors Emerson Baker and John Reid suggest that an added motive for Phipps taking off for London was a wish to appear there before the defeated commander of Port Royal. De Menneval proved more persistent in pursuing Phipps for return of his personal money and belongings than he had in defending Port Royal. He had been given permission to leave Boston, something Phipps was able to delay temporarily by having the proud Frenchman arrested for breaching his surrender agreement. Phipps clearly wanted to get his defence in early. He was also still being pursued by Robert Bronson for money he said was due him in respect of the loan of a servant to the *Golden Rose*. When his claim came to court, Bronson had an initial success but lost on appeal.

20.8 *Acts of the Privy Council (Colonial)*, James II, 30 July 1687. Accessed via LLMC Digital.

20.9 *Dictionary of Falkland Biography*, www.falklandsbiographies.org/biographies/falkland_anthony.

20.10 Hopkins, Leon, *The Pirate Who Stole Scotland*, Pen & Sword Books, England, 2023.

20.11 *Acts of the Privy Council (Colonial), William III, Vol l,* 14 May 26 February 1689. Accessed via LLMC Digital.

20.12 *Acts of the Privy Council (Colonial)*, William III, *Vol 2,* 14 May 1691. Accessed via LLMC Digital.

20.13 'America and West Indies: November 1691' in *Calendar of State Papers Colonial, America and West Indies: Vol 13, 1689–1692*, ed. J. W. Fortescue, London, 1901, pp. 563–572.

20.14 'America and West Indies: September 1691, 1–15' *in Calendar of State Papers Colonial, America and West Indies: Vol 13, 1689–1692*, ed. J. W. Fortescue, London, 1901, pp. 527–542.

20.15 *The acts and resolves, public and private, of the Province of the Massachusetts Bay,* Massachusetts Archives ((M-Ar)A001-A092), item A027, v. 1.

20.16 'America and West Indies: September 1691, 16–30' in *Calendar of State Papers Colonial, America and West Indies: Vol 13, 1689–1692*, ed. J. W. Fortescue, London, 1901, pp. 542–549.

20.17 The whole passed under the Great Seal 12 Dec., 1691, 14 pp, Board of Trade. New England, 5. No. 207; and *Col. Entry Bk., Vol. LXII*, pp. 353–364.

20.18 Three Decks, https://threedecks.org/index.php.

20.19 'America and West Indies: April 1693, 18–30' in *Calendar of State Papers Colonial, America and West Indies: Vol 14, 1693–1696*, ed. J. W. Fortescue, London, 1903, pp. 86–95. Short's submission was described by Fortescue as 'a rambling restatement, extremely ill-spelt, of the principal grounds of his complaint'.

20.20 *On the report of the Customs on the petition of Henry Rycroft and Matthew Ryder (masters of the* Jeremy *and the* Thamer*)*, 11 Feb, 1692, in *Acts of the Privy Council (Colonial) Charles II, Vol 16, l June, 1680–31 May, 1683.* Accessed via LLMC Digital.

Chapter 21: Short Shrift

21.1 'America and West Indies: June 1692' in *Calendar of State Papers Colonial, America and West Indies: Vol 13, 1689–1692*, ed. J. W. Fortescue, London, 1901, pp. 644–663.

21.2 'America and West Indies: July 1692' in *Calendar of State Papers Colonial, America and West Indies: Vol 13, 1689–1692*, ed. J. W. Fortescue, London, 1901, pp. 663–679.

21.3 Church, Thomas, *Benjamin Church. The History of Philip's War: Commonly Called the Great Indian War, of 1675 and 1676. Also, of the French and Indian Wars at the Eastward, in 1689, 1690, 1692, 1696, and 1704,* J. & B. Williams.

21.4 'America and West Indies: February 1693, 2–15' in *Calendar of State Papers Colonial, America and West Indies: Vol 14, 1693–1696*, ed. J. W. Fortescue, London, 1903, pp. 13–26.

21.5 'America and West Indies: February 1693, 2–15' in *Calendar of State Papers Colonial, America and West Indies: Vol 14, 1693–1696*, ed. J. W. Fortescue, London, 1903, pp. 13–26.

21.6 'America and West Indies: February 1693, 16–28' in *Calendar of State Papers Colonial, America and West Indies: Vol 14, 1693–1696*, ed. J. W. Fortescue (London, 1903), pp. 26–36.

21.7 'America and West Indies: February 1693, 2–15' in *Calendar of State Papers Colonial, America and West Indies: Vol 14, 1693–1696*, ed. J. W. Fortescue, London, 1903, pp. 13–26.

21.8 'America and West Indies: April 1693, 1–15' in *Calendar of State Papers Colonial, America and West Indies: Vol 14, 1693–1696*, ed. J. W. Fortescue, London, 1903, pp. 70–86.

21.9 'America and West Indies: May 1693' in *Calendar of State Papers Colonial, America and West Indies: Vol 14, 1693–1696*, ed. J. W. Fortescue, London, 1903, pp. 95–111. In May 1693 Connecticut and Rhode Island refused to send the 200 men that Phipps had ordered them to march to New York's assistance. The same month Phipps' authority over the Connecticut militia was revoked and command returned to New York governor, Benjamin Fletcher. This was a seeming admission by the Lords of Trade that they had got things wrong in this respect.

21.10 Historical Society of New York Courts, https://history.nycourts.gov/figure/joseph-dudley/.

21.11 'America and West Indies: April 1693, 18–30' in *Calendar of State Papers Colonial, America and West Indies: Vol 14, 1693–1696*, ed. J. W. Fortescue London, 1903, pp. 86–95.

21.12 'America and West Indies: September 1694, 1–13' in *Calendar of State Papers Colonial, America and West Indies: Vol 14, 1693–1696*, ed. J. W. Fortescue, London, 1903, pp. 341–354.

21.13 'America and West Indies: September 1694, 1–13' in *Calendar of State Papers Colonial, America and West Indies: Vol 14, 1693–1696*, ed. J. W. Fortescue, London, 1903, pp. 341–354.

21.14 'America and West Indies: February 1693, 2–15' in *Calendar of State Papers Colonial, America and West Indies: Vol 14, 1693–1696*, ed. J. W. Fortescue, London, 1903, pp. 13–26.

21.15 Three Decks, https://threedecks.org/index.php?display_type=show_ship&id=5495In.

21.16 'America and West Indies: January 1693' in *Calendar of State Papers Colonial, America and West Indies: Vol 14, 1693–1696*, ed. J. W. Fortescue, London, 1903, pp. 1–13.

21.17 'America and West Indies: January 1694, 17–31' in *Calendar of State Papers Colonial, America and West Indies: Vo 14, 1693–1696*, ed. J. W. Fortescue, London, 1903, pp. 232–244.

Chapter 22: Double, Double Toil and Trouble

22.1 Roach, Marilynne, *The Salem Witch Trials: A Day-by-Day Chronicle of a Community Under Siege* Taylor, Trade Publishing p. 94.

22.2 Pope, Charles Henry, *The Pioneers of Maine and New Hampshire 1623 to 1660*, Charles H. Pope, Boston, 1908, pp. 42–43.

22.3 New England Historical Society, https://newenglandhistoricalsociety.com/cotton-mather-joseph-dudley-allies-enemies-1695/.

22.4 Mather, Cotton, *Memorable Providences, Relating to Witchcrafts And Possessions*, R. P., Boston, 1689. Accessed via the Text Creation Partnership. https://quod.lib.umich.edu/e/eebo/A50139.0001.001?rgn=main;view=fulltext.

22.5 Gaskill, Malcolm, *Witchfinders: A Seventeenth-century English Tragedy*, John Murray Press.

22.6 Gaskill, Malcolm. *Witchfinders: A Seventeenth-century English Tragedy,* John Murray Press, p. 323.

22.7 Roach, Marilynne, *The Salem Witch Trials: A Day-by-Day Chronicle of a Community Under Siege,* Taylor Trade Publishing, p. 518.

22.8 Roach, Marilynne, *The Salem Witch Trials: A Day-by-Day Chronicle of a Community Under Siege*, Taylor Trade Publishing, pp. 101–102.

22.9 Mather, Cotton, *A Midnight Cry, a discourse given on a day of prayer kept by the North Church in Boston*, Printed by John Allen, Samuel Phillips, 1692. Accessed via Text Creation Partnership.

22.10 Roach, Marilynne, *The Salem Witch Trials: A Day-by-Day Chronicle of a Community Under Siege*, Taylor Trade Publishing, p. 528.

22.11 Holmes, C., *The Opinion of the Cambridge Association, 1 August 1692: A Neglected Text of the Salem Witch Trials, The New England Quarterly*, 89(4), pp. 643–667 www.jstor.org/stable/26405817.

22.12 Mather, Increase, *Cases of conscience concerning evil spirits personating men, witchcrafts, infallible proofs of guilt in such as are accused with that crime,* Printed, and Sold by *Benjamin Harris* at the London Coffee-House, Boston, 1693. University of Michigan. Accessed via Text Creation Partnership.

22.13 'America and West Indies: October 1692' in *Calendar of State Papers Colonial, America and West Indies: Vol 13, 1689–1692*, ed. J. W. Fortescue, London, 1901, pp. 717–731.

22.14 'America and West Indies: January 1693' in *Calendar of State Papers Colonial, America and West Indies: Vol 14, 1693–1696*, ed. J. W. Fortescue, London, 1903, pp. 1–13.

22.15 'America and West Indies: February 1693, 16–28' in *Calendar of State Papers Colonial, America and West Indies: Vol 14, 1693–1696*, ed. J. W. Fortescue, London, 1903, pp. 26–36.

22.16 'America and West Indies: September 1693' in *Calendar of State Papers Colonial, America and West Indies: Vol 14, 1693–1696*, ed. J. W. Fortescue, London, 1903, pp. 154–167.

Chapter 23: London Calling

23.1 Preface in *Calendar of State Papers Colonial, America and West Indies: Vol 14, 1693–1696*, ed. J. W. Fortescue, London, 1903, pp. vii–xlvi.

23.2 '*America and West Indies: August 1693*' in *Calendar of State Papers Colonial, America and West Indies: Vol 14, 1693–1696*, ed. J. W. Fortescue London, 1903, pp. 136–154.

23.3 Jarvis, Michael J., *In the Eye of All Trade: Bermuda, Bermudians, and the Maritime Atlantic World, 1680-1783*, Omohundro Institute of Early American History and the University of North Carolina Press, p. 70. Governor Fletcher augmented his income by granting licences to 'privateers' involved in the Red Sea piratical round, Governor Andros required landowners to re-register their deeds for which he charged enhanced fees, Sir Nicholas Trott, governor of the Bahamas, sold free pardons to criminals, and Bermuda governor Sir Robert Robinson stole from the public treasury, sold several public slaves belonging to the Crown for his personal profit, and pocketed a considerable sum in royal duties on treasure salvaged from shipwrecks.

23.4 'America and West Indies: September 1693' in *Calendar of State Papers Colonial, America and West Indies: Vol 14, 1693–1696*, ed. J. W. Fortescue, London, 1903, pp. 154–167.

23.5 'America and West Indies: March 1692' in *Calendar of State Papers Colonial, America and West Indies: Vol 13, 1689–1692*, ed. J. W. Fortescue, London, 1901, pp. 605–616.

23.6 'America and West Indies: September 1695' in *Calendar of State Papers Colonial, America and West Indies: Vol 14, 1693–1696*, ed. J. W. Fortescue, London, 1903, pp. 583–593.

23.7 'America and West Indies: September 1693' in *Calendar of State Papers Colonial, America and West Indies: Vol 14, 1693–1696*, ed. J. W. Fortescue, London, 1903, pp. 154–167.

23.8 *Appeals to the Privy Council,* Report No 05-1692-00, Jahleel Brenton v George Lawson (In re *The Two Brothers*), Jahleel Brenton v Thomas Wilkinson (In re *The Three Brothers*), Jahleel Brenton, appeal of (In re *The Mary*). Accessed via James Foundation, Harvard University, https://amesfoundation.law.harvard.edu/ColonialAppeals/index_new.php?report_no=05_1692_00.

23.9 'America and West Indies: September 1693' in *Calendar of State Papers Colonial, America and West Indies: Vol 14, 1693-1696*, ed. J. W. Fortescue, London, 1903, pp. 154–167. The *Mary* in this instance was a brigantine and not the sloop of the same name that was with Phipps in Port Royal and later used by him to sail to and from Pemaquid and perhaps for some personal trading. But it may very well have been the barque *Mary* (barque at the time being a generic description for a small square-rigged vessel) which Phipps complained had been seized by Usher 'in Piscataqua River, for no cause known to the owner'. He told Usher that 'this fresh complaint, with former ones of the same nature, make me ask for what offence this vessel is detained. If you claim jurisdiction over both banks of the river I should be informed thereof, that the matter may be adjusted by the two Governments or by the King, for it is contrary to the royal instructions that there should be [no] hindrance to trade or misunderstandings between Governments'. Phipps was on thin ice making this threat since the barque *Mary* was almost certainly engaged in illicit trading, avoiding Navigation Act taxes and paperwork by unloading cargo on the banks of the Piscataqua River.

23.10 'America and West Indies: November 1693' in *Calendar of State Papers Colonial, America and West Indies: Vol 14, 1693–1696*, ed. J. W. Fortescue, London, 1903, pp. 201–215.

23.11 'America and West Indies: January 1694, 2–15' in *Calendar of State Papers Colonial, America and West Indies: Vol 14, 1693–1696*, ed. J. W. Fortescue, London, 1903, pp. 222–232.

23.12 'America and West Indies: February 1694' in *Calendar of State Papers Colonial, America and West Indies: Vol 14, 1693–1696*, ed. J. W. Fortescue, London, 1903, pp. 244–254.

23.13 'America and West Indies: January 1694, 2–15' in *Calendar of State Papers Colonial, America and West Indies: Vol 14, 1693–1696*, ed. J. W. Fortescue, London, 1903, pp. 222–232.

23.14 'America and West Indies: July 1694' in *Calendar of State Papers Colonial, America and West Indies: Vol 14, 1693–1696*, ed. J. W. Fortescue, London, 1903, pp. 301–315.

23.15 'America and West Indies: September 1694, 17–29' in *Calendar of State Papers Colonial, America and West Indies: Vol 14, 1693–1696*, ed. J. W. Fortescue, London, 1903.

23.16 'America and West Indies: November 1694, 1–15' in *Calendar of State Papers Colonial, America and West Indies: Vol 14, 1693–1696* ed. J. W. Fortescue, London, 1903, pp. 390–399.

23.17 'America and West Indies: November 1694, 1–15' in *Calendar of State Papers Colonial, America and West Indies, Vol 14, 1693–1696*, ed. J. W. Fortescue, London 1903, pp. 390–399.

23.18 'America and West Indies: November 1694, 1–15' in *Calendar of State Papers Colonial, America and West Indies, Vol 14, 1693–1696*, ed. J. W. Fortescue, London 1903, pp. 390–399.

23.19 'America and West Indies: October 1694, 16–31' in *Calendar of State Papers Colonial, America and West Indies: Vol 14, 1693–1696*, ed. J. W. Fortescue, London, 1903, pp. 377–390.

23.20 'America and West Indies: February 1695' in *Calendar of State Papers Colonial, America and West Indies: Vol 14, 1693–1696*, ed. J. W. Fortescue, London, 1903, pp. 429–434.

23.21 Mather, Cotton, *Cotton Mather: Magnalia Christi Americana*, Vol 1 (of 2), 1702, pp. 155–156.

Chapter 24: Curse of the *Concepcion*

24.1 Jarvis, Michael J, *In the Eye of All Trade: Bermuda, Bermudians, and the Maritime Atlantic World, 1680-1783*, Omohundro Institute of Early American History and the University of North Carolina Press, p. 8.

24.2 Ward, Estelle Frances, *Christopher Monck, Duke of Albemarle*, John Murray, London, 1915.

24.3 *The Duke of Albemarle's will*, The History of Parliament blog, ed. Paley, Ruth, https:// TheHistoryOfParliament.wordpress.com/2016/10/19/ The-Duke-of-Albemarles-Will/.

24.4 Baker, Emerson W. & Reid, John G., *The New England Knight*, University of Toronto Press, 1998, pp. 185 & 248–250. See also *Will of Sir William Phips of Boston County of Suffolk Province of Massachusetts Bay New England*, 29 January 1697, National Archives PROB 11/436/181.

24.5 Sewall, Samuel, *Diary of Samuel Sewall 1674–1729, Vol I 1674–1700*, Massachusetts Historical Society. Accessed via Internet Archive, https:// archive.org/details/diaryofsamuelsew01sewaiala.

24.6 Sewall, Samuel, *Diary of Samuel Sewall 1674–1729, Vol 1 1674–1700*, editors' note, Massachusetts Historical Society. Accessed via Internet Archive, https://archive.org/details/diaryofsamuelsew01sewaiala.

Chapter 25: Unintended consequences

25.1 *Statute of Monopolies 1623*, Acts of the English Parliament, 1623, www. legislation.gov.uk/aep/Ja1/21/3/introduction.

25.2 Woodcroft, Bennet, superintendent of specifications, indexes, & C, *Invention, From March 2, 1617 (14 James I), to October 1, 1852 (16 Victoria), Part 1 – (A to M)*, George Edward Eyre & William Spottiswoode, London, 1857.

25.3 Kitson, Frank, *Prince Rupert, Admiral and General-at-Sea*, Constable, London, 1998.

25.4 Anderson, Adam, *An historical and chronological deduction of the origin of commerce : from the earliest accounts to the present time*, A. Millar, J. & R. Tonson, London, 1764.

25.5 The difference between a 'public' and a 'private' company is that the number of shareholders in a private company is limited by law. Public companies are not to be confused with present day listed companies: those whose shares are traded on and listed by a recognised stock exchange. In the seventeenth century there was nothing to stop any joint-stock company advertising its shares for sale or accepting any number of shareholders.

25.6 Defoe, Daniel, *An Essay Upon Projects,* written in 1692 or 1693, but not published until 1697, p. 20.

25.7 Petram, Lodewijk, *The World's First Stock Exchange*, Columbia Business School Publishing, Columbia University Press.

Chapter 26: Not Without Honour

26.1 Macleod, Christine, *The 1690s Patents Boom: Invention or Stock-Jobbing? The Economic History Review*, vol. 39, no. 4, 1986, pp. 549–571. Accessed via *JSTOR.*

26.2–26.9 Woodcroft, Bennet, superintendent of specifications, indexes, & C, *Invention, From March 2, 1617 (14 James I), to October 1, 1852 (16 Victoria),* George Edward Eyre & William Spottiswoode, London 1857. Patent numbers listed by Woodcroft: 26.2 – 298; 26.3 – 271, 302, 331; 26.4 – 271; 26.5 – 306; 26.6 – 186, 270, 272, 273, 292; 26.7 – 308; 26.8 – 279; and 26.9 – 333.

26.10 Scott, William Robert, *The Constitution and Finance of English, Scottish and Irish Joint-Stock Companies to 1720*, Vol II, Cambridge University Press, 1912.

26.11 *Williams v Williams, plaintiff Joseph Williams, defendants: Daniel Foe and Thomas Williams,* National Archives, reference C 7/373/22, 1692. And see O'Brien, John, 'Union Jack: Amnesia and the Law' in *Daniel Defoe's 'Colonel Jack', Eighteenth-Century Studies*, vol. 32, no. 1, 1998, pp. 65–82. Accessed via *JSTOR.* Daniel Defoe apparently invested £200 in the company owning the diving engine invented by Joseph Williams, of which he managed to get himself appointed treasurer and secretary. In an early example of Defoe's crooked ways, he used company funds to pay off some of his own debts. He did this by getting his hands on promissory notes, endorsed by Joseph Williams and intended to be used for the benefit of the company. Defoe sold these to London goldsmith/

banker Thomas (yet another) Williams. But when the London Williams presented the notes to Cornish Williams for settlement, the Cornish Williams refused payment, saying he had been defrauded. London sued Cornwall and Cornwall sued London. Defoe was named in both cases, but Cornwall seems to have lost out on the grounds that he had effectively signed blank cheques, perhaps at Defoe's behest.

26.12 *Parties: Thomas Jett of London, citizen and merchant taylor, Sir Stephen Evance of …*, National Archives, reference E 214/1124, 30 June 1693.

26.13 Halley's Log, https://halleyslog.wordpress.com/.

26.14 *The Trial of Joseph Dawson, Edward Forseith, William May, Wm Bishop, James Lewis and John Sparkes, at the Old Bailey, for Felony and Piracy: 8 William III, AD 1696, Cobbett's Complete Collection of State Trials and Proceedings, 8 William III*, pp. 451–484. And see Hopkins, Leon, *The Pirate who Stole Scotland, Chapter16*, Pen & Sword History, 2023.

26.15 *Cochrane v Houblon*, 1696, National Archives ref C 8/357/93. See also *Humphrys v Houblon*, 1702 and 1703, National Archives ref C 8/593/62 and C 9/216/22.

26.16 Scott, William Robert, *The Constitution and Finance of English, Scottish and Irish Joint-Stock Companies to 1720*, Vol 1, Cambridge University Press, 1912, p. 327.

26.17 Scott, William Robert, *The Constitution and Finance of English, Scottish and Irish Joint-Stock Companies to 1720*, Vol II, Cambridge University Press, 1912, p. 489.

26.18 The Bank of England and the Million Lottery were both successful attempts to raise money for the government in its war effort. They had similarities. The Bank sold over £1 million worth of shares to the public which it lent to the government at a healthy rate of interest and no repayment date. On the security of its guaranteed income, it then issued its own bills, the first bank notes.

Like the Bank, initiated in 1694, the Million Lottery also raised in the order of £1 million. There were prizes but the essence of the scheme was that ticket holders received payment of £1 per ticket per year for 16 years. This meant the tickets themselves had a value and could be exchanged (as paper money). The projector William Paterson was much involved in formation of the Bank of England, while inventor and prolific projector Thomas Neale was behind the Million Lottery.

26.19 Defoe, Daniel. *An Essay Upon Projects*, p. 14.

Bibliography

Allison, Robert J., *A Short History of Boston*, Commonwealth Editions, 2004.

Andra-Warner, Elle, *Hudson's Bay Company Adventures: Tales of Canada's Fur Traders*, Heritage House, 2009.

Andrews, Charles McLean, *The Fathers of New England: A Chronicle of the Puritan Commonwealths*, Project Gutenberg, first published 1918.

Backscheider, Paula R., *Daniel Defoe: His Life*, John Hopkins University Press, 1989.

Bailyn, Bernard, *The New England Merchants in The Seventeenth Century*, Read Books Ltd, 1979.

Baker, Emerson W. & Reid, John G., *The New England Knight*, University of Toronto Press, 1998.

Ball, Robert Stawell, *Great Astronomers: Edmund Halley*, first published 1907, Feedbooks, 2017.

Banks, Charles Edward, *Topographical Dictionary of 2885 English Emigrants to New England 1620–1650*, Genealogical Publishing Co., 1976.

Besse, Joseph, *A Brief Account of Many of the Prosecutions of the People Call'd Quakers in the Exchequer, Ecclesiastical, and Other Courts, for Demands Recoverable by ... of Tithes, Church-rates, &c: Humbly*, first published by J. Sowle in 1736, HardPress, 2017.

Bryce, George, *The Remarkable History of the Hudson's Bay Company*, first published by Sampson Low, Marston & Co. in 1902, bz editors, 2013.

Buchan, John, *Oliver Cromwell*, first published by Houghton Mifflin Co. in 1934, Lume Books, 2018.

Campbell, Richard J. ed, *The Voyage of Captain John Narbrough to the Strait of Magellan and the South Sea in his Majesty's Ship* Sweepstakes, *1669–1671*, The Hakluyt Society, 2018.

Cawthorne, Nigel, *Witches: The History of a Persecution*, Arcturus Publishing, 2019.

Charles River Editors, *The Hudson's Bay Company: The History and Legacy of the Famous English Trading Company in Colonial America*, Charles River Editors, 2017.

Charles River Editors, *The Massachusetts Bay Colony: The History and Legacy of the Settlement of Colonial New England*, Charles River Editors, 2015.

Charnock, John, *Impartial memoirs of the lives and characters of officers of the navy of Great Britain, from the year 1660 to the present time*, London, R. Faulder, 1794 (From Imprint Collection, Library of Congress).

Church, Benjamin, *The History of Philip's War: Commonly Called the Great Indian War, of 1675 and 1676. Also, of the French and Indian Wars at the Eastward, in 1689, 1690, 1692, 1696, and 1704*, HardPress, 2017.

Craven, Wesley Frank, *The Virginia Company of London, 1606–1624*, first published by the Corporation of Williamsburg in 1957, HardPress. 2016.

Cundall, Frank, *Historic Jamaica*, Gutenberg, 2017 (original 1915).

Defoe, Daniel, *An Essay Upon Projects*, printed by R.R. for Tho Cockerill, 1697.

Dillon, Patrick, *The Last Revolution*, Pimlico, 2007.

Duguid, Charles, *The Story of the Stock exchange: its history and position*, HardPress, 2017.

Dyer, Florence E, *The Life of Admiral Sir John Narbrough*, Philip Allan, 1931.

Earle, Peter, *The Treasure of the* Concepcion, Viking Press, 1980.

Firth, C. H., *Oliver Cromwell and the Rule of the Puritans in England*, first published in UK by Putnam's Sons in 1900, Lume Books, 2018.

Francis, John, *History of the Bank of England: Its Times and Traditions from 1694 to 1844*, *The Banker* magazine, 1852.

Fraser, Antonia, *Cromwell, Our Chief of Men*, Orion, 1973.

Gaskill, Malcolm. *Witchfinders: A Seventeenth-century English Tragedy*, John Murray Press, 2008.

Gerson, Noel B., *The Magnificent Adventures of Henry Hudson,* Sapere Books, 2021.

Giuseppi, John, *The Bank of England*, Evans Brothers, 1966.

Hacke William, *A Collection of Original Voyages*, John Carter Brown Library, 1699 (1993 reprint).

Hall, Michael Garibaldi, *Edward Randolph and the American Colonies 1676–1703*, Norton Library, 1969.

Hopkins, Leon, *The Pirate Who Stole Scotland*, Pen & Sword History, 2023.

Hourly History, *Salem Witch Trials: A History from Beginning to End*, Hourly History, 2021.

Jardine, Lisa, *Going Dutch*, Harper Press, 2008.

Jarvis, Michael J., *In the Eye of All Trade: Bermuda, Bermudians, and the Maritime Atlantic World, 1680–1783*, Omohundro Institute & UNC Press, 2010.

Jenks, Tudor, *Captain John Smith*, first published by The Century Co. in 1904, Hard Nosed Press, 2019.

Karraker, Cyrus H., *The Hispaniola Treasure*, University of Pennsylvania Press, 1934.

Kitson, Frank, *Prince Rupert, Admiral and General-at-Sea*, Constable & Co., 1998.

Mandell, Daniel R., *King Philip's War: Colonial Expansion, Native Resistance, and the End of Indian Sovereignty* (Witness to History), Johns Hopkins University Press, 2010.

Mather, Cotton, *A Family Well Ordered*, first published 1699.

Mather, Cotton, *Cotton Mather: Magnalia Christi Americana*, The Library of Early American Literature, originally 1702.

Mather, Cotton, *Diary of Cotton Mather: 1681–1708*, HardPress, 2017.

Mboma, Lievin Kambamba, *Pilgrims and Puritans in Colonial America*, 2021.

Miller, Lee, *Roanoke, Solving the Mystery of England's Lost Colony*, Pimlico, 2001.

Minto, William, *Daniel Defoe*, Harper & Brothers, 1879.

Novak, Maximillian E., *Daniel Defoe*, Master of Fictions, Oxford University Press, 2001.

Palfrey, John Gorham, *History of New England during the Stuart dynasty* Volume 2, first published by Little, Brown in 1860, HardPress, 2017.

Paterson, William, *The Writings of William Paterson ... Founder of the Bank of England,* HardPress, 2017.

Petram, Lodewijk, *The World's First Stock Exchange,* Columbia University Press, 2011.

Pond, Enoch, *The Lives of Increase Mather and Sir William Phipps*, Massachusetts Sabbath School Society, 1847.

Pope, Charles Henry, *The Pioneers of Maine and New Hampshire 1623 to 1660*, Charles H. Pope, 1908.

Pritchard, R. E., *Captain John Smith and His Brave Adventures*, Haus Books, 2008.

Randolph, Edward, *Edward Randolph: His Letters*, The Prince Society, 1909.

Roach, Marilynne K., *The Salem Witch Trials: A Day-by-Day Chronicle of a Community Under Siege*, Taylor Trade Publishing, 2002.

Rose, Craig, *England in the 1690s, Revolution, Religion and War*, Blackwell Publishers, 1999.

Savage, James. *A Genealogical Dictionary of the First Settlers of New England*, Vol 3, Jazzybee-Verlag, 2016 reprint.

Seymour, William, *Battles in Britain 1066–1746*, Sidgwick & Jackson 1975.

Spencer, Charles. *Prince Rupert: The Last Cavalier*, HarperCollins, 2020.

Warburton, Eliot, *Memoirs of Prince Rupert, and the Cavaliers*, First Published from the Original Manuscripts, HardPress, 2017.

Ward, Estelle Frances, *Christopher Monck, Duke of Albemarle*, John Murray, 1915.

Whitmore, William Henry, *A Memoir of Sir Edmund Andros, Knt., Governor of New England, New York and Virginia*, DigiCat, 2022.

Williams, Glyndwr, *The Great South Sea, English Voyages and Encounters 1570–1750*, Yale University Press, 1997.

Winsham, Willow, *England's Witchcraft Trials*, Pen & Sword Books, 2018.

Index

About the Author

AFTER A SHORT career as an accountant and financial analyst, Leon Hopkins moved into journalism. In the years that followed he worked for national newspapers and wrote for, edited and published numerous magazines, newsletters and websites. Leon's non-fiction books include *The Hundredth Year*, *The Audit Report* and *The Landlord's Handbook. The Pirate Who Stole Scotland* was his first book for Pen & Sword History, and *There's Only One Henry Green* was his first novel. There is more information about Leon's books on his Amazon author's page. After a few years in France, he now lives happily in Cornwall with his wife Jo, where he writes most days. Besides reading and writing, his other interests include sailing, playing chess and walking.

Acknowledgements

I THANK THE publishers, Pen & Sword History, and especially commissioning editor Sarah-Beth Watkins, copy editor Chris Cocks and production editor Laura Hirst for their work on this project. Thank you also to my wife Jo for hardly complaining at all about the many hours I have spent staring at a computer screen while tapping away at a keyboard.